Praise for

Promote Yourself: The New Rules for Career Success

"A smart, practical guide on navigating the world of work today."
—*USA Today*

"*Promote Yourself* is a perfect read for young people starting their 'real' job, or veterans who want to up their game. Think of Dan Schawbel's new book as everything you always wanted to know about building a career but didn't know how (or whom) to ask."
—Daniel H. Pink, #1 *New York Times* bestselling author of *To Sell Is Human* and *Drive*

"Outlines a process for building a successful career in an age of ever-changing technologies and economic uncertainty." —*INC.*

"This is a book about freedom. The freedom to chart your own path, make your own ruckus, and stand up and say to the world, 'Here, I made this.'" —Seth Godin, *New York Times* bestseller and author of *The Icarus Deception*

"Career book of the year: *Promote Yourself* . . . Schawbel offers not only inspiration and challenge but also shores up his advice with a menu of resources to conquer unfamiliar digital recruiting and workplace landscapes . . . GOLD MEDAL CAREER BOOK. I've received countless career books from publishers over the decades and also written quite a few, a background that gives me the confidence to suggest that this year's gold medal for career management books should have Dan Schawbel's name on it for *Promote Yourself.*" —*Chicago Tribune*

"A sweeping guide on how to spread your influence in the modern workplace." —*Parade*

"*Promote Yourself* gives you the tools you need to excel in the workplace. Schawbel demonstrates exactly how to take your career into your own hands and push forward. It's the perfect instruction book to help Millennials get the edge they need."

—*The Huffington Post*

"If you're just standing around waiting and hoping for the boss to notice you, I've got bad news: It's probably not going to happen. High-performing leaders are attracted to activity. You've got to get moving! In *Promote Yourself,* Dan Schawbel shows you what to do to get noticed— and get promoted—inside the company you're already with."

—Dave Ramsey, *New York Times* bestseller
and nationally syndicated radio host

"*Promote Yourself* is a tactical and practical guide to navigate the new world of work. It will inspire you to create your own career path and control your own destiny."

—Guy Kawasaki, former chief
evangelist of Apple, *New York Times* bestselling
author of *Enchantment* and *APE*

"Suggests a variety of strategies to help Generation Y succeed and thrive professionally."

—*Forbes*

"Don't let the title fool you—*Promote Yourself* is not about blowing your own horn in any kind of an arrogant way. It's about harnessing your strengths and making them evident in your workplace. Dan Schawbel shares his expert formula for career success in a way that inspires a level of confidence and a desire for success that didn't exist before. Read this book and let Dan introduce you to your best self."

—Ken Blanchard, coauthor of
The One Minute Manager® and *Trust Works!*

"Schawbel provides simple and effective tips to use your online presence to grow your career instead of destroy it." —*The Boston Globe*

"If you want to promote yourself with power—but also with grace—this is the book for you."
—Susan Cain, *New York Times* bestselling author of *Quiet*

"With *Promote Yourself*, Schawbel turns his considerable talents to advising Millennials about how to succeed in today's increasingly competitive marketplace." —*TechCrunch*

"Reveals the new rules of the modern workplace that young people must learn to get ahead." —*Business Insider*

"A book to watch." —*800-CEO-Read*

"Universally helpful." —*SUCCESS* magazine

"Focuses on the mind-sets you need and the powerful actions you can take to make yourself indispensible in the workplace."
—*Psychology Today*

"A handbook of how to navigate the challenges in growing your career through a multigenerational workplace." —*San Francisco Chronicle*

"Dan Schawbel offers up terrific ideas on promoting yourself and your skills that will translate into promotions in any field. And while he targets Millennials with his wisdom, workers of all ages will benefit from his advice." —Harvey Mackay, author of
the #1 *New York Times* bestseller
Swim with the Sharks Without Being Eaten Alive

"Schawbel's book is a game changer for any employee who is looking to get ahead at work. It reveals the skills and strategies that will turn you into a future leader."　　　　　—Stephen R. Covey, *New York Times* bestseller and author of *The 7 Habits of Highly Effective People* and *The 3rd Alternative*

"Most career self-help books are written by pretenders for pretenders. Dan Schawbel's *Promote Yourself* is the opposite. Keen, insightful, and written by a realist and for the talented."

—David D'Alessandro, bestselling author of *Career Warfare* and former CEO of John Hancock

"Packed with research, real-life examples, and practical, concrete suggestions for action, *Promote Yourself* is an invaluable guide for anyone considering how to succeed better inside—and outside—of work."

—Gretchen Rubin, #1 *New York Times* bestseller of *The Happiness Project* and *Happier at Home*

"Check out Schawbel's book, *Promote Yourself,* for way more career success secrets, including exclusive research on using social media at work, how managers view Millennials, and what skills those managers look for come promotion time."　　　　　—*Women's Health*

"In this remarkable book, Schawbel gives you all the resources, advice, and inspiration you need to take charge of your own career and get ahead at work. Read *Promote Yourself* if you want to achieve your dreams and have fun doing it."

—Jack Canfield, cocreator of the *New York Times* bestselling *Chicken Soup for the Soul®* series and *The Success Principles*™

"A *Fast Company* article, 'The Brand Called You' changed Dan's life. I promise that if you read Dan's book, it will change your life!"

—Alan M. Webber, cofounder, *Fast Company* magazine

"If you want to get promoted, read this book. Schawbel's fresh, compelling writing style will keep you immersed in the pages of *Promote Yourself* as you learn timely ways to advance your career."

—*T + D* magazine

"[*Promote Yourself* offers] the reader the unique skills and strategies they'll need to get ahead (and get a job) today and for the rest of their careers. . . . Dan has become the spokesperson for the Gen Y cohort and has built quite the career out of knowing, understanding, and advising our next generation of leaders."

—*Small Business Trends*

"*Promote Yourself* is a very engaging and extremely thought-provoking read. The topic is both timely and highly relevant, and Dan sets the foundation with the facts and stories, distilled with both actionable and practical insights. I learned a lot from it and so will you!"

—Brad Smith, CEO of Intuit

"*Promote Yourself* is loaded with so much terrific, valuable, usable information for getting ahead—and staying there—I'm embarrassed to admit that I learned a lot myself. This is a book not only for every college grad but for anyone who wants to take their career to an awesome new level."   —Kate White, former editor-in-chief of *Cosmopolitan* magazine and *New York Times* bestselling author

"Schawbel's book contains valuable, not-so-obvious insights to getting ahead in making your mark in today's competitive workplace. The book is based on Dan's solid research, provides sound advice, and just might be one of your most valuable reads."

—Michael Feuer, founder of OfficeMax

"Promote Yourself is a book I wish I had when I first started my career. It will help you enhance your skills, deal with different generations in the workplace, and become the leader that your company needs you to be."　—Doug Conant, former CEO of Campbell Soup Company, founder and CEO of ConantLeadership and *New York Times* bestselling author of *TouchPoints*

"Promote Yourself is a fascinating read and also a practical guide, for anyone entering the job force. Right on! Thank you Dan for giving us inspiration, and a solid blueprint for building a successful career."

—Richard Thalheimer, founder and former CEO of The Sharper Image

"The world of work moves fast. Today's professionals need to stay relevant by traversing the corporate lattice, continually acquiring transferable skills and experiences—and the networks that form along with them. *Promote Yourself* provides savvy ways for GenYers to build and enhance their personal brand calling cards."

—Cathy Benko, vice chairman, Deloitte LLP, and bestselling author of *Mass Career Customization*

"This should be the last book a young person bent on success should have to read. Dan melts the concept of success into an action plan. What you will learn is that everything you need is something you already have, or have access to, and the only thing left to do is to tap these resources to be the successful person you are by getting done what it takes for the world to notice."　—Mel Ziegler, founder of Banana Republic and author of *Wild Company*

"Having spent years moving up inside a large organization, I can attest that Dan's book contains the essential secrets to promote yourself to the top." —Terry Jones, founder of Travelocity and chairman of Kayak.com

"*Promote Yourself* is an insightful and inspiring book that will help navigate you through obstacles such as personal branding, promotions, and how to take charge of your career." —Daymond John, business mogul and celebrity branding expert

"I love this book. *Promote Yourself* is absolutely the best all-around book I've read about and for Millennials. From the very first paragraph to the last, Dan Schawbel offers clear insights, persuasive facts, compelling examples, and practical tips on what you need to do to be successful in the new world of work. And not only that, it's exceptionally well written. *Promote Yourself* is straight from the heart and direct from Dan's own experiences in practicing what he preaches. You really need to read *Promote Yourself* now. . . . and to put it to use as soon as you have. And one other thing: If you're not a Millennial, you've got even more reasons to read this book. You need to know how they're thinking, and *Promote Yourself* is the best place to start learning just that." —Jim Kouzes, coauthor of *The Leadership Challenge* and the Dean's Executive Fellow of Leadership, Leavey School of Business, Santa Clara University

"Schawbel will help you navigate the new workplace with ease and give you all the tools you need in order to stand out at work and get promoted faster than your peers!" —Barbara Corcoran, founder of The Corcoran Group, investor/shark on ABC's *Shark Tank,* and author of *Shark Tales*

PROMOTE
YOURSELF

ALSO BY DAN SCHAWBEL

Me 2.0: 4 Steps to Building Your Future

PROMOTE YOURSELF

THE NEW RULES FOR CAREER SUCCESS

DAN SCHAWBEL

Bestselling author of *Me 2.0*

FOREWORD BY MARCUS BUCKINGHAM
New York Times bestselling author of
Now, Discover Your Strengths

 St. Martin's Griffin ✖ New York

www.stmartins.com

The Library of Congress has cataloged the hardcover edition as follows:

Schawbel, Dan.
    Promote yourself : the new rules for career success / Dan Schawbel ;
foreword by Marcus Buckingham. — First edition.
        p. cm.
    Includes bibliographical references and index.
    ISBN 978-1-250-04455-6 (hardcover)
    ISBN 978-1-250-02567-8 (e-book)
    1. Career development.   2. Success in business.   3. Career changes.
4. New business enterprises—Management.
    HF5381 .S2853 2013
    650.14

                                                    2013024881

                ISBN 978-1-250-02568-5 (trade paperback)

St. Martin's Griffin books may be purchased for educational, business, or
promotional use. For information on bulk purchases, please contact
Macmillan Corporate and Premium Sales Department at 1-800-221-7945,
extension 5442, or write specialmarkets@macmillan.com.

First St. Martin's Griffin Edition: September 2014

                10   9   8   7   6   5   4   3   2   1

DEDICATION

This book is dedicated to my incredibly supportive parents, who believed in me in the best and worst of times. Through all the stress and obstacles, they made sure I kept my head up and had a positive attitude. I feel very privileged to have them both in my life because having great parents makes it that much easier to "Promote Yourself" and achieve your dreams. The best advice they've given me is to not take life too seriously, always be yourself, and not to let anything get you down. This book is written in honor of them because without them, I wouldn't be here.

CONTENTS

Contents

FOREWORD

BY MARCUS BUCKINGHAM,

NEW YORK TIMES BESTSELLING AUTHOR OF *NOW,*

DISCOVER YOUR STRENGTHS AND *STANDOUT*

Change is constant and certain. We may flatter ourselves into thinking that we feel the pressure of change more keenly than our ancestors did, but it seems especially easy to notice flux and uncertainty in our time. Technology has made the world a smaller place—people and companies are intimately interconnected. Economic bubbles and recessions have left corporations and communities repeatedly having to adjust to new realities. Jobs are more variable and skills more quickly obsolete than ever before. Organizations are hiring less, for less, replacing humans with technology and outsourcing or offshoring jobs whenever they can.

Generation Y will come to dominate the workforce, but they are entering it at a particularly difficult time. While they are often—and rightfully—considered to have a pioneering, we-can-change-the-world outlook, they are also a more delicate cohort than the stereotypes might suggest.

We all know that members of Gen Y are accustomed to constant, immediate feedback. Forget annual reviews; they want weekly or daily check-ins with their supervisors. And we know they're used to that feedback being overwhelmingly positive. They are accustomed to being praised for their uniqueness. The result is a challenging set of expectations. Nearly 40 percent of Gen Y respondents to a 2012 Trendera[1] survey believed that they should be promoted every two years. An even more eye-opening statistic: Only 9 percent believed that their promotions needed to be warranted by their performance.

What will help them, on the other hand, is that all they know is a world of constant change. It's their normal. When the Baby Boomers entered the workforce, they sought jobs at corporations where they envisioned staying for the next thirty years. Now, Gen Y is entering the workforce knowing they are likely to have at least seven jobs during the course of their careers. In fact, 60 percent of Gen Y respondents recognized their current position as a mere stepping-stone.

Given these realities, the most critical skill anyone can have is awareness of his or her unique, transferable strengths. My research involving literally hundreds of corporations and millions of people has demonstrated that top performers are those who focus on their strengths the majority of the time. That may seem obvious—play to your strengths and you'll succeed. But, even more than preceding generations, Gen Y needs to learn that simple truth. For all the analysis indicating that they are praised and self-entitled, they show a marked tendency to overlook their strengths. Asked whether they will succeed professionally by fixing their weaknesses or by enhancing their strengths, an astounding 73 percent of Gen Y respondents (as compared to 55 percent of people overall) chose fixing their weaknesses.[2]

So what does all this mean for Gen Y in the workforce at large? It means that they need to learn how to double down on their strengths. Winning in the workplace mandates that you know who you are, where your greatest strengths lie, and how to differentiate yourself. When your job could shift tomorrow and technology is constantly making old skills obsolete, your strengths are your constant. You must understand

and promote your greatest strengths, your edge that can be applied in every situation. Is your strength strategic thinking? Competitive spirit? Empathy? Ability to bring people together? All of those ingrained talents will travel with you, regardless of technological or societal change. These strengths are multipliers, adding value to what you do in any situation. Specific skills may become irrelevant with change, but strengths are infinitely transferable.

In the chapters that follow, Dan will help you figure out how to take your strengths and uniqueness and turn them into your personal brand. Promoting yourself doesn't mean getting promoted. Instead, Dan will show you how to communicate your unique contribution, so that you make yourself indispensable. In this competitive world, he will ensure that you highlight your strengths for all to see. As the workplace continues to transform, your personal brand is the key to your success. Be the best version of you—and let everyone else marvel at that value.

PROMOTE
YOURSELF

Thinking Inside the Box

> If everyone has to think outside the box, maybe it is
> the box that needs fixing.
>
> —MALCOLM GLADWELL,
> BESTSELLING AUTHOR
> OF *THE TIPPING POINT*

M eet Jason, a typical twentysomething college grad. He's at the office, working hard on his latest project—and doing a great job. Like many of his peers, Jason is pretty good at multitasking, so while he's working he's got his earbuds in and is listening to music on his smartphone, texting and IMing his friends (some of whom are only a few cubicles away), and checking Facebook status updates. Jason has been working for his employer for about a year, and he's getting itchy feet. His manager has been out at an offsite meeting and Jason is waiting for her to come back so he can ask her about working at home or that promotion he thinks he deserves. A year in the same job is a long time, he thinks. It's time to move up or move on.

As recently as five or six years ago, Jason's move-up-or-move-on calculation would have been a good one. The economy was chugging along nicely, unemployment was low, and newly minted college grads were getting jobs right away—and if you couldn't get a job, you could at least get a paid internship that would most likely lead to one fairly quickly. Bonuses were big, and recruiters were always calling. But today, the economic situation is pretty grim. Millions are out of work, and it doesn't look like things are going to get much better anytime soon.

But that's just the beginning. Jason and most of today's young workers are competing for jobs and promotions not only against other young people, but also against experienced older workers who've lost their jobs and highly trained workers in other countries. And internships, if you can get one at all, are usually unpaid.

In other economic times, Jason might have quit his job to start his own company. But small businesses that were created just a few years ago by young aspiring entrepreneurs who had been attracted by the prospect of making millions blogging and doing social networking, are failing because of the lack of resources, mentorship, and funding. Banks aren't lending, venture capitalists are only investing in new companies with a track record, and established companies are cutting back.

As I see it, one of the biggest problems is that while schools are giving out degrees as quickly as they can print 'em, they aren't doing a particularly good job of actually preparing young workers for the real world. There are probably hundreds of job functions today that didn't even exist five years ago, but schools are still preparing students to step into those old jobs, not the new ones. And kids who are starting college today are being taught only how to do today's jobs instead of how to adapt to a changing world and acquire the kinds of skills that will help them land the jobs of the future—jobs that probably don't even exist today.

So here's the situation: The economy sucks, which leaves a lot of people afraid to quit their jobs because they worry that they won't be able to find a new one; even in the best of times, entrepreneurship isn't easy; and a traditional college education isn't the guarantee of future success that it once was. The good news is that there are a lot of other ways to take control of your career without quitting your job, striking out on your own, or burning your diploma. The fact is that companies need young entrepreneurs working on the inside if they're going to stay in business let alone succeed. The challenges of rapid globalization and constant technological disruption in the midst of a global economic downturn that has tightened up the credit markets and slowed down mergers and acquisitions has put companies under many of the same pressures that their employees are under, They need to grow from within, and the only way they can do that is with you. That means that now, more than ever, in order to advance in your career, it's essential that you become indispensable at work. You can't just sit back and wait for things to happen. If you're going to get ahead and be happy with your career, you need to be in the driver's seat, constantly seeking out opportunities and being persistent. When you do, your manager, your coworkers, and the executives will view you as a valuable asset, and you'll get those raises and promotions that you've been killing yourself to get. Today's workplace doesn't tolerate slackers. Either you rise to the top' or you don't survive. The problem is that most people don't know how to get started. But I'm going to show you exactly how, and by the time you finish this book, you'll be an expert at using your current job as a springboard to success and using thinking-inside-the-box skills—rather than outside-the-box skills—to realize your potential, maximize your success, and take your career to a whole new level.

I know, I know, that's an awfully big promise. But let me tell you how I got to a place where I can make—and deliver on—those promises. To start with, I'm not some kind of Internet genius/billionaire. I've definitely always been interested in tech (I once started a James Bond Web site), but school was never easy for me.

During college, I got an internship at an event promotions company doing grunt work—printing, scanning, and I even got the CEO's coffee a few times. This was about to be another "I-don't-want-to-do-this-job-again" episode, but I noticed some of my coworkers creating flyers and doing design work. The next day, I showed my boss the Web sites

I'd created and was running as a hobby. He saw that I was pretty tech-savvy and he gave me a chance to work on the company's Web site and design brochures. *Lessons learned: Just doing my job wasn't enough. In order to get ahead I had to really stand out, and the skills I learned outside the workplace could help me get promoted* inside.

On March 14, 2007, I read an article that changed my life: "The Brand Called You," by Tom Peters. In it, Peters talked about the power of personal branding and the art of crafting your ideal career. It hit me that that's exactly what I had been doing during college—I just didn't have a term for it. I knew that I enjoyed helping other people with their careers and it was something that I was good at. At the same time, I saw that career management was shifting to online brand management and that it was increasingly possible to use the Web to build a career. I did a quick Internet search to see whether anyone else my age was talking about personal branding online. There wasn't, so I jumped in.

The first thing I did was change the name of the blog to Personal Branding Blog (I know, not terribly inspiring, but it gets right to the point). And I set about learning as much as I possibly could. Then I turned things around a little and used what I knew and was learning to teach others (which helped me learn even more). Every night, when I came home from work, I'd write a new blog post and I'd comment on every article on the Web that was even remotely connected to personal branding. No more weekends or free evenings for me, and I found that it was a terrific way for me to show what I knew and to get feedback at the same time. Slowly, slowly, the blog began to grow and I became an expert people were contacting for help. After a few months, I was able to get an article published on another site. And then, after I'd been pitching them for months, *Fast Company* did a profile of me as a young leader in the personal branding space.

Someone at EMC saw the *Fast Company* piece and gave it to a VP who was just getting into the social media space. I worked with the VP to create a new position in the PR department: social media specialist.

All of a sudden, people were coming to me, asking for my help with social media. I had shown my employer what made me special and unique in the marketplace—my personal brand—and become a high-value employee. Lessons learned: *If you work really hard, make yourself an expert on something, and pursue your passions, you* will *be able to achieve what you want.*

Over the years, I've seen way too many people of my generation working in jobs that make them miserable (according to MetLife's tenth annual Study of Employee Benefits Trends, a third of Americans would like to be working for a different employer within the next twelve months). Many of my fellow young professionals have contacted me, asking for advice on how to move up in their company—talented people who felt stuck and who didn't learn what they needed to know in school (largely because it isn't taught). They aren't using their talents to their full potential. They know they'd like to move to another position in their company, but they lack the necessary skills and don't know how to get them. Some have great ideas but don't have the backing to develop them on their own. Almost all of them want to make a change, but they don't know how to evaluate their options or where to get started.

So, here's the deal. I've been there. I know exactly what it's like to feel frustrated and unfulfilled. But more important than that, I know what to do to move beyond those obstacles and position yourself for real success. Over the course of this book, I'm going to show you how to do the same.

Before we go on, a quick point of full disclosure. By 2010, my Personal Branding Blog had become much more than a hobby—it had helped me land a deal for my first book and had brought me a number of speaking and consulting gigs. So I decided that leaving the corporate world to form my own company was the next logical step. My friends and coworkers were stunned. They couldn't believe that a twenty-six-year-old would quit a well-paying, nine-to-five job and start a business without any corporate backing. They said it was a risky move, and some even said that I was crazy. The most senior leader in my department predicted, "Before you know it, you'll get bored and join McKinsey or another consulting firm."

As it turns out, they were wrong. I wanted to be in control of my own destiny and I had the right mix of passion, expertise, ambition, and confidence that allowed me to make my new company, Millennial Branding, a success. Now, while I'm an evangelist for entrepreneurship, I recognize that this path is not for everyone, nor should it be, especially at the start of your career. That said, resist the urge to start thinking that working for a company is somehow "settling." I've discovered that entrepreneurship is now accessible to everyone regardless of age or occupation. You don't need to own a business to be an entrepreneur, but you do need the entrepreneurial mindset to be successful in business. In a study in partnership with oDesk.com, we found that 90 percent of people say being an entrepreneur is a mindset instead of someone who starts a company. It's also a set of skills: selling, motivating others, working with teams, persistence, among others. You can learn and perfect all of those skills by being entrepreneurial *within* your company, taking advantage of your employer's deeper pockets and corporate structure. (This is especially important if you've got a lot of student loan debt, little or no access to capital, and/or you're still living with your parents.) Frankly, I'm happy I worked for a big company. What I learned there made me a better entrepreneur later. Now, I'd like to bring some of the lessons I've learned as an entrepreneur—both on the job and on my own—back to the young employees who are working at the kind of company that I worked so that they can succeed at any job, in any market, and pursue their passions to the fullest no matter where those young workers set out from or where those passions lead.

New Workplace, New Rules

The workplace of today is quite different from what it used to be. And, as I mentioned earlier, schools aren't preparing their grads for it. For example, a lot of colleges are telling their students to wait until the summer between junior and senior years to get internships. Really? That may sound good, but I guarantee that the less work experience you have, the harder it will be to get an internship when you really want one. There's also not nearly enough communication between academic departments and the career services offices. Someone needs to be communicating with actual employers to find out what skills they're looking for. But that's not happening. And here's the result: Intel, which has a very generous tuition reimbursement program, recently cut 100 colleges from their list because their internal audits showed that employees who graduated from those programs didn't perform at the level expected for their degrees. Ouch. At the same time, the number of Web sites that offer training in topics that really matter in today's workplace has exploded. If schools were doing their jobs, those places (which we'll talk about in Chapters 2 and 3) wouldn't exist. You'll need to learn how the new economy works in order to be successful at navigating it. All of these factor into how you develop your career in order to get noticed and get ahead. This is the new reality of the workplace.

All in all, if you want to succeed in today's workplace—to develop your career and get noticed—you'll need to learn how to navigate your way through an economy that seems to be changing every day. Here's a brief guide to some of those changes. We'll explore them and a lot more as we go through the book.

1. You job description is just the beginning. If you want to succeed in today's workplace and make a name for yourself, you'll have to do a lot more than what you got hired to do. In fact, your job description is just a scratch on the surface of what you should be doing. Always be on the lookout for new projects and collaborations with other groups, and do as much training and development as possible. This will position you to better compete for bigger roles when they come up. Andrew Goldman, VP, Program Planning and Scheduling at HBO/Cinemax, put it nicely when he said, "We live in a world where you can't just be doing the bare minimum unless you're working for your dad."

2. Your job is temporary. As the world changes, so does the workplace. Companies are acquiring or being acquired, merging with other companies, or crumbling. Your team could be eliminated, your position outsourced, or you might lose interest in your job altogether. It's no surprise that according to the U.S. Bureau of Labor Statistics, the average American will have about eleven jobs between the ages of eighteen and thirty-four. The job you're in now is just one stepping-stone along your path.

3. You're going to need a lot of skills you probably don't have right now. A recent Department of Education study shows that companies are having trouble finding and retaining the right talent. The DoE estimates that 60 percent of all new jobs in the twenty-first century will require skills that only 20 percent of current employees have. Soft (interpersonal) skills have become more important than hard (technical) skills. It's never been easier to acquire hard skills—and those skills will only get you so far. Companies are looking for leadership, organizational, teamwork, listening, and coaching skills.

4. Your reputation is the single greatest asset you have. Titles might be good for your ego, but in the grand scheme of things what really matters is what you're known for, the projects you're part of, how much people trust you, whom you know, who knows about you, and the aura you give off to people around you. Sure, what you do is important, but what others *think* you do can be just as important if not more so. If you build a strong reputation, the money and opportunities will find you.

In 2011, when I polled 450 of my blog readers at Personal-BrandingBlog.com, 92 percent said that knowing how people perceive them at work would help their career. Employees are begging for feedback. But in my experience working with corporations and individuals, most people are either too afraid to ask for feedback or they aren't getting enough of it to make a difference.

5. Your personal life is now public. According to a study by my company and identified.com, the average Gen Y employee is connected to sixteen coworkers on Facebook. What that means is that when you leave work, you're still connected through the relationships you have with your coworkers online. As a result, even things you do on your own time can affect your career—in a big way. The fifteen seconds it takes you to tweet about how much you hate your boss or to post a pic of you passed out with a drink in your hand could ruin your career forever. Even the smallest things—how you behave, dress, your online presence, body language, and whom you associate with can help build your brand or tear it to the ground.

6. You need to build a positive presence in new media. There are plenty of benefits to new media and the convergence between your personal and private lives. Your online social networks enable you to connect with people who have interests similar to yours. Your online presence can help you build your reputation, and the educational opportunities available online can help you dig deeper into the things you're passionate about and want to become an expert in. And, as we'll talk about in later chapters, expanding your social network will eventually help you in your career by putting you in touch with people who know what you can do and are in a position to help you get ahead.

7. You'll need to work with people from different generations. Because the combination of economic need and increasing life spans is keeping people in the workplace longer, you will undoubtedly find yourself working shoulder to shoulder with people of all different ages. (In some professions, experienced workers are competing for entry-level jobs with recent graduates, since they are willing to take a pay cut to stay employed.) There are now four distinct generations in the workforce: Gen Z (interns), Gen Y (employees), Gen X (managers), and Baby Boomers (executives). Each of these generations was raised in a different period of time, has a different view of the workplace, and communicates differently. By learning how to manage relationships with those in other generations, you will be more successful.

8. Your boss's career comes first. If your manager is unsuccessful, his frustrations will undoubtedly rub off on you, and the chances you'll ever get a promotion are pretty slim. But if you support your manager's career, make their life easier, and earn their trust, they'll take you with them as they climb the corporate ladder—even if that means going to another company.

9. The one with the most connections wins. We have moved from an information economy to a social one. It's less about what you know (you can find out just about anything within seconds with a simple Google search), and more about whether you can work with other people to solve problems. The rapid pace of technology, information, consumer demand, and the constant shifting of organizational hierarchies is going to impact how you manage your career at work. If you don't get—and stay—connected, you'll quickly become irrelevant to the marketplace.

10. Remember the rule of one. When it comes to getting a job, starting a business, finding someone to marry, or just about anything else, all it takes is *one* person to change your life for the better. People may be saying no all around you, but as long as one person says yes, you're on your way. Successful people get what they want because they understand that it only takes one opportunity to get to the next level, and when they reach that level, it takes only one more to get to the next level. It's up to you to get those people on board to support your career.

11. You are the future. By 2025, 75 percent of the global workforce will be Gen Y. That means that even though you may be early in your career, in the not too distant future you'll be at the forefront. Right now, you have to position yourself to take one of these major leadership roles when the workforce shifts and older generations retire. More on this in Chapter 1.

12. Entrepreneurship is for everyone not just business owners. A lot of people define *entrepreneurship* as starting a business, but in recent years the meaning has broadened to include someone who's accountable, who's willing to take risks, and who sells him- or herself. If you want to get ahead, start looking at your company's management as a venture capital firm. Be persistent, sell your ideas to them, and come up with innovative solutions no one else has thought of.

13. Hours are out, accomplishments are in. If you want to keep your job and move up, stop thinking that you have to put in a ridiculous numbers of hours per week. Instead, realize your value, deliver on it, measure your successes, and then promote yourself.

14. Your career is in *your* hands, not your employer's. No matter what they say, companies are looking out for themselves. And while you should definitely try to make your company successful, you need to make sure that you're getting something out of the deal too. If you aren't learning and growing, you aren't benefiting anymore and that's an issue that you will have to resolve. Don't rely on anything or anyone: Be accountable for your own career and take charge of your own life.

I f you want to succeed, you'll need to master these new rules. I wrote this book to help you do exactly that. While *Me 2.0*, was about how to get a job through social media, this one is about what happens *after* you have a job. How do you get the skills you need to advance in your career? How do you prepare yourself to deal with any problems that may come up in this incredibly uncertain time? How do you network with executives and managers? How do you manage relationships between people from different generations? How do you create a personal brand that showcases your uniqueness, will make people take notice of you at work, and will help you promote yourself faster than your peers are promoting themselves? In short, that's what this book is all about. And instead of telling you to quit your job and start your own company or break corporate rules, I'm going to instruct you on how to stay within the corporate policies, while reaching your true potential at work.

This book is written for all you high-potential young workers like Jason, who have no clear career roadmap, but are willing to put the effort in to make a difference for your company, and yourself. Of course anyone who's looking to get ahead at work or in their career will benefit from reading this book as well. And you're going to get a unique blend of my experience and the experiences of hundreds of people just like you from interviews I conducted with more than 100 employees, managers, and executives at major companies like Intel and PepsiCo, as well as the results of a proprietary study my company did in partnership with American Express, where we surveyed 1,000 young employees and 1,000 managers. The results will surprise you and shed much needed light on the trends, tips, statistics that are the secrets to getting ahead.

This book contains eleven chapters, each one aligned to the "think inside the box" method that's required to be successful at work. As the workplace changes, you need to know the new rules and how to navigate through them. I also realize that even though most people are and will continue to work for companies, some of you will be drawn toward entrepreneurship. So even if you know you'll be on your own someday, it's often extremely helpful to get some corporate experience under your belt before you turn in your office keys. Whatever your path, this book will serve you as both an instruction manual and reference guide.

In the first section, I'll show you how to get the skills you need to succeed. We'll talk about hard (technical) skills, soft (interpersonal) skills, and social media skills. You will learn about the skills you need, how to go about obtaining them, and how to use them to advance.

In the second section, we'll move on to how to get yourself known for those skills, how to build a following, how to make yourself more visible, and how to boost your influence within your organization—all without being too self-promotional.

In the third section, we'll focus on the results of the study I mentioned, which will unveil what managers are looking for when retaining and promoting young talent (and what the young professionals think the managers are looking for; hint: the two lists aren't always the same). When you understand corporate needs, you'll make fewer mistakes, advance faster, and feel more confident in the workplace.

In the fourth section, we'll talk about activities you should be doing outside the workplace to advance your career on the inside. I'll show you how to take the ideas you're most passionate about and use them to move to different positions within your company. We'll also talk about how you can essentially start your own business while you're still on the job—and how to get your managers and executives to support you—and give you the resources you'll need to make it happen. Employees are becoming more entrepreneurial at work. And many companies are acting kind of like venture capitalists, seeking out high-potential employees and rewarding innovation *inside* the box, funding projects that might have died on the vine if you had to go out and get your own funding.

Finally, in the last section, we'll talk about making changes. Chances are you won't be at the same job your entire career. So we'll talk about how to assess whether to stay with your current employer or move on; what to do if you hate your job but can't afford to leave; how to handle recruiters, ask for a raise, and much more.

Corporate America may be changing quickly, and we can't count on the economy to turn around anytime soon. But if you follow the steps I've laid out in this book, you have every reason to be optimistic. In each chapter, I'll help you through the process of identifying the skills you'll need to move ahead in your career—and how to get them. Knowing that will give you a tremendous advantage over your peers who will be spending a huge amount of time floundering around learning what you'll already know. It will also make you more successful and fulfilled in your current position, and give you the tools you'll need to move confidently into your next position.

I'll leave you with this final thought before we set out: Although the focus of this book is on thinking inside the box—succeeding and advancing *within* your organization—it's critical that you be open to new possibilities. In an ever-changing job market, you need to be able to change right along with it. Throughout this book, I'm going to show you the possibilities and help you take advantage of them. Your career is in your hands and I'm here to support your ambitions and help you promote yourself. Let's get started!

Cheers to your success,

Dan Schawbel

1

The Future Is YOU

Millennials hold the keys to unlocking the secrets of tomorrow.

—BARRY SALZBERG,
GLOBAL CHIEF
EXECUTIVE OFFICER,
DELOITTE TOUCHE
TOHMATSU LIMITED

We are Millennials. We are eighty million strong and we're taking over the world. I am fully confident that this generation will transform business as we know it for the better. We've lost trust in organizations, we're pushing them to align with social causes, and we want them to support our local communities. We aren't fond of corporate hierarchies and don't want to feel constrained by a nine-to-five workday. We believe that companies shouldn't judge performance by tenure, age, or hours worked but on results achieved. As more of us enter the workforce, change will happen rapidly and companies that don't adjust will lose out on the most in-demand talent pool in history. In 2014, 36 percent of the U.S. workforce will be Millennials (aka Gen Y). By 2020, we'll be up to 46 percent, and we'll account for 75 percent of the *global* workforce by 2025.[1] We have the power to change corporate America because a decade from now we will *be* corporate America. We have the power to change corporate America because a decade from now we will *be* corporate America. Valerie Grillo, Chief Diversity Officer of American Express, understands the full potential and magnitude of Millennials. "We live in a world where digital and social media have completely changed the way we connect with and market to our customers. Attracting and retaining the best available talent is critical to long-terms success—Millennials are a key component of that strategy."

But this isn't a story only about the future. A recent study by my company and PayScale concluded that 15 percent of Millennials are already in management positions.[2] As our influence continues to grow, I believe that we'll force companies to be more transparent in the workplace, have a more honest recruitment process, and become more collaborative. Hierarchies will collapse, mega corporate buildings will consolidate and turn into optional coworking spaces. Employees will be able to work anywhere at any time and will be judged only on the results they produce.

The workplace will become more like a game instead of a chore, and will have a culture that looks more like a start-up than an old-school enterprise. This is great news for workers and for any and all companies that adapt to these changes. But don't just take my word for it. Cynthia Trudell, Chief Human Resource Officer at PepsiCo, also sees the tremendous impact Millennials will have on the workplace. "Many of the operating changes we're making today are designed to move ourselves to a flat hierarchy and away from the old traditional command and control. If you envision the future and you watch the way Gen Y works as a team, it's because they're trained to do that in school, and that's the way of the future."

So why am I telling you all of this? Simple: I think that by understanding the impact your generation will have on the workforce in the years to come, you'll know what you need to do now to get noticed at work and get people interested in your ideas. Once that's in the bag, you're well on your way to becoming a leader at your company.

Some companies have already begun changing their culture to

make it more Millennial-friendly. The same PayScale study I worked on shows that the average tenure for Millennials is two years (five for Gen X and seven for Baby Boomers). Chegg Inc., an online textbook rental service based in Silicon Valley, had trouble retaining its Millennials for even the two-year average.[3] The company created an unlimited paid-vacation policy, something that HubSpot, Netflix, and a few others implemented years before. Employers that offer these plans find that besides being a good recruiting tool, they also increase employees' productivity by eliminating stress from their lives that could impact their job performance. Some employers have gone even further, actually giving employees spending money to use during their vacation, but with the caveat that they can't do *any* work and have to be completely disconnected from technology while they're away. Employers say that when employees get back they're more refreshed and ready to go.

The annual turnover rate of Millennials at Chegg has fallen by 50 percent each year for the last two years as a result of the program. Another company, software maker Aprimo, guarantees recent college grads an increase in responsibility within a year, a policy the company credits with increasing their Millennial retention rate by 85 percent.[4] Bottom line: Companies that demonstrate to employees that they care about them and their careers (in part by making the workplace more Millennial-friendly and providing opportunities to take on more responsibility) will retain them. Everyone else will lose the battle for talent. But we still have a long way to go.

Here are a few more examples of the tremendous impact Millennials will have on the workplaces of today and tomorrow:

- **We'll take down the firewall.** Millennials are always connected through technology, and use social media tools and their smartphones to keep in touch with family, friends, and coworkers. Smart companies will allow for social usage at work because it makes workers more productive, allows for fast and cheap communication across the world, and makes their employees happy. On the other hand, companies that block social media sites in the workplace and limit our mobile device choices will have trouble recruiting and/or retaining Millennials. When Millenials take charge of the workplace, all companies (with a few exceptions in highly regulated industries) will allow for open technology use. Thirty-three percent of Millennials would choose social media freedom and device flexibility over a higher salary. And according to Cisco, 56 percent wouldn't work at a company that banned social media use.

• **We will turn work into more of a game than a chore.** Millennials grew up playing video games, and we're constantly pursuing our dream jobs. We aren't willing to settle, are highly optimistic, and believe that our job should reflect our lifestyle. When we're bored with our job, we end up leaving. In the future, Millennials will turn the way that work gets done around. Gamification in the workplace is already starting to gain traction now but will become standard in the future. Gamification is a new way to train and develop employees using games. One example of a company that's already used gamification to cultivate a loyal millennial employee base is BlueWolf Consulting.[5] Employees at BlueWolf earn points by posting new topics for discussion or responding to coworker posts, which keeps the company innovative and increases engagement. In addition, they are encouraged to share posts, white papers, and other materials through their own social network profiles. They earn points when their posts are clicked, which can be cashed in for different prizes such as iPads or lunch with the CEO. As a result, their Web site traffic increased by 45 percent, and traffic on their corporate blog went up by 80 percent. Gartner predicts that by 2014, more than 70 percent of companies will have at least one gamified application.

• **We will work with our friends.** Millennials want work to feel more like home, and we're more likely than workers of previous generations to choose a job just to be with our friends. This is why so many of us start businesses and choose our friends as business partners. We see the lines between personal and professional blended and feel that it's easier to bring our social life with us to work that way.

• **We will build a collaborative organization.** Millennials are big on collaboration. And if we're going to have a more collaborative workplace, the actual physical structure of the workplace has to be redesigned (individual cubicles, for example, are quite isolating). So instead of traditional office space, we will have social spaces customized to our own needs. Two examples of this are Unilever's Hamburg office and Microsoft's office in Amsterdam, where employees don't have permanent desks and are encouraged to move around and find the place they can be most productive.[6] In the workplace of the not too distant future, you'll see offices designed without cubicles, more extensive use of open spaces and round tables, virtual offices, and more companies using coworking spaces instead of enormous corporate buildings with thousands of employees in them. Technology will be a major part of how employees collaborate and we're seeing this already through internal social networks and social media tools that allow for blogs, forum posts, video, and so forth. The goal in all of this is to facilitate employee-to-employee communication and interaction.

• **We will have a positive influence over older generations.** Actually, this is already happening. For example, we were the first to adopt social networking. Older generations came on board later often because they wanted either to keep in touch with or spy on their children. Since Millennials are so different from previous generations in how they act, behave, make purchasing decisions, and see the world, they will start to change the perceptions and behavior of their elders (74 percent of Millennials already believe that they influence the purchase decisions of their peers and those in other generations).[7] "We can actually see Gen X changing their perception of brands and what they expect of products and services and experiences because Millennials are raising the bar for everybody and that plays out in the workforce," says Ross Martin, Executive Vice President at MTV Scratch at MTV Networks. Part of the issue is that Gen Yers don't just want to be marketed to, they want to be part of the branding and product creation process and engaged with online.

Gen Y's influence extends to the offline world as well. Traditional retailers such as Macy's have begun to offer completely new fashion brands—and are even redesigning their brick-and-mortar stores—to make them more attractive to younger shoppers. And in the workplace, younger workers are reverse mentoring Boomers, making them more tech-savvy, and helping them better use technology to do their jobs.

• **We'll give corporate America a better reputation.** In many circles, corporate America is still seen as impersonal, out of touch, and driven by the bottom line. But 92 percent of Millennials believe that business should be measured by more than just profit and should focus on a societal purpose.[8] Millennials are all about giving back to communities, making a positive difference in the world, and we're known to place meaning over money when it comes to making decisions about where to work. In this way, we're going to have a positive influence on the way business is done, support global charities and nonprofits, and paint a better picture of corporate America in the future.

• **We will change the way workers are promoted.** Promotions typically come after a certain length of time on the job. But Millennials want faster promotions and often aren't willing to wait years to get to the next level at a company. We believe that promotions should be more aligned to accomplishments and results instead of based on age and years of experience. Traditionally, promotions tend to happen at the beginning of a company's fiscal or calendar year. But as our influence grows, promotions will happen anytime they're deserved. The key word here is *deserved*. You're still going to have to work hard and produce results to constantly add value to your team and your company.

By understanding the impact your generation will have on the workforce in the years to come, you can better prepare for it now and become a leader at your company. This will help you get noticed at work, make people interested in your ideas, and even give you more confidence.

Sounds pretty great, doesn't it? The future is bright and the future is you!

2

Discover What You Were
Meant to Do

We are all born with extraordinary powers of imagi-
nation, intelligence, feeling, intuition, spirituality, and
of physical and sensory awareness.

—KEN ROBINSON

Most of us who fall into the Millennial demographic grew up hearing our parents tell us over and over that we're special, that we could be anything we wanted to be. And they tried to help us along by praising everything we did whether we deserved it or not. We got trophies for just about everything, win or lose (when I was a kid, I was the goalie on my soccer team and let through more goals than I stopped. But I've still got a closet full of trophies). I hate to break it to you, but as special as you are, life in the real world is a little more complicated than our parents made it out to be. While there are plenty of opportunities for success, there are also obsta-cles. Lots of them. In this chapter we're going to be taking an honest look at both with the aim of helping you figure out a solid career path.

Who Are We, Anyway?

For the most part, we Millennials are a pretty optimistic bunch. 84 percent of us believe we're going to get where we want to be in life.[1] We expect to find our life's calling, and in the pursuit of meaningful work, we're willing to make sacrifices—including lower pay—to get it. We also expect to retire at age sixty-three (just two years older than today's average retirement age).[2]

Unfortunately, it doesn't look like we're going to be able to get by on optimism alone. Thanks to a tough job market, student loan debt, low starting salaries, and a low savings rate, it's going to take us longer to reach adulthood than previous generations. We're getting married, buying our first homes, and having children later than our parents did. In my research with PayScale.com, we found that only 71 percent of Millennials are living on their own after starting their career. Compare that with 88 percent of Gen X and 96 percent of Boomers when they were our age. Put a little differently, 21.6 million of us were still living with our parents in 2012.[3] That's a lot.

We've also had to rethink the definition of "career." Back in 1980, young workers were twenty-six years old when they hit a median wage of $42,000 per year. The average Millennial won't hit that benchmark until age thirty.[4] Fewer than a third of us are working in jobs that are related to our undergraduate college major, and only 62 percent are in jobs that even require a college degree at all.[5] That means that the career you set out to create might not be the same one you end up with. You'll have to accept that and adapt if you want to be successful.

Given that, it's not much of a surprise that 38 percent of Millennials who are currently working are actively looking for a different role and 43 percent are "open to offers." Only 18 percent expect to stay with their current employer for the long term.[6] This is both a generational trend as well as a global economic one. Millennials don't want to settle for a job they aren't passionate about, and workers see both financial and career development opportunities by moving around.

Another way to look at this is that our generation is the first ever to have a lower quality of life than their parents did. How low? One study estimates that by the time we reach age sixty-five, our generation will be 25 percent less well off than our parents.[7] Despite our optimism, we're not actually going to be able to retire until age seventy-three.[8]

So what does all this mean? On the most basic level, it means that we're going to need to be better at adapting to change. When it comes to the workplace, there's no promise of a "greater tomorrow." The days of going to college, having a few good internships, graduating, and landing a nice job are long gone. These days being special isn't enough; neither are those trophies you got for just showing up. Companies are down-sized, merged, or can disappear more quickly than ever before as entire industries are now disrupted by new technologies no one had even thought of a few years—or months—before. And, as mentioned above, what you study in college may not have anything to do with what you do in your career so don't waste your time on regrets if, when looking back, you chose the "wrong" major.

It also means that our definition of "family" is going to change. Besides telling us how great we were (and still are), our parents tend to be very involved in our personal and professional lives. I'm sure you've seen stories (which, sadly, are true) about parents who call a college professor to complain about their child's grades, or about the 8 percent of college grads who actually bring their parents to job interviews.[9] Despite (or maybe because of) that intrusiveness, 37 percent of us say a parent is our mentor (compared with 28 percent who say it's a professor, 21 percent who say it's a friend, and 17 percent who say a current or former employer.[10])

Perhaps because we've relied so much on our parents, we tend to look at the workplace as a kind of second home. Eighty-eight percent of us want a fun, social work environment. Seventy-one percent want our coworkers to be a second family[11], with our manager as a kind of work "parent." It has also become much harder to separate what we do at work from our personal lives because technology has made it hard to tell where one ends and the other begins.

The problem here is that the workplace is not a place for parents—especially the biological kind. It's nice to have mentors and get advice from people you trust, but ultimately, it's about independence. If you get a job because it's something your parents think you should be doing, you'll be less happy, less engaged, and more likely to quit or get fired.

So, what do you do?

Be Who You Want to Be

Okay, now that you know what you're up against, let's talk about how to get you to where you want to be. You'll want to start with a personal mission statement that succinctly captures your values. Some mission statements are public facing—in other words, the companies make their mission statements public, usually in an attempt to show prospective customers how well their values and the company's values mesh. For example:

- Facebook: "To give people the power to share and make the world more open and connected."
- ConocoPhillips: "To use our pioneering spirit to responsibly deliver energy to the world."
- Nike: "To bring inspiration and innovation to every athlete in the world."

In your case, the mission statement you're going to create is for your use only. It's going to be all about what you represent and strive for. The goal is to clearly articulate your values so you can make sure your career aligns with them. Mine, for example, is "To support my generation with inspiration and career advice as they go from college to leadership positions."

So grab a piece of paper and write down a list of your values, the things you most care about in life. It's easy to come up with a quick list—truth, justice, and the American way—but I encourage you to spend some time on this. Here is a sample list of values you can use to help you get started: ambition, comfort, compassion, faith, family, health, influence, leadership, loyalty, mastery, openness, originality, pride, professionalism, reputation, resilience, responsibility, sincerity, spirituality, wealth[12].

The list you compile—and the mission statement you create—will help you decide which jobs to get, what companies to work for, or the company you end up starting yourself. Keep in mind that your values can change over time (things that may seem completely unimportant to you now might be incredibly important when you become a parent). But don't worry about that now. Start with what's important to you today because it'll give you a direction to go in.

Three Career Must-Haves: P, S, M

If you're buying something, there are three critical factors: Price, Quality, and Speed. You can have only two. For example, you can get great quality at a great price, but you can't get it quickly. Or you can have quick and cheap, but the quality will suck. Or you can have a great product quickly, but it'll cost you.

When it comes to thinking about a satisfying career, there are also three critical factors, but in this case you need all three to have a fulfilling career: Passion, Strengths, and Market. Having only two won't cut it. For example, if you're passionate about something, you'll work hard and turn that skill or knowledge of a subject into one of your strengths. But if employers don't care about that particular skill, you'll have a tough time finding a job that will put food on your table. If you're really good at something but you don't really like it, building your career around it will give you ulcers—even if you're making a lot of money.

Hopefully, your passion, strengths, and market will all come together, as they did for David Olivencia, director, IT Strategy & Planning at Verizon. "Throughout my youth and into my high school years I was pretty good at math. I also liked electronics, radios, music, computers, and video games. I looked at careers that utilized math, enabled these technologies, and did cool things with computers. It was about my sophomore year in high school that all of these came together for me and engineering shot to the top of the list as a career I wanted to pursue."

Of course, finding a career that satisfies all three conditions isn't easy. Remember the 38 percent of Millennials who are actively looking for a new job, and the 43 percent who are open to offers? Clearly something's missing there. Given how much time we spend at work, it's no wonder that not being excited about your job can take a real toll on your mental and physical health and your relationships. "When I first started out at J.P. Morgan, I was more concerned about the pay than what I was actually doing. After nine months, I dreaded each second to the point where I would be in tears," said Gerly Adrien, who's currently a business analyst/controls officer at JPMorgan Chase. "It was one day in April, when I said I couldn't take it anymore and told myself I was going to quit. Right then, I was offered a new opportunity doing what I love to do. Instead of focusing on the pay, I loved coming into work, even when I had to work weekends. It was all worth it because I was truly smiling. And I'm still smiling."

Pew Research did a survey recently and found that 30 percent of college students pick majors that may satisfy the passion and skills parts of the equation, but have very poor job prospects. These include social sciences (11 percent), education (6 percent), psychology (7 percent), and visual/performing arts (6 percent). By contrast, only 2.4 percent of students pick computer science, 5 percent go for engineering, and 1.4 percent for physical sciences—three career areas with particularly high demand. In fact, despite high unemployment in the U.S., there are nearly four million job openings in STEM fields (science, technology, engineering, mathematics) that are going unfilled (at least by Americans) because there aren't enough qualified applicants.

At this point you may be remembering your parents' advice to pursue your passions and forget about everything else. While there may be some truth to the old adage that "If you do what you love, the money will follow," the odds are against you. Don't get me wrong: I'm all for pursuing your passions. Unfortunately, the reality is that very few musicians and artists make enough money to support themselves, and those who *have* found success in the arts or other "soft" fields, have partnered with others who have strong business skills. So, if your passion is for philosophy, Greek literature, or papier-mâché, it's important that you pursue it with your eyes wide open and with a clear strategy in mind.

Uncovering Your Passion and Picking a Career

By the time I graduated from college, I had a pretty clear image in my mind of the kind of career I wanted to have. But I recognize that not everyone is so lucky. In fact, most of the young people I work with aren't completely sure what their passions are—even after they've graduated. While I can't pick a passion for you, I want to spend a few minutes talking about how you can identify your own. After that, we'll discuss some of the basic steps that will help you design a career that's right for you.

It all starts with being self-aware and jotting down what you enjoy doing and what you're good at. Keep in mind that while there may be some overlap, those two lists may not be the same. So I suggest that you create your "I'm good at" list first, then rank those activities in order of how much you like doing them. If you're stuck, the following questions may help get those introspective juices flowing:

- When have you been the most committed and passionate toward something in your life?
- What talents do you use the most and what are your strengths?
- Which jobs did you like and dislike in the past?
- What aspect of those jobs did you like the most and least?

This is exactly the kind of list that Danny Groner, manager of blogger partnerships and outreach for Shutterstock.com, put together. "I decided very early on that I wanted to do something that required good writing, reading, and analytical skills," he told me. "I was drawn to all of the new forms of communication and the ease with which you could access information. At the time, I had no idea what kind of doors that would open up by way of a career. But I knew that if I stuck to what I was good at, and passionate about, I'd find my way." And he certainly did.

After you get your list together, get some feedback from people close to you, including parents, friends, neighbors, coworkers, and teachers. Ask them to give you their take on what you're good at and what you enjoy. That outside perspective can be incredibly valuable. For example, if several people tell you that every time they see you doing a-b-c, you're smiling and work efficiently, but that every time they see you doing x-y-z, you look miserable and drag your feet, you'll be a few giant steps closer to figuring out what your passions are (and aren't).

These same people may also be able to help you filter through what can sometimes seem to be an overwhelming number of possibilities. "I was interested in thinking about scientific problems through a business lens, but wasn't sure what the range of opportunities could look like for me," said Heather Bowerman, management consultant at McKinsey & Company. "Talking to people—professors, graduate students, family, and friends—unlocked a whole world of ideas. For example, I realized I could work on the commercialization cycle of pharmaceuticals, do business development at a biotech company, or become a market analyst for a scientific company."

If you're still not quite able to articulate your passion(s), don't worry. Try one or more of these popular assessment tools.

- **Strength Finder** helps you discover your top five strengths and learn how you can use them to excel and perform at a higher level. gallupstrengthscenter.com/purchase

- **StandOut** will tell you how to make the most of your natural-born strengths with the goal of helping you become a high performer and develop a unique leadership style that's best for you. tmbc.com/store/standout_assessment

- **MBTI (Myers-Briggs Type Indicator)** is one of the most famous career assessments in existence and does an excellent job of identifying your personality type so you can connect it to the right career/profession. It can also help you better relate to others and become more self-aware. mbticomplete.com/contents/learnmore.aspx

- **Career Key** helps you to identify careers and even college majors that match your set of interests, traits, skills, and abilities. careerkey.org/your-personality/take-career-test-career-assessment.html

- **Career Path "Job Discovery Wizard"** by CareerBuilder helps you identify the right jobs to take based on your skills, attitudes, and preferences. careerpath.com/career-tests/skills-assessment/

Hopefully, at this point you'll have identified at least one passion candidate. If not, no need to panic—there's still one more great approach, which might be the best ways to figure out what your passions are: Trial and error. Sometimes, you'll need a lot of it. I had eight internships in college, each in a different discipline of marketing and sales, including Internet marketing, PR, advertising and market research. Having such a wide variety of experiences helped me hone in on what I really wanted to do, so I started a consulting company where I created Web sites for small businesses. I ended up focusing on Internet marketing at large companies because I was best at it and enjoyed it the most, plus I saw that more companies were paying attention to online media and Web sites, so there was an increasing opportunity/market that I could enter.

I thought I'd had a lot of internships in college—and I did—but Eddy Ricci Jr., Regional Director, Training & Development, at Northwestern Mutual edged me out. "I did nine internships," he said. "They ranged from writing fantasy football articles to investment banking. . . . I thought it was more important to have an idea of the attributes of the career I wanted versus title or set path. How many people say they want to be a "doctor or lawyer" but then the qualities of the job don't match the career and lifestyle they hoped for? I knew I wanted to do something that helped people, was challenging, had great income potential, was fun, and allowed me to have ownership and autonomy over the tasks at hand as well as my outside life."

A lot of young people worry that by trying a lot of different things, they'll have wasted a lot of time on the bad options. I couldn't disagree more. Learning what you don't want to do is a lesson that's at least as valuable as learning what you *do* want to do. You'll also pick up many new skills, experiences, and connections as you move around using this try-a-lot-of-things approach. Plus, you'll have had a chance to see what a job is actually like before you make a commitment.

Connecting Your Passion to Opportunities

Once you *have* identified a passion, you'll want to learn something about the kinds of jobs that are available in that field and what's required to get one of them. "I studied bioengineering, so my background was a mile wide and an inch deep across several disciplines: engineering, medicine, technology, biology, chemistry, materials, etc.," said McKinsey's Heather Bowerman. "It was my job to focus that on something I cared about, and carve out a niche."

In later chapters, we'll talk about specific ways you can build your skills to stand out and move up in your company, but right now, the 10,000-foot overview is enough. In order to match your passions and strengths with the right job, you need to know what skills are in high demand and the available jobs that require those skills. This way you can see if you are qualified for positions or if you need to acquire new skills to become a stronger candidate. A good place to start is Skills Profiler (careerinfonet.org/Skills/), which takes your list of your skills and matches them to jobs that require those skills. After that, career infonet.org/Occupations will give you occupation profiles such as a "Budget Analyst" and then break them down by state, number of open jobs, and the knowledge, skills, and abilities you'll need for each job. It will also show you the typical tasks you'll be doing, the software programs you'll need to know, and the level of education required.

Reading about a job—even on excellent Web sites like the ones I just mentioned—is very different from actually seeing a real, live person actually *doing* that job. And the best way to do that is to find someone who works in the field you're considering and shadow him or her. If you already know the right person, great. Call or e-mail and ask for an informational interview. If you don't know the right person, put the word out to your network of friends and family. Chances are that someone knows someone who knows someone you could talk to. It's important to remember that your goal here is *not* to get a job—it's to find out what it's like to do that job so you can make a relatively informed decision about whether it's something you'd like to do.

Another time-honored way of testing the waters before you plunge headlong into a career is to become an apprentice, learning under someone else who's been there and done that and is willing to help you follow in their footsteps. The word "apprentice" conjures up images of medieval craftsmen (or, if you've seen Disney's *The Sorcerer's Apprentice,* of Mickey Mouse schlepping buckets of water). While apprenticeships have a long history, they are anything but outdated. For example, back in 2008, marketing guru Seth Godin, created a one-time-only, six-month "Alternative MBA Program" to demonstrate that people can learn everything they need to know under a mentor (him). The program included an hour-long class, four hours of projects, three hours working on a personal project, and five hours living and connecting—every day.

And Peter Thiel, best known for cofounding PayPal, created the Thiel Fellowship where ambitious young people compete to bring their world-changing ideas to life. If they win the competition, they're granted $100,000 to skip college and focus on their work, research, and self-education. They're also mentored by extremely successful entrepreneurs and end up getting the experience they couldn't even have dreamed of from a traditional university.

If you're lucky, you or someone in your network will know the perfect person to apprentice for. If you're like most of us, you'll have to do a little digging. There are a number of excellent options.

Go to industry conferences and try to hit up some of the speakers. If they can't help you, they may know someone who can. You might not think that anyone would even talk to you, but most people are quite flattered at being asked to mentor someone who's really interested.

Go to PivotPlanet.com or LivePerson.com and search for advisors in your desired profession, such as "Sales Account Executive" or "Insurance Broker." You can pay an advisor by the hour to learn about them, their field, and how you can go about breaking in.

Another approach is to volunteer at a nonprofit where you can learn more about jobs that interest you while making a positive impact on your community. You won't get paid, but you'll have a chance to try out numerous job functions, make industry contacts that can help you as you build your career, and develop some valuable skills. For Verizon's David Olivencia, volunteering has been incredibly valuable, personally as well as professionally. "I have taken on leadership roles in several nonprofits: National Society of Hispanic MBAs, HITEC (Hispanic IT Executive Council), and CHLI (Congressional Hispanic Leadership Institute)," he told me. "Each has not only helped me give back to make the world a better place but they have also helped grow my leadership."

I know you're trying to launch a career here and you want to start bringing in some money, but don't get hung up on the lack of pay. Eighty percent of executives would be more likely to hire a graduate with skilled volunteer experience than one without—but fewer than 50 percent of college seniors have thought about volunteering to increase their marketability.[13] More specifically, PepsiCo, HP, and Morgan Stanley (to name just a few) have programs that train emerging leaders using international volunteering. PepsiCo, for example, has the PepsiCorps program, which is a one-month assignment for employees to use their skills and expertise to solve global problems such as water scarcity and access to affordable nutrition, while at the same time allowing them to develop leadership skills. Today, more than twenty-four major companies send more than 1,700 volunteers abroad to tackle similar issues[14].

Now you may find yourself in a situation where you've got a pretty good idea what direction you want to head, but you're not completely sure what you want to do for your career. In this case don't wait for the perfect job to come along. Go on and throw yourself into a job situation and, chances are, you'll learn a lot. Let me give you an example of what I mean. Shradha Agarwal was studying at Northwestern University and she and her friends didn't know what to do for their careers. So they created a student peer group called "The Institute for Business Education" to help them figure that out. The group was divided into five different types of paths that they wanted to explore: recruiting, investing, entrepreneurship, marketing, and consulting. As one of their first entrepreneurial projects was to launch a new business magazine called *Northwestern Business Review,* a magazine that highlighted how businesses can be agents for positive change. They were able to sell advertising to big companies like Target and Goldman Sachs, which wanted to target business-minded students from a leading school like Northwestern—especially since the magazine launched with 10,000 subscribers.[15] By creating and taking on projects, they were able to see for themselves what the right path was for them—with a focus on work that was meaningful to them individually. The design editor of the magazine ended up running her own startup in the music industry, while others went to work at banks, consulting firms, and companies like Target. These projects helped them develop a sense of ownership and they've taken that into every experience they've had in the real world. The organization still exists at Northwestern (both the magazine, which is now distributed biannually to sixty college campuses and student organizations), and many high school students choose Northwestern over other colleges because of it. Shradha chose the entrepreneur path as the chief strategy officer and cofounder of Context Media, a company that operates a suite of digital healthcare networks that deliver condition-specific programming at point-of-care hospitals nationally.

The idea here is to create something out of nothing and use it to gain the kind of experience that will help you decide on a career path moving forward. The good news is that you don't need to be an A student to do this or have a wealthy parent; anyone can create projects out of thin air if they want to.

The Culture Club

One of the most important—and most overlooked—elements of your search for your perfect job is the culture of the organization. It's absolutely essential that you get a sense of the people you'll be working with *before* you take a job. That's why some of the other strategies we've discussed, such as shadowing or informational interviews, are so important. You need to find out what a typical day is like for someone in the job you're considering, what their responsibilities and challenges are, what their benefits are, how flexible they are, maybe even what the dress code is. Taking a job where your prospective coworkers are too laid back or too straight-laced for you is a recipe for failure. Even the simplest things can make a big difference. For example, if social media is important to you but the company you're considering blocks it, that's a big red flag.

Keep in mind that culture is a two-way street. At the same time as you're evaluating a company's culture, they're evaluating you to see how well you'd fit in. Half of employers say that the biggest predictor of whether a Millennial will stay at their company is a good cultural fit. The top reasons why Millennials leave their companies are because they received a better offer from another company (30 percent), their career goals aren't aligned to their company (27 percent) and a lack of career opportunities (13 percent).[16]

Understanding the Job Market

Okay, that gets you through the Passion and Strengths parts of the equation. Now you need to figure out whether anyone will actually pay you to do what you're good at and love doing. And no, I'm not suggesting that you sell yourself out. I'm suggesting that you be strategic in the way you pick your career.

Identify the market need by doing research online on Indeed.com to see how many positions are open in your profession and industry. Check out lists of the top jobs from *U.S. News*—money.usnews.com /careers/best-jobs/rankings to see which ones are the most in demand, pay good salaries, and provide job satisfaction. For the business jobs in 2013, the top job was "Market Research Analyst" and then "Financial Adviser" and "Accountant." LinkedIn found that out of 259 million profiles, the most in-demand skills were social media marketing, mobile development, cloud and distributed computing, pearl/python/ruby, and statistical analysis, and data mining[17]. This type of information can show you what the market demand is for skills that you can obtain through training, whether formally or self-taught.

Everyone Needs an Entrepreneurial Spirit

Entrepreneurs are known for taking risks, failing, and adapting to change. And whether you decide to start your own company or you'd feel more comfortable in a large organization, you'll need to think like an entrepreneur. Here's what I mean:

Risk taking is (or should be) an essential part of any career move—even if it's your first job. Obviously, if you're starting your own company, you're taking a risk, and so is anyone who's investing in you and your ideas. Even though we tend to think of taking a corporate job as low risk (when compared to being an entrepreneur or a freelancer/consultant), that isn't always the case. Let's say that you've identified a prospective employer that you really want to work for. But they don't have an opening for the position you'd like. There is, however, an opening in the mailroom. Do you take the job in the hope that you'll be able to prove yourself and eventually move into your ideal job? Possibly a risky move. But that's the kind of thing that has paid off for a lot of ambitious young people, including Bianca Buckridee, vice president, Social Media Operations, at Chase.

"I was waitressing my last couple of years in college at a hotel/restaurant and the general manager asked if I'd be interested in taking on a role to help out as an executive assistant," she told me. "Scheduling and providing great service was easy for me but I also recognized that this was a great opportunity to build an office management program from scratch. I started creating structure to help make the managers lives easier without asking the GM, and luckily it turned out well. While the initial criteria was to get a job to pay the bills, I didn't look down on myself for not getting a role right out of college that matched what I'd studied."

What happens if your attempt to parlay a less-then-ideal job into an ideal one fails? You'd better think about that before you take any job. Failures happen. A lot. But if you've thought through the likely (and unlikely) scenarios and developed good contingency plans, you'll recover from your failures (which I believe are actually just learning experiences in disguise) a lot more quickly than someone who had no plan b, c, or d.

Of course, it's not possible to plan for every possibility, so you need to be flexible enough to deal with the completely unexpected. For example, while you might have a contingency plan that would cover you if you got laid off, what if you wake up one morning and that skill you've become such an expert in has suddenly become irrelevant? What if one day you just decide that you've totally lost your passion? What if your business partner raids your bank account to the tune of $1.5 million and bolts? Or what if someone in your family gets incredibly sick? You're going to have to quickly retool if you want to keep eating.

That's exactly what happened to Ann Miletti, a mutual fund manager for Wells Fargo. "I graduated college with a teaching degree—a path that I thought about from the time I was young," she told me. "What I couldn't foresee is that my first child was born with a serious heart defect, which put my career on hold, as I focused on his health. My husband and I had tough decisions about what to do for our future, given the fact that we had a son that needed an extra amount of care, and the fact that we were left with a tremendous amount of debt, which we obviously didn't plan for. So we did what we had to do and I readjusted from there. I took a job at Strong Funds (a mutual fund company that Wells Fargo acquired) working the midnight-to-eight shift, so I could be with my son during the day. I needed to reeducate myself and also had to acquire a few securities licenses to keep that job, and from there I created a new path."

Sudden changes—although they're not usually quite as extreme as these examples—happen all the time. So often, in fact, that the ability to adapt to change is a trait a lot of managers look for in young employees. And just so you know, flexibility isn't just for young people. The Bureau of Labor Statistics recently reported that the average person changes careers (not just jobs) three to five times during their lifetime.

Before you start sending out resumes, there's one more important step that most people forget about. You need to figure out whether you want to work for a company (as an employee), for yourself (as an entrepreneur), or somewhere in between (do freelance or consulting work). This isn't a decision to make lightly—and it's not a decision you're stuck with forever. Plenty of people move from one role to another. But right now, when you're trying to design a career that best leverages your passions, strengths, and marketability, it's a good idea to know where you're starting from.

As an employee, you're working for someone else. The smaller the company, the broader your job description will be. In other words, at a small company, you'll probably have a chance to do more things than you would at a large company. That could be a good thing, especially if you're still not 100 percent sure of what you want to be doing long term. On the other hand, people who work at smaller companies typically work longer hours than those at big companies. If you're working for a startup—unless it's a very well-funded one—you'll typically put in the most hours for the least pay. But if the company hits big, you may make up for all that in valuable stock options.

As a freelancer, you're exchanging your skills for money—just as you would be doing as an employee. The difference is that you get to pick how many clients you'll take on (as an employee, you only have one), and you can fire your clients any time you want. You also get to decide how you get paid: by the hour, by the project, or on a regular retainer. Another advantage to freelancing or consulting is that your clients will be hiring you based solely on what you can deliver, instead of your age or education—factors that can sometimes limit upward mobility within companies. Plus, in many areas, you can work from anywhere.

As an entrepreneur, your business is generally self-funded or backed by angel investors or venture capitalists. Unless you're able to hire people to run the company, you're in the hot seat, leading and managing the company, finding and landing customers, and responsible for the success or failure of the venture. More students are becoming entrepreneurs while they're still in college, and when they graduate, they see the entrepreneurial path as a viable alternative to a traditional job.

The path you take—whether it's as an employee, a freelancer/consultant, or an entrepreneur—depends on a number of factors. For example, what kind of lifestyle do you want? If you want to work from home and have the flexibility to travel regularly, freelancing and/or consulting is your best bet. If you'd rather have an office to go to and you want a clearer separation between your work and personal lives—including having some actual free time—you might be happier working for a big company as an employee.

Think about how many hours you're willing to work and how much control you want over your work. If you want a straight nine-to-five, working on projects that someone else assigns, you'll be happier as an employee. But if you want to develop your own ideas and you're willing to work 24-7, you may have what it takes to be an entrepreneur.

Think about how you work with other people and your risk tolerance. If you love collaborating, you're a good team player, and you want to wake up every morning knowing you've got a job, the employee route may be best for you. If you want to run the show and you're willing to risk everything you've got to develop your ideas, you may want to be an entrepreneur. And if you prefer to work on your own, set your own hours, and you're willing to beat the bushes to find clients, consulting could be best for you. Niels Ganser started freelancing as a systems administrator while he was doing the same thing for his employer in Sydney, Australia. He started off charging twenty-eight dollars per hour and after eighteen months of balancing both jobs, he was doing so well that he was able quit his corporate job to work for himself. Niels now commands up to $100 per hour and he's got more work than he can handle. His favorite thing about working for himself versus a corporation? "Determining your quality of life and how much you enjoy your job far outweighs the lack of vacation time or traditional benefits," he told me.

Connecting Your Career Path to Your Skills

This chapter was designed to set you on a career path that leverages your skills and your passions. In future chapters, we'll talk more about honing, refining, and expanding your skill sets so you can advance in whatever path you've chosen.

One final thought. Don't leave your career to chance—it's up to you to get yourself hired and to promote yourself. And while it's always a good idea to get input from people you trust, the ultimate decision needs to be yours. Doing something that you're good at but don't feel passionately isn't sustainable over the long haul. Neither is doing something you feel passionate about but doesn't bring in enough to put food on the table. So plot your own path. You'll be glad you did.

3

Hard Skills: Be More Than Your Job Description

In today's knowledge-based economy, what you earn depends on what you learn.

—BILL CLINTON

Stay Current to Stay Employable

As we've discussed, one thing that's certain in any organization is that change is constant—companies get sold, management teams get fired, job functions get outsourced or automated, and any number of other things could happen that are equally unexpected and beyond your control. People who adapt, survive; people who don't, don't. If you don't do everything you can to keep up with the way the world is changing, you'll soon find yourself irrelevant—and out of a job. Remember Blockbuster? They had a huge market share of the video rental business, but they didn't keep up with the growing demand to have videos delivered right to your house. But Netflix did, and they snapped up most of Blockbuster's market share. Now Netflix has to compete with the nearly endless supply of free media streamed by companies like Hulu and YouTube. Charles Darwin captured this idea perfectly when he said, "It is not the strongest of species that survives, nor the most intelligent, but the one most responsive to change."

Makes sense, doesn't it? A graphic designer trained in HTML, Flash, and the 2002 version of Adobe Photoshop and Illustrator—but who hasn't kept up with innovations—won't be nearly as valuable as someone right out of school who has mastered the latest and greatest design software. And it's always cheaper to hire a young person who has current skills than to keep an older person whose skills aren't as up to date. Something to keep in mind, since at some point you're going to be one of those older workers and your job may be threatened by someone who's still in diapers today but who, in a few years, will be the master of skills that haven't even been invented yet.

Ultimately, you're the one who decides which skills to master and how you spend your time; the more time you invest in learning skills that are in high demand, the more valuable you become. When you master the right hard skills that relate to your profession and industry, people will notice your talents and ask you to work on projects with them. You'll become the go-to employee. But none of that is going to happen unless you're persistent in letting people know what it is you can do and where you can make the biggest contribution to your company (this is so important that I've devoted an entire chapter to self-promotion). All that added attention will earn you more respect from the people you work with, and more confidence—along with even more visibility and important projects—from the people you work for.

The American Society for Training and Development (ASTD) estimates that by 2015, 60 percent of new jobs will require skills that only 20 percent of the population currently has. So how do you know which skills you'll need in the future? Hard to say exactly, but there are some current trends that will give you some basic direction:

THE SKILLS GAP. Despite some of the highest unemployment rates in fifty years, there are currently three million job openings in this country.[1] In fact, a recent survey by the ManpowerGroup found that 52 percent of U.S. companies have trouble filling jobs. The most difficult jobs to fill? College-level positions in engineering, accounting and finance, and IT. According to Manpower, the biggest problem is that too many applicants lack the hard skills they need to do the job. Clearly we need more college grads in this country, but the Georgetown Center on Education and the Workforce projects that demand for college-educated workers will outpace supply in the U.S. by over 300,000 per year. So who's going to fill those jobs? Workers in India, Pakistan, Eastern Europe, and Asia, where engineers are valued as much as doctors and where young people are flocking to acquire the skills needed to work in the new economy. To give you a sense of how important engineers are these days, in September 2009, when unemployment was nearly 10 percent—its highest level in decades—the rate for engineers was 6.4 percent.[2] And as I write this, the nationwide unemployment rate is over 7 percent—but for engineers, it's under 2 percent.[3]

GLOBALIZATION. Remember the 300,000-jobs-per-year gap I mentioned just a second ago—all those jobs that are going overseas. The news only gets worse. According to Knight Frank Research, and Citi Private Bank's Wealth Report, by 2050, India will bump China out of the number one spot on the list of the world's biggest economies. By then, the U.S. will have been out of first place for thirty years.

AUTOMATION. All around the world and in every industry, machines are doing jobs that used to be done by people. Just think of the self-checkout lines at stores where you scan your own items, run your own credit card, and bag your stuff. That used to be someone's job, and this gets us to one of the main points of this chapter: It's not enough to simply adapt to change. You need to find a way to become invaluable, a way to ensure that you're doing things that can't be automated. That means keeping up with trends and everything else that could affect the job you're in and the one you'd like to be in. It means making yourself an expert today but always learning new skills that will make you an expert tomorrow. In some cases, you might have to change jobs—it's hard to predict which of today's seemingly essential skills will be completely unnecessary tomorrow.

AVERAGE IS OVER. Here's a great quote from *New York Times* columnist Thomas Friedman: "In the past, workers with average skills, doing an average job, could earn an average lifestyle. But, today, average is officially over. Being average just won't earn you what it used to. It can't when so many more employers have so much more access to so much more above average cheap foreign labor, cheap robotics, cheap software, cheap automation and cheap genius." Being average won't get you noticed. It doesn't matter what field you're in. As I said above, you need to find a way to make a unique contribution, add value, and stand out. That's the only way to survive.

The days of working at a company for twenty years with no worries about job security and retiring with a nice pension are long gone. And so is loyalty to one's employer. Today, the trend is toward collaborative environments and hiring people who can work independently.

The message here is pretty simple: The skills you have right now might not be relevant tomorrow. So you'd better get trained for the skills you need while enhancing the ones you already have. Justin Orkin, a sales executive at AOL's Advertising.com, put it beautifully: "I read a lot of blogs, have weekly meetings with our team," he says. "I'm also a council member of the advertising board. You have to do lots of reading and listening to stay fresh and current. The past is great, but everyone wants to know about the future. The future is today."

So are you up for the task? I know that this may sound a little daunting, but the truth is that if you're willing to put in the work, you will be able to find a job in the new economy. And you will be able to keep that job from being outsourced. Of course, whether you decide to do this or not is up to you, but I can guarantee you that it's far better to be seen as someone who is actively contributing and managing their career than someone who is just sitting back and praying for something to happen. By acquiring all the necessary skills and using them to make meaningful contributions, you can't help but get ahead in your career. Management won't promote you until you promote yourself first—by acquiring the right skills and marketing them. You need to give them a reason to pay attention to you. And you'll do that by making yourself so good that they can't avoid you. Remember, the people higher up in the org chart than you are looking for all-stars like you, people whose skills can help push the company forward (and advance the manager's career in the process).

The Indispensable Employee: Hard Skills

Hard skills are the practical, technical skills you need to fulfill your job description; they're about getting the job done. Without them, you'd never be able to get an interview, let alone an actual job. Hard skills are measurable—how many lines of code can you write in a week? How good are you at Excel? How fast can you type? And you'll be able to use them in a variety of positions and companies. For example, if you're in accounting, generally accepted accounting principles (GAAP) will apply whether you're in a bank or a bakery. Because hard skills are easy to quantify, it's often possible to earn certificates and awards for acquiring them.

Here's a quick list of hard skills, quite a few of which are technology-related, but as technology changes, so will the hard skills required. A lot of the skills that are absolutely essential to running today's businesses (coding, Web site design, and social media just to name a few) didn't exist ten years ago. And ten years from now, there will be a huge demand for people with skills no one has ever heard of today. I partnered with oDesk.com on a study that found that 94 percent of freelancers believe that learning new skills throughout your career is either very or extremely important. As we go through this chapter, be aware that learning hard skills isn't something you do only once. Keeping your skills current is an ongoing process.

- Project management
- Financial management
- Budgeting
- Contract negotiating
- Sales forecasting
- Engineering (mechanical or software)
- Using office software
- Proficiency in a second language
- Web design
- Business writing

So how important are hard skills? Let me give you a few numbers. My company surveyed 1,000 managers and 1,000 young workers about hard skills. Here's what we found:

- Sixty-five percent of managers and 61 percent of young workers said that having technical ability is a "very important" or "the most important" factor when considering employees for management roles.

- Eighty percent of managers and 79 percent of young workers said that having strategic thinking and analytical skills is a "very important" or "the most important" factor when considering employees for management roles.

Besides helping you get and keep jobs, hard skills also allow you to move within your organization. Say you're an administrative assistant at a large company. You hate what you're doing but you need the paycheck and the benefits. There's a job open in IT, and you're thinking of applying—even though you have no formal training. I can pretty much guarantee that you won't get the job unless you can demonstrate some significant hard skills in IT. But if you *do* have those hard skills, well, that's a completely different story.

Oana Kelsay, who's a Global Logistics Planner at Johnson & Johnson, was able to leverage her hard skills—which she'd developed on her own—to move quickly out of her entry-level job. As a college student, she took a job at Johnson & Johnson in their Customer Service department as a way to pay for her education. She says, "I was quite the techie from high school on, so when I joined J&J I quickly became known as the unofficial IT, and my fellow CS reps would call on me to help them solve their problems. Thankfully, I had a great manager who understood my skill set, and when the Customer Service department launched SAP to replace its old AS400, she quickly had me trained on the new system so I could become an SAP power user, assist in solving issues, test the new system, and train my colleagues. I ended up moving to the department I'm currently in, Strategic Planning."

And none of that would have happened if Oana hadn't developed hard skills outside and in addition to her basic responsibilities.

Identifying the Skills You Need— Especially if You're Eying a New Position

If you're going to do your current job well, you have to know which hard skills are required. And if you're thinking about making a lateral—or upward—move within your company, you'll need to find out the hard skills your *new* job requires. There are a few ways to do this.

The most logical place to start is by reading the job description, since most job descriptions include a list of required skills. But because job descriptions don't always prioritize required skills in a useful way, you should also talk to your manager and drop in to visit the friendly folks in HR. Ask them what skills you'd need to have to do the job you've got your eye on. If you'll need more than one skill, which one should you start with? And how can you go about learning those skills—does the company have in-hours training? Will they pay for you to take classes elsewhere, or are you on your own?

It's also a good idea to talk with people who are doing the job you want to do. HR or managers may give you a list of officially required skills, but someone who's in the trenches every day will have a much better idea of what's *really* needed to succeed, and the two lists may or may not overlap. Paul Di Maria, a senior manager at a leading market research firm, does a fantastic job of learning by listening. "I ask around for best demonstrated practices when I feel like my work is getting stale," Paul says. "I also latch on to any opportunity where I get to listen to people that are tops in my field. That interaction is precious. I hope to know a quarter of what they do, and they never stop learning and developing themselves."

All that face-to-face talking sounds a little old-school. So don't forget about online resources. LinkedIn has become a media company and is now, in a sense, an extension of the face-to-face conversation: LinkedIn captures the most shared content in their system—these are the topics that people feel are the most important—and organizes it by category on linkedin.com/today. Depending on your interests, you can customize the type of content and news you see. LinkedIn also has a service called "Thought Leaders" that features exclusive blogs from big-name people like Richard Branson. It's a great opportunity to learn from the best.

If you're interested in a particular job, Onetoline.org will tell you the exact skills you'll need to be successful. It's a great resource whether you're hoping to move up in your department or are planning to change fields entirely. You'll get a clear picture of what life is like for people currently in that position, including what they do over the course of any workday, and classes you'll need to take to stay current. For example, if you're interested in being a financial analyst, you'll need to be able to evaluate the quality of securities, be proficient in financial analysis and spreadsheet software, and have a good working knowledge of finance and accounting. You'll also be able to find out the education requirements, median salary, and even the number of current and projected openings.

A Brief Pause . . .

Once you know the skills you need, there's an important step that you have to do before you can get out there and start acquiring them. What I'm talking about is doing an honest assessment of your strengths and weaknesses, what you're best at and what you might need to improve. The goal is to home in on the hard skills you can develop that will help you become the subject matter expert you want to be—the go-to person on a particular topic, the one people come to whenever they've got questions, whether it's because you're a Microsoft Excel power user, you're a whiz at creating smartphone apps, or you're the only one in your office who knows the obscure Indian dialect that is the only language your supplier speaks. The more people seek you out, the more in-demand your skills, the more valuable you'll be to your company.

Strengths or Weaknesses?

Whenever I talk about strengths and weaknesses, I always get the same question: Is it better to focus on developing strengths or overcoming weaknesses?

Unfortunately, there's no absolute right or wrong answer; you need to do what you feel most comfortable doing. Some people find it more effective to develop their strengths. Some, like Lisa Stewart, Assistant Vice President, e-Exchange, at State Street—a Fortune 500 financial services company—find it better to work on overcoming weaknesses. "I focus more on finding my weaknesses so I can improve them before someone else finds them. I don't want to give management any reasons to want to replace me." And still others put an equal emphasis on both. "I need to know and exercise my strengths to ensure that I won't lose them," says J&J's Oana Kelsay. "I need to acknowledge and work on my weaknesses so that I can quickly turn them into strengths. I have this obsessive need to be the best at everything, and I know I can't do that unless I know both my strengths and weaknesses."

While the choice is yours, I recommend that you develop your strengths. When you focus on developing your strengths, you'll see results sooner than if you had spent the same amount of time on overcoming your weaknesses. That will give you more confidence. Plus, it's generally more fun to do and learn about things you're already good at. And when you're enjoying yourself, you're likely to want to keep learning and developing your skills even more. There are exceptions though. For instance, if you know you've got a weakness that could potentially hurt or limit your career (in terms of hard skills, that might be something like wanting to become a financial analyst without knowing anything about statistics), your first priority should be to resolve that weakness. What I want you to do here is identify your hard skills. Not all of them, of course, just the ones that could affect your performance, give you an advantage, make you stand out on the job, or that could affect your ability to get a job in the first place.

So, ask yourself the following questions and come up with a list of your top five to ten strengths:

- What am I the best at?
- What do others say I'm good at? (In a lot of ways, this is more important than what you think of yourself.)
- What does my job require me to be good at?
- What matters at the job and do I have the right skills to excel?
- What skills do I need to have to get me my next promotion or raise—whether it's where I'm working now or somewhere else?
- What else do I need to know to get to the next level in a career here or at any other company?
- Am I playing to my strengths in team settings and making my team more successful?
- Do my coworkers and managers know what my strengths are and do they see them as contributing to the team's success?
- Are my strengths being underutilized? If so, why, and what can I do about it?

Got a pretty good handle on your strengths? Great! Now let's take a quick look at areas where you could improve. Yes, I know I've been saying to focus on your strengths, but we all have weaknesses, and ignoring them could undermine your performance and limit your career mobility. Ask yourself these questions and put together a list of five to ten weaknesses (the ones you want to focus on are the ones that could—or do—affect your current or future job):

- What could I improve on? What do I think I should be better at?
- Are my weaknesses preventing me from doing my job correctly or from excelling on the job?

- Has my manager given me feedback about my weaknesses?
- Which weaknesses do I need to focus on in order to improve at work?

If you're having trouble with compiling lists of strengths and weaknesses, don't be shy about asking the people you work with to help you. Consider it a kind of informal peer review. Two important caveats: Ask for feedback only from people you trust. Second, don't do this too often. This may sound a bit silly, but a lot of employers I work with complain that too many of their young workers are constantly asking, "How'm I doing?" If you're constantly trying to get people to tell you what they think, you run the risk of being perceived as someone who can't work independently, who needs too much hand-holding, and who's not leadership material.

Instead of indiscriminately hounding your manager or your coworkers for feedback on your performance, try to find the proper time. For instance, if your manager brings up a certain skill of yours that you aren't confident about, ask how you can improve it. Similarly, if you've used Excel to put together a financial projection but a colleague comments that your numbers are off, that's the perfect time to ask for some guidance on what you can do to improve your Excel skills.

Another creative way to get feedback is to have a weekly conversation/meeting with your manager to review your progress. Tell him what you're working on and be honest with what you're having trouble with. People usually like being asked for help—as long as you don't go overboard.

Well, that's how things would be in an ideal world. In reality in most cases, unless it's an official performance review, most people won't come right out and tell you about your weaknesses (your strengths, maybe) even if you ask. It seems too rude. So you may have to play sociologist. If you pay close attention to the way people respond to what you say and do, you'll get a lot of nonverbal feedback—facial expressions, body language, tone of voice. (Since reading people is a soft skill, we'll tackle it in the next chapter.)

And while you're talking to people, if you know you've got some skills that they aren't aware of, speak up! For example, John Gerzema, Executive Chairman of BrandAsset Consulting, who oversees strategy for Young & Rubicam Companies, told me a great story about an employee who took the initiative to let John know about some skills that were being underutilized. "Recently I had a young and promising analyst approach me about training. As the company I run specializes in brand strategy steeped in analytics, I assumed that he wanted more mentoring in quant and data. But as we sat down, he explained to me that in his off-hours he's a photographer and documentary filmmaker, and he felt that this side of him wasn't being used in the company. 'We're a branding company after all, so why wouldn't we want to access these skills?' he told me. Moreover, by working all day crunching numbers, he felt his creative side was beginning to atrophy." Impressed by this young analyst's passion, John did two things. First, he transferred the employee to Chicago (where the company's film, photography, and graphic design offices are) so he could be closer to a creative community. Second, John restructured his job so he was using his filmmaking and photography skills. "But the main thing I took away from all this," John added, "is that Millennials aren't defined by their jobs. Their jobs are merely one part of a bigger mosaic. In Hollywood, the more hyphens you have, the more power. Someone who's an Actor-Writer-Director-Producer, for instance, is going to get more walks down the red carpet than someone who wears only one hat. And that's what my analyst was telling me: 'There are more sides to me than you understand or can empathize with. And if you don't see them, you might not be seeing me for long.'"

What a powerful example of the need to make absolutely sure that your managers and coworkers know about your skills.

Acquiring Hard Skills

As I mentioned earlier, the goal of developing hard skills is to become a subject matter expert and proficient at specific functions that relate to your job. The best way to identify the skill or skills to focus on first is to sit down with your manager and ask which are important for your profession and which you'll need to have if you want to move up. (If you want to dig a little deeper, ask the same questions of an industry mentor or a colleague with more experience than you.) Make sure your manager helps you list them in order of importance. Then, select the skills that you want to develop and become an expert at. Ideally, you'll start with one or two that in some way play to your strengths, the ones that will allow you to distinguish yourself relative to others in your company and your industry. When you're doing something you're already pretty good at, it's natural to want to spend more time doing it. As a result, you'll get better even faster. If the top skills on your list don't play to your strengths, go down the list until you reach one that does. This doesn't mean that you should ignore all the skills that don't utilize your strengths. Not at all. I'm just saying that it's a lot easier to become an expert at one thing at a time. That said, there is often overlap between skills, so working on more than one at a time—as long as they complement each other—is fine. Ultimately, anything you do and any skill you develop will help you get ahead faster. It's just a question of getting the most bang for your buck. If you try to do too much you'll spread yourself too thin and might get distracted and not get anywhere.

There are many different ways to acquire hard skills, but for the most part they all fall into one of two broad categories: skills you learn through your company and skills you learn on your own. Let's look at each of these in detail.

Company-Sponsored Education

Smart companies have learned that in order to attract and retain young people, they have to provide opportunities for advancement. Otherwise, young workers are going to move on to an employer that values them more. Many large companies offer in-house courses—sometimes with instructors in the room, sometimes via webinar or some other technology. Sonie Guseh, an Account Manager at Google, takes advantage of every learning opportunity the company offers. "Workshops, webinars, and conferences are some of my favorite ways to continue to be knowledgeable about new innovations, creative best practices, and develop new skills that are relevant for current and future roles," says Sonie. "Some of my favorites have been on developing leadership skills and on understanding the ever-changing face of media consumption."

Other companies offer online training courses that can be taken onsite or remotely. Some employers will pay for you to take courses someplace else, say at a local college or an online university. And just about all companies will pay for you to attend professional conferences or specialized events as long as you're going to learn something that will benefit them. But you'll never know any of this unless you ask about it.

When David Roman, a Business Systems Analyst with American Express, asked he got an enthusiastic thumbs-up. David was preparing to take the PMP (project management professional) exam, and Amex paid for him to take two week-long classes to develop his project management skills. "They also allowed me to rearrange my work schedule because the classes were only taught during the day," he adds.

Unfortunately, it's not always easy—especially if you're a relatively new employee—to find out about the kinds of company-sponsored education and training that may be available. So your first step will be to tap into your network—your manger and coworkers—to find out what they're doing to stay relevant and what they suggest that you do. They'll undoubtedly give you some great advice on opportunities that shouldn't be missed and some that you shouldn't bother with.

But don't forget about your HR department, which can be your most powerful resource. Most people have contact with HR during the hiring and orientation process, but once they're on board, they never come back. Big mistake. One of HR's primary roles is to develop talent within the company, and they'll have a good handle on in-house and outside training that would be appropriate for someone in your position.

And if your company has an active intranet, that's probably the first resource HR will suggest that you look into. In case you haven't heard of an intranet, it's a proprietary computer network that shares information among employees of a particular company internally. If you don't work for the company that owns it, you can't access it. Every company's intranet has different types of content. Some have little more than their corporate newsletter. Others may offer online, in-house training and job postings—which usually include a detailed description of the skills required. When you have some free time, spend a few minutes browsing those listings—especially positions that you think you might be interested in at some point.

Keep in mind that the quantity and quality of company-sponsored education is all over the map. Ford pays up to $5,000 per year in tuition and fees for employees pursuing degree programs. They also cover up to $200 per year for books. When I was at EMC, I took a whole bunch of courses and trainings through EMC University: writing, EMC products and technology, Six Sigma, and many more. These were not lightweight courses. Six Sigma, for example, was an intense six months and included a lot of work that I had to do on my own time. Many of the courses I took through EMC University had little to do with my job. But because I was adding to my skill set and making myself a more valuable employee, the company was completely on board, which included giving me time off if I needed it and covering all the expenses. Many other companies have similarly robust programs, while others offer considerably less. The best way to figure out where your employer is on that continuum is to ask HR and your manager what's available.

If your company is either providing education in-house or paying for you to get it elsewhere, they'll be looking at their return on that investment in you, which means that you may have to put together a convincing pitch for your manager. As with any pitch, you'll start by doing some research. If you want to attend an expensive out-of-town conference, for example, find out what other companies will be attending, who's speaking, who's sponsoring, and what specific courses or lectures will be offered. If you're considering taking a formal course— whether in-house or outside—talk to people who've taken it to make sure it actually helped them in their career. Before you make your pitch, make sure you've got strong answers to the questions your manager might ask (and that you would if you were in his place). What will you learn and how will that improve your job performance, make you a more valuable employee, and benefit the company? Essentially, you'll need to demonstrate that the benefit to the company is more than the price of the conference and the opportunity cost of having you miss a few days of work.

A few important warnings: Sometimes company-sponsored training comes with strings. For example, if they have a tuition reimbursement program, you may have to sign an agreement promising to stay at the company for a certain number of years after getting your degree (otherwise you'd have to pay back the cost of the education). And never sign up for an employer-sponsored course if you think you might drop it. Doing so will make you look like an unreliable flake (instructors almost always take attendance, and if you don't sign in, your boss will know about it, and he'll be a lot less likely to approve the next course you want to take). So, do all of your research before you sign up.

This can all be something of a balancing act. As I've said, the more you learn, the more valuable you'll be to your employer—and that will enable you to move up in your organization and command higher salaries along the way. But don't take on so much additional work that your performance on the job you were hired to do suffers.

Learning on Your Own

If your company doesn't provide internal or external training, you'll still need to continually upgrade your hard skills to stay relevant. The difference is that finding and taking advantage of the right resources is 100 percent up to you. The good news is that there's really no end to the number of ways you can acquire hard skills on your own.

If your company isn't paying for you to acquire hard skills, I'm also going to assume that you'll be doing it on your own time. So before you dive into something, I want you to think very carefully about two questions: How are you going to keep yourself motivated? and: How are you going to find the time to do hours of extra studying, continue to be a top performer in your job, *and* still maintain a social life? I know, I know, this is a book about your career, but there's a lot more to life than work. Letting work dominate your life is simply not healthy. Besides having fun, hanging out with friends, and going camping on the weekends, having a life outside the office will keep you from burning out on the job and will make you a more effective employee.

One more factor to consider as you think about learning skills on your own is that it can sometimes be a challenge to prove that you've actually acquired a new skill or improved an old one. One ingenious way around this problem is to check out Acinet.org/certifications_new, which is a one-stop shop for finding certifications in your field. You can search by name, organization, occupation, and industry. They've got exams where you can test your knowledge and your skills, and best of all, you can get a certificate that shows that you're as good as you say you are.

Consider all of these factors as you think about how to discover and refine the hard skills you'll need to advance in your career. In the next section you'll find a number of valuable resources that I've broken down by category. Because I know that money can be an issue for a lot of people who are just entering the workforce (or haven't been there that long), I've included only free resources.

FREE OR LOW-COST EDUCATIONAL TOOLS. Okay, you've got a pretty solid idea of the skills you want to develop. Of course, it's always nice if your company will pick up the tab, but that's not always going to happen. In this section I want to give you some great resources—most of which you can access from home or pretty close by—where you can learn new skills or improve those you already have. I'm focusing here on resources that are free or very inexpensive. So whether you want to find out how many keywords you need to have in a blog post to maximize its SEO effectiveness or how to pass the CPA exam, start the process here.

CONFERENCES AND WORKSHOPS are great places to acquire skills and network. You'll learn the latest information from people who are successful in your field, and you'll have a chance to meet other people who share the same interests. We'll talk more about networking later in the book, but for now, just remember that the more contacts you have, the more people you'll have available to ask for help if you need it and the further you'll be able to advance your career.

• Check with Eventbrite.com to see what's available in your area. Eventbrite.com is a Web site that lists events of all types.

Search by industry and location to find the ones closest to you. You can even register online.

• Check with Conferencealerts.com. They've got searchable lists of conferences all over the world by topic. If you find one that's relevant to your job or the job you're eyeing, ask your manager if the company will pay for it.

EDUCATIONAL WEB SITES. Here are just a few of the many sites that offer free or low-cost courses in any subject you can think of:

• Skillshare.com is a community education marketplace where you can learn from subject matter experts. If you're an expert in another area, you might be able to barter by teaching someone what you know in exchange for what he or she knows.

• Udemy has free and low-cost courses on a variety of topics, including operations management, product development, and even Twitter. You can also find my courses on personal branding and the companion course for this book on how to get ahead at Udemy.com/u/danschawbel.

• KahnAcademy.org is a not-for-profit company whose mission is to change education for the better. They have a library of over 4,000 world-class educational videos on a wide range of topics, which are available to anyone anywhere for free.

• Quora is a Q&A site where you can ask questions and get answers from a large community of experts in a wide variety of fields. Information is organized by interest area (math, finance, marketing, and so on), and you can search their extensive archives for questions other people have asked or ask your own.

• Big think (Bigthink.com) is a great source of big ideas from a network of 2,000 experts on a huge variety of topics from around the globe.

• iTunes U (Apple.com/education/itunes-u/) is the world's largest digital catalog of free education content. You'll be able to take complete courses created and taught by instructors from leading schools, see assignments and updates from instructors, take notes and highlight text in iBooks, and access multimedia course materials.

• TED.com. Every year there are two TED conferences which bring together the world's most inspiring and creative minds. Many of the TED sessions are available online either at Ted.com/talks or on YouTube. Explore the site and discover your own favorites. Unlike the other options in this section which offer ongoing courses, Ted.com offers individual lectures.

• Textbookrevolution.org is a student-run site dedicated to increasing the use of free educational materials by teachers and professors. You can search for free books and textbooks.

Open Courseware (Ocw.mit.edu) and Venture Lab (Venture-lab.org) are run by MIT and Stanford, respectively, and give you access to undergraduate and graduate level courses on an amazing variety of topics from C++ and microeconomics to media studies and foreign languages. Coursera (Coursera.org) is similar to the other two, but offers free courses from more than thirty colleges and universities. Treehouse (Teamtreehouse.com) focuses only on web design and development, and Codeacademy.com allows anyone to learn how to code. Besides software, you can learn to build Web sites, games, and apps. One neat feature is that you can take a course with friends and keep motivated by monitoring each other's progress. Why coding? Because it's a highly specialized skill that's always in demand. And that generally translates into higher earning power.

As the world gets smaller, having foreign language skills is also becoming more and more important. For instance, my friends who are fluent in Japanese and Chinese have never struggled to find work. Language skills also open up new opportunities for work and travel. With busuu.com you can start that process for free. Pick a language and start learning in a very interactive way—either on the Web or via a mobile app. You can also connect with a community of other people learning the same language so you can practice your skills.

General Learning About Your Field

Although we've been talking about learning hard skills, don't overlook the importance of more general knowledge—especially about what's going on in your industry. In our research, we found that 76 percent of managers and 80 percent of young employees said that having industry knowledge is a "very important" or "the most important" factor when considering junior people for promotion into management roles. There are a number of ways to gain knowledge about your industry. Most are free or close to it—all you'll need is an Internet connection. So I encourage you to explore as many of the following as possible. Every piece of knowledge you pick up will help you do your job better right now and position you to move ahead.

• **Business media.** One of the best is the *Harvard Business Review* (Hbr.org) for general business knowledge, but you can get a bird's-eye view and learn a lot from *The Wall Street Journal*, *Forbes*, and *The New York Times*.

• **Industry-specific publications.** Every industry has trade publications. Find yours. Ask your manager what she's reading. Take the elevator to whatever floor the CEO is on and ask his administrative assistant what the CEO is reading.

• Blogs are a great way to develop skills and knowledge about specific topics or entire sectors. While you can Google the topic you want to learn about, you can also find out which ones are the most popular by visiting sites such as Alltop.com (which categorizes the top blogs) and Technorati.com (a blog search engine).

• Web sites. There are quite a few excellent sites that offer great advice on career, entrepreneurship, and more. 30 Second MBA (Fastcompany.com/mba) is one of the best (the CEOs of *Time* magazine and Nintendo are there, so is Mark Zuckerberg from Facebook). Score.org offers free, confidential mentoring from industry experts via e-mail. This is an especially good resource if you're thinking about starting your own business one day.

• Books. Earning your degree is great. But getting your diploma doesn't mean you can stop learning. And while a lot of knowledge is being acquired through digital means, books still play an important role in learning (and yes, Kindle and iPad versions still count as books).

Becoming the Subject Matter Expert

Once you've identified the hard skills you need to do the job you aspire to, and you've figured out the best ways to acquire them (whether that's on your company's time and dime or your own), the only thing left to do is start putting those skills to work. In today's job market, simply meeting the skill requirements in your job description isn't enough. Not even close. If you're going to have any hope of getting promoted and moving up in your organization, you'll need to think beyond the job title on your business card (that's assuming your company even gives you business cards) and start adding real value to your department or company. The most effective way to do this is to make yourself the go-to expert on a specific topic or skill, the first name that pops into your coworkers' or supervisors' minds when they need help, the one they have on speed dial for special projects. In other words, you want to be just like David Trahan, a consultant at Interbrand. "I'm known as 'one of the digital guys,'" he says. "But more specifically as the 'social media guy.' I'm part of a small cross-functional task force that's developing our digital capabilities, training different departments on how to integrate digital into our business. I get called in a lot for brainstorms, client calls, and special projects related to digital and social media."

The Web site Talentdrive.com, which has a proprietary sourcing tool that helps recruiters find résumés online, did a report recently and found that 71 percent of hiring managers are trying to fill specialized positions, but 67 percent of job seekers consider themselves to have "broad skill sets." In other words, they're trying to be generalists, to satisfy everyone. Big mistake!

The most successful brands—whether they're individuals or huge corporations—try to be known for one very specific thing. And that's exactly what you need to do. The bottom line is that if you're too much of a generalist, you won't be known for anything. When projects come up, there'll be no reason for whoever it is that's staffing it to call you instead of someone else. So if you want to get ahead, you need to be a specialist, a subject matter expert. Specialists generate value and attention. When you're the expert and people know it, managers will seek you out. You'll become an invaluable asset to the company.

Now, just to be clear, I'm not saying that you shouldn't be good at a wide variety of things. You definitely want to protect yourself by having skills in a number of important business functions. That'll help you better adapt to change. But you can't be a superstar at everything. You can, however, excel at one thing. And that's especially important early in your career when you need the most visibility.

If you're working for someone like Mike Proulx, Senior Vice President and Director of Digital Strategy at Hill Holliday, one of the top ad agencies in the U.S., and you're not a specialist, your career will stall pretty early on. "We absolutely need specialists," says Proulx. "While my team is responsible for social media, it's simply not possible for everyone to have deep and intimate knowledge with every social platform, policy, and best practice. We want everyone to specialize in areas that they are most passionate about and we rely on each other to share across the team, with our clients, and on our company blog."

Bottom line: Being a specialist helps you add value to whatever you do. But because the job landscape is constantly changing, you may have to change your specialization once in a while to ensure that you're always adding value. Plus, you'll have an easier time adapting if you've got a good understanding of the big picture as well.

Your Career Plan

The world is changing so quickly, and there's so much uncertainty out there that it's really hard to keep up with what's going on—especially what's changing in the workplace environment. For that reason, if you're going to succeed, you'll need to be able to adapt quickly to the constantly shifting landscape.

To do that, you'll need to create a plan and identify a goal—something concrete and measurable. Interbrand's David Trahan is a firm believer in having a concrete plan. "I know where I want to go in my life, but I also have a plan for my current company," he says. "I have a one-year plan in place, and an idea of what the next year would be if I attained my goals. I know what I need to do to accomplish my goals. I have developed an understanding of internal politics, egos, and goals, so that I can extend and tailor myself to have maximum impact in all my projects."

Start with setting your short-, medium-, and long-term goals—you should absolutely have some of each. I've found that the most success-ful plans start with the end goal in mind and work backward from there, outlining in as much detail as possible the specific steps you'll need to take to reach that goal. For example, "Within the next three years, I'm going to be in a new position as Assistant VP of X. In order to do that, I'll get certified in Y and master Z skills. I'll make time to take one of the company-offered courses throughout the year. I'll also attend two industry conferences per year, go to monthly meetings of the Z networking group, and every week I'll have lunch with an indus-try colleague." For people in your parents' generation, a long-term plan might go out as far as ten years, while short-term might be a year or two. But for today's young workers, long-term is probably no more than three years, and short-term could be as little as six months. Of course, you'll also want to build some flexibility into your plan: Your com-pany could go out of business, you might have to quit your job to care for a sick relative, or a technological advance might come along that could make your goal obsolete before it happens. In cases like those, you'll need to adjust your plan on the fly, set new goals, and plot a new course.

You should let your interests, passions, and maybe even a little luck drive your plans too. Mary Pilon, a sports reporter for *The New York Times*, figured out what she wanted to do based on her experi-ences and shared some great advice with me that you can also benefit from. "I've been fortunate to work at places with people who are pas-sionate about what they do and their enthusiasm has proven conta-gious," she says. "I don't think there's any secret to making it in a career. Work hard, see 'No' as a starting-off point, and do what you love. And be open-minded. I don't think a younger version of me ever saw myself as a financial reporter or a sports reporter. But by giving these things a try, I realized I loved these different areas of storytelling. I love that journalism can help people in direct and indirect ways. I love that the core of my job is getting things right, learning, and teaching others. I don't know what I'm going to wear tomorrow or what I'll be doing in one year, five years, or beyond that. As great as it can be to set goals sometimes, obsessing over them can blind you from the opportunities right in front of you."

Getting to be a reporter with *The New York Times* is no easy feat, so it's hard to argue with Mary. That said, while she may not have a firm plan, she definitely has goals and ways of measuring her progress as she moves toward those goals. Make sure you do the same.

Become the Expert Your Company Can't Live Without

The four most important things you can do throughout the process of making yourself the go-to subject matter expert are:

- **Pay attention to what's going on around you.** What skills seem to be in more demand now than before? And don't forget to check in with yourself too: What skills are you using less frequently than you did in the past?

- **Keep communicating.** No matter how much you pay attention to what's going on, there's no way you'll be able to absorb everything. So, talk to people: coworkers, managers, people in jobs you'd like to be doing. And ask lots and lots of questions: What are the skills they value most? Least? What jobs are most in demand now? What jobs do they think will be most in demand in the future? We'll talk about how to network in the next chapter.

• **Make a plan.** How are you going to get the skills you need? You should always be learning, acquiring knowledge and skills that will benefit you as you advance in your career.

• **Stay flexible.** Remember, things change constantly. What's important today may not be tomorrow, and what will be important tomorrow may not even have been invented yet.

As you've seen in this chapter, obtaining hard skills and getting known for them can position you to get a job and can enable you to function efficiently while you're there. But if you really want to get to the next level, to be a manager, or to advance your career at all, you'll also need soft skills. That's exactly what we'll be exploring in the next chapter.

4

Soft Skills: Make Every
Impression Count

We are being judged by a new yardstick: not just
how smart we are, or by our training and expertise,
but also by how we handle ourselves and each
other.

—DANIEL GOLEMAN,
AUTHOR OF
*EMOTIONAL
INTELLIGENCE*

Job results are king, right? Make your numbers, land the con-
tracts, finish on time and within budget. Do those things and
it'll be smooth sailing toward the top. Isn't that how it's supposed to work? Anyone who's been in the corporate world for even a
little while knows that's not the way things always play out. You've seen
deserving people skipped over for promotion (hopefully you weren't
one of them). You've seen underperformers advance. You've wondered
how the guy who can't think his way out of a paper bag got to be a
manager. So you know that there's more to career advancement than
job results. So what's the missing ingredient? Soft skills.

On the most basic level, soft skills—sometimes called *emotional
intelligence*—are nontechnical skills. But it's a little more subtle than
that. They're interpersonal skills, skills that enable you to form rela-

tionships with coworkers, fit into the corporate culture, and communicate successfully. Hard skills, which we talked about in the previous chapter, are what will help you navigate the technical elements of your job, but it's soft skills that will enable you to move ahead. Soft skills are generally very apparent to the people around you, and if those skills are sharp, people will notice. By gaining and mastering communication and other soft skills and developing your own emotional intelligence, you'll become the person everyone wants to work with. You'll become an influencer and a leader. You'll also be very much in charge of managing the way you're perceived by others. Don't wait to be judged by others. Instead, focus on highlighting your abilities in a way that clearly demonstrates (as opposed to you having to say anything) the skills you have and the value you and those skills bring to your team and your employer.

The difference between hard skills and soft is kind of like the difference between a single computer and a network. You can do a lot of stuff with the computer, but the network allows you to communicate with other computers, access the company's intranet from home, and print a document from the other side of the building. One computer gets the job done, but the network lets you get so much more out of every device that's connected. I asked a number of managers at Fortune 500 companies to tell me about the soft skills they think young employees will need if they want to move up in their careers. Here's what they said:

- Strong work ethic
- Optimism/positive attitude
- Good communication skills
- Good conversation skills
- Storytelling abilities for presentations
- Time management abilities
- The ability to listen and to speak to the "human needs" of

coworkers and customers and make them feel understood and respected

- Being good at reading people
- Ability to build relationships and connect with others on a deep level
- Exercise tact when delivering a message
- The ability to propose solutions to problems, not just talk about problems
- Meaningfully contribute to brainstorming
- Ability to write well
- Problem-solving skills
- Team player
- Being likable
- Self-confidence
- Can accept and learn from criticism
- Flexibility/adaptability
- Can work well under pressure
- Empathy
- Integrity
- Sense of humor

How Important Are Soft Skills?

To be perfectly blunt, people with hard skills are a dime a dozen. A high school kid can probably learn most of the hard skills that would be required to do just about any job, but it's doubtful that he or she would have the emotional maturity and people skills to make it in a Fortune 200 company. In Chapter 2, we talked about how important it is to stand out. Well, nothing will make you stand out more than the ability to bring out the best in yourself and others. So how important are soft skills? In a word, they're critical.

"Sufficient soft skills enable the employee to learn the hard skills: they see the value, and they see the bigger picture," Susan Langill, Food & Nutrition Director at Sodexo, told me. "A successful employee has enthusiasm, drive, social filters, interpersonal skills, and an eagerness to learn and succeed. This employee will advance your team and your organization and with these transferable skills is capable of learning most or all the hard skills needed to perform most of the job tasks within an organization."

Let me give you a few more examples:

• 71 percent of employers say they value emotional intelligence over IQ, according to CareerBuilder.com. Fifty-nine percent would not hire someone with a high IQ but low emotional intelligence.

• When my company interviewed employers about the most important traits they look for when hiring students, 98 percent said "communication skills," 97 percent said "positive attitude," and 97 percent said "teamwork."

• 89 percent of people who get fired within the first eighteen months on the job are let go because of attitudinal reasons; only 11 percent because of a lack of skills, according to Mark Murphy, founder and CEO of Leadership IQ.

• When evaluating an employee's performance, 32 percent of employers say hard skills are the most important, 7 percent say digital/tech skills, and 61 percent say soft skills, according to our study.

The bottom line here is that being able to do your job isn't enough. The big question is: How well do you fit in with the corporate culture?

Can you build relationships with the people you work with and for? Do you have the skills to overcome personality conflicts, motivate your team members, and sell your ideas to your managers?

Now that you know how important soft skills are, all you have to do is get out there and learn them, right? Unfortunately, that's a lot easier said than done. Unlike hard skills, soft skills are hard to teach—and they're even harder to measure. And unlike hard skills, where you can take what you've learned in a lab setting and put it to work right away, with soft skills it's all about putting yourself in situations where they're needed and slowly getting better and better. But before we can start turning you into a soft skills expert, we need to identify your strengths and weaknesses.

Assess Your Soft Skills

Let's do a quick self-assessment. This isn't intended to be a scientific analysis—you can get that with any number of tools, including Myers Briggs, many of which are available for little or no cost online. What we're doing here is trying to get a rough idea of where you stand. On a scale of 1–5, where 1 is Not Good at All and 5 is Spectacular, rate the following statements:

- I am willing to be an active listener   1   2   3   4   5
- I am a good negotiator   1   2   3   4   5
- I am confident in group settings   1   2   3   4   5
- I work well under pressure   1   2   3   4   5
- I willingly accept criticism   1   2   3   4   5
- I am good at managing my time   1   2   3   4   5

• I am good at relating to coworkers and others	1	2	3	4	5
• I am accountable for my own actions	1	2	3	4	5
• I am good at taking initiative	1	2	3	4	5
• I am good at resolving conflicts with others	1	2	3	4	5

Okay, now add up your total. If you got anything more than 45 points (the max is 50), you can skip the rest of this chapter—you're a soft skills genius. If you're somewhere between 30 and 45 (which is where most of us are), you're going to want to take advantage of every opportunity to polish your soft skills. Anything less than 30, and you've got some serious work to do.

Ways to Improve Your Soft Skills

Now that you have a rough idea of your soft skills strengths and weaknesses, let's get into the specifics of how to improve (or develop) soft skills. Learning to communicate effectively is the most important soft skill of all. It's also probably the most misunderstood. Communication involves more than just talking. A lot more. Just think of all the e-mails and texts you send every day, the way you order your coffee in the morning, the smile you give to the cute guy or gal on the subway on the way to work, the face-to-face meetings with coworkers, and even when you're standing silently next to people in the elevator. Just about everything we do—even the way we sit, walk, eat, or play—communicates something to someone. For the next few pages I want to take you through some excellent ways of improving your communication skills.

LISTEN. If you don't listen carefully, you can't possibly know what people want, what their state of mind is, why they're doing what they're doing, and how you can help them achieve their goals (as opposed to how you can convince them to do what you want them to do).

The most important part about listening is not talking. I know that sounds pretty basic, but a lot of people are in such a hurry to get their opinions heard that they interrupt others, talk on top of them, and sometimes just won't shut up—especially when they're nervous. One way to tell whether you might be too chatty is to think about how you start conversations. Do you launch into a long story about something that happened to you or that you did, or do you start by asking a few questions and listening to *their* stories?

When you're talking with someone really be there and ask a lot of questions—but don't make it into a cross-examination. If they say something interesting, explore it a little deeper. Base your follow-up questions on their response to the initial question. The more you let people talk about themselves, the more they'll be interested in you and support your ideas.

And if you're easily distracted, practice focusing. One method I've used to test my focus is to try to recall the details of a conversation after it's over. If I've got some paper handy, I'll jot down a quick summary of what the other person said. Or I'll dictate those notes into my phone. I know this sounds like something you'd hear in Psych 101 or from one of those tech support people who've been trained to repeat back what you've said, but it actually works. First of all, it demonstrates that you were actually listening; second, it can clear up any misunderstandings; and third, it can give you a chance to ask follow-up questions so you can dig deeper into what the other person is trying to get across. If you find that you can't remember what the person you're talking with said, that's a big red flag that you need to be paying more attention.

Being a good listener is a critical communication skill on its own.

But it also affects the way you communicate in other areas. For example, your ability to listen will have a direct effect on your ability to write summaries of meetings, follow-up e-mails, and even thank-you notes.

WRITE WELL. "If I had to give our young leaders one piece of advice, it would be to work on your writing skills," Nancy Altobello, Vice Chair of People at Ernst & Young LLP, told me. So while you may spend a fair amount of time tweeting and texting, as you move through your organization, you'll also need to be writing reports, white papers, newsletters, and, of course, e-mails. Being able to produce well-structured, intelligent, concise, written materials that people will want to read is essential. "When it comes time to deliver that tough message to a client or coworker, chances are it will take more than 140 characters," Altobello adds. Whatever you're writing be sure to get to the point quickly and have a strong call for action. People who read what you're writing (and that includes e-mail subject lines) should come away knowing exactly what you want them to do. At the very least, this will save you having to deal with a hundred questions asking you to explain things that you left out of the original document.

It's also essential to know your audience. The e-mail lunch invite you send to your boss should be very different from one to a friend. And everything should be proofread before it goes out. Bad grammar, spelling, punctuation, incomplete sentences, and endlessly long and rambling text will make you look sloppy and unprofessional. It's extremely difficult to proofread your own stuff, so having an extra pair of eyes may be necessary for some documents. And since you never know where your paper or e-mail or whatever will show up (people routinely hit Reply All or accidentally forward documents that they shouldn't), I suggest that you always write imagining that someone you're really trying to impress is going to be reading it.

Writing is a bit of an exception to the soft-skills-can't-be-taught rule, meaning that if your writing isn't what it should be, you can take classes and improve your spelling, grammar, punctuation, sentence structure, and other basics. But what's harder to teach is exactly *what* to say in all those perfectly spelled, beautifully structured words.

All of our communications skills are connected. We've just seen how listening affects writing. Well, writing, in turn, affects other areas. For example, knowing how to put your ideas down on paper in a logical, well-organized way will make it a lot easier to present those ideas to others.

PRACTICE PRESENTING.   The further you move up in an organization, the more presentations you'll have to do. Unfortunately, the prospect of talking in front of others is frightening. So, aside from taking beta blockers or sedatives (which, of course, you would only do if your doctor told you to), the only way to calm the butterflies in your stomach is to practice. The more you practice, the easier it'll be. For instance, give a two-minute presentation at dinner and a five-minute monologue to the mirror before bed. Opportunities to do presentations are all around. You could even go so far as to stand up and present everyone's orders to the server when you're out to lunch with your friends. If you can't find any opportunities to practice, you aren't looking hard enough. If you want more practice, join a group like Toastmasters (Toastmasters.org), an international organization that helps people develop speaking and presentation skills.

The biggest fears people have around presentations are making a fool of themselves in front of a bunch of strangers, and having to sway others to your point of view. The easiest solution is to make sure you have some allies in your audience, and the easiest way to do this is to go around and meet with some of the people you'll be presenting to. Give them an overview of what you'll be talking about and get some feedback. If they like what you're doing, they'll be in your corner, and you won't have to convince them. If they don't like what you're doing, ask what their concerns are and try to resolve them. You may be able to incorporate some of their thoughts into your presentation. Nothing makes people feel more important than taking their advice. And the ability to make others feel important is invaluable.

Body Language: Observing and Using the Unspoken

In the workplace—and everywhere else—you're communicating all the time, whether you know it or not. You've probably read or heard somewhere that 80 or 90 percent of communication is nonverbal. The exact percentage doesn't matter—the point is that it's a lot. People will judge you based on all sorts of nonverbal cues—how you carry yourself, the way you nod your head when you're listening to others, how you walk through the office. Managers do this a lot, particularly when they're evaluating people for promotions. Sure, they want someone with the right skills and abilities. But they also want someone who dresses and acts the part.

A few pages back I talked about improving verbal (written or spoken) communication by learning to listen better. In much the same way, I want to start talking about nonverbal communication by encouraging you to "listen" to others' body language.

OBSERVE OTHERS. You're going to do this for two reasons. First, by observing others' oral and body language, you'll get some insights into what's motivating them, what they're concerned or excited about. That will allow you to tailor your approach to their unique situation. With a tentative person, for example, you'll want to be less aggressive than you might be with someone who's aggressive. Observing others in this way applies to both customers and fellow employees and managers. "Change is not easy and is often met with resistance and uncertainty. Social media and technology are so rapidly progressing, as is the way people consume content, that adapting to these changes, and getting people on board, can be challenging," says Royale Ziegler, Social Media Manager at E! Entertainment. "It's extremely important to consider how an individual will best receive my message and then deliver it accordingly."

Second, it's essential that you know how others perceive you and how they react to what you say and do. Sometimes those reactions will be verbal, other times they'll be behavioral. Sometimes they'll be obvious, other times they'll be very subtle. Someone who asks you a lot of questions is probably interested in you and wants to hear what you have to say. Someone who's doing a lot of eye rolling, foot tapping, looking around the room, saying a lot of "Oh, really's" and never asks you a follow-up question is telling you very clearly that you're not connecting and you will need to find out why or probe the issue by taking another tack. While many people don't have any problem reading others' cues, not everyone does. If you can't get a pretty accurate handle on how others perceive you, that's a skill you need to work on. If this is you, you'll need to make a concerted effort to pay closer attention to the way people respond to what you're saying and doing. Stop every once in a while and ask yourself how you're doing.

WATCH YOUR BODY LANGUAGE. Remember what I just said about most communication being nonverbal? Think about what you do with your body when you're involved with others. Do you lean backward in your seat and cross your arms? Do you find yourself standing with your hands on your hips? Do you have "restless leg syndrome" (yes, that's an actual condition)? Do you face people head-on or do you sit or stand at an angle (research shows that people tend to focus on whatever it is that their feet are pointing to)? Do you straighten paperclips, twirl pens, or fidget in some other way? Simple behaviors like these can make a huge difference in your ability to communicate with others, hear what they have to say, put them at ease, and build relationships with them.

MAKE EYE CONTACT IN ONE-ON-ONE AND TEAMWORK SITUATIONS. If you've ever tried to have a conversation with someone who's not looking at you, you know how frustrating and annoying it can be. And you know how nice it is—and how important you feel—when the person you're talking with looks directly at you. Keep your eyes on the person you're with and don't let your eyes wander around the room looking for someone better to talk with. If you have a habit of looking around while others are talking, stop it.

Soft Skills for Remote Workers

According to a recent study done by Cisco, 70 percent of college students and young professionals don't think it's really necessary to go into an office. Surprisingly, more and more employers seem to agree. And chances are that you're already doing it. Another study, this one by the software company Wrike, found that 83 percent of employees work remotely at least part of the day. All that time you spend reading and answering e-mails on your commute, before bed, at breakfast, and even on the way to the bathroom in the middle of the night counts, as it should.

Here's the problem, though: Even as working from home becomes more acceptable and the rigid command-and-control office model becomes more outdated, remote workers (and by that I mean anyone who does work someplace other than his or her employer's office) worry that their coworkers or bosses will see them as slackers, and that the lack of face time with the boss could hurt their careers.

For Andre Obereigner, an HR Professional with IBM in Malaysia who supports the company's HR business in Germany and Europe, the face time

---

issue is his number one concern. Certainly, not being in the same place at the same time makes it harder to communicate with each other. "And even when you do communicate, you're missing the facial expressions and body language that convey information that can be vital in the decision-making process," he says.

Unfortunately, some remote workers do, in fact, turn into slackers and wind up getting fired. And even if you're not a slacker (and you wouldn't be reading this book if you were), remote workers have a harder time forming strong emotional bonds with coworkers (no chance for after-work cocktails, obviously), and they don't get that invaluable face time with senior management. "There isn't the opportunity to pop into someone's office and ask how they're doing, talk about what they're working on, etc.," says Sherri Hartlen-Neely, an Associate Director at Computer Sciences Corporation who manages remote workers. It's also a lot harder to get people to notice your hard skills if you're not in the office. But the things that could get you fired—and the things that will make you a success—are the same for remote workers as they are for in-house workers.

MAINTAIN CONTACT.

This is huge. The old expression "out of sight, out of mind" is definitely true in the corporate world. If people don't see you, they won't think of you when a new opportunity comes up. So you need to make sure your manager sees your name or your face or hears your voice every day. Sherri Hartlen-Neely suggests that managers reach out to their staff for the occasional chitchat that happens naturally when you are all located in the same physical space. "As a manager (and I would argue as an employee) you have to make a concerted effort to reach out at various points throughout the week to just say 'Hey there! What's happening?'" Use Skype, Google Talk, or some other video conferencing system. IM, text, or tweet, and don't be afraid to pick up the phone. But make sure you know your manager's preferred method of communication. Age-based stereotypes are sometimes true: If your boss is much older than you, a phone call might be the way to go. If they're your age or younger, newer technologies may work better, but ask anyways.

NETWORKING

Network as much as you can, especially with coworkers and other people in your industry. Go to your company's offsite training programs and holiday parties, and participate in as many networking events and conferences as you can. Building strong relationships can be a challenge for a telecommuter, but it's incredibly important.

PUT IN SOME FACE TIME WHEN YOU HAVE THE CHANCE.

Many companies will have onsite meetings every year or so. If you get an invite to one of these, don't turn it down. "We generally pick a couple of days in the year when the entire team can fly in and get together for some face-to-face team building and learning, says Hartlen-Neely. "And, of course, there is the team dinner at that onsite meeting that we all look most forward to. There's something to be said about breaking bread together that lets you feel a little closer to someone and understand them better."

Making the Right Impression

The old expression "You never get a second chance to make a first impression" isn't quite correct, and we'll get to that in a minute. But there's no question that first impressions are really, really important. Researchers at Princeton found that first impressions are formed in one-tenth of a second.[1] Pretty scary. But even scarier is the fact that longer exposures don't significantly alter those first impressions. That means that you don't actually even have to meet someone to form an impression, which is why you need to think long and hard about how you come across.

So, let's talk about the various components to making an impression.

MIND YOUR MANNERS. "In my opinion, the soft skill that Gen Yers lack the most is manners," Mark Kuta, Value Chain Planning Sales

Manager at Oracle, told me. "How to conduct yourself at a lunch meeting, how to follow up with people, how to use your class to differentiate yourself. I've purchased books on manners for several of my young employees." This will sound awfully basic, but the kinds of manners I'm talking about here are the same ones your parents taught you when you were little: Be polite, say "please" and "thank you," listen respectfully and don't interrupt when others are talking. And yes, even though your parents didn't say anything specifically about texting, let me assure you that texting or checking your e-mail in the middle of a meeting or a business lunch is extremely rude.

DRESS THE PART.   As trite as it sounds, you really do need to dress for success. Forty-one percent of employers say that people who dress better or more professionally are more likely to get promoted than those who don't dress as well. A recent study done by CareerBuilder.com took a look at the dress-for-success issue but from the opposite angle. They found that things that might seem superficial to you can make a big difference to managers. The top factors that make them less likely to promote a candidate were: piercings (37 percent), bad breath (34 percent), visible tattoos (31 percent), clothes (29 percent), and a messy desk (27 percent). Other factors included having chewed fingernails, being too suntanned, or wearing too much perfume.[2] Research shows that when women dress in a masculine way for a job interview, they're more likely to get the job, and if they're in a prestigious job and dress provocatively, people think they're less competent.

Feeling outraged? Fair enough. But even though it seems inappropriate for someone to consider how you look, that's just the way it is, like it or not. As Dean Lawyer, Senior Area Manager, State and Local Government Mobility Solutions, at T-Mobile, told me, "Looking down on a co-worker with strange hair, body piercings, tattoos, etc., without getting to know the person behind the package may not be right, but it is a reality. So if your hair isn't the most interesting thing about you, you should consider the kind of attention it demands." The goal is to look polished and professional but not to lose your personality. The most important thing to consider when deciding how to dress at work is what the standards are. If you're in a start-up and everyone's wearing jeans, great, wear jeans. If they're all wearing jeans and you show up in a suit, you'll look like a brownnoser. But if you're an investment banker where the standard is suits and you show up in jeans, you'll look like an idiot.

So here's the deal. Dress for the position you want to have, not the one you do have. As Melanie Mitchell, Senior Vice President, Search Marketing Strategy at Digitas, explained, "If your peers wear jeans to work every day and most managers wear business casual attire, it is easier for someone in management to perceive you as manager material if you dress up at least a few days each week."

I suggest that you dress one level up from whatever the office standard is. If the dress code is jeans, wear khakis. If it's business casual, wear a jacket but no tie. You get the point. You also need to be prepared. Bottom line: By dressing professionally and appropriately, you're sending the message that you're ready for more responsibility and upward movement.

Getting That Second Chance

As I mentioned earlier, first impressions are incredibly important, which is why you need to do everything you can to make a good one. A bad first impression is hard to recover from. But definitely *not* impossible. It's going to take some work, though. "Making a great first impression by being prepared, engaged, and authentic, is essential," says Todd Davis, the Head of Recruitment, NA Fulfillment at Amazon. "If you can get back to demonstrating those qualities, you've got a good chance." John Bell, Global Managing Director of Social@Ogilvy (the advertising giant), told me that while anyone can stub a toe in a single encounter, "what we do consistently over the first ninety days of a job or engagement is what people will remember most."

Recovering from a bad first impression is all about exceeding expectations. In some ways that'll be easy—after your first screwup, you have the chance to beat expectations the next time around. But you need to think carefully about what went wrong and consider how to correct it. Does it have to do with your image? Was it something you did? Something you said? The most important step in recovering from a bad first impression? As Todd Davis told me, "You need to own your bad first impressions. Follow up with the person you think you missed the mark with. They'll appreciate it."

Don't take anything I'm saying here as an invitation (or permission) to not take first impressions seriously. Erica Tremblay, Director, Market Intelligence & Marketing Development Program at EMC, says that while it's possible to recover, there's no guarantee that you'll actually get the chance. "People are busy, they may move on to another project and never work with you again so you never get the opportunity to right the ship," she says. "It's best to focus on making a solid first impression."

The reason for that is pretty simple: The first meeting sets expectations for future interactions. And the second is also important because it either confirms or overrides whatever happened during the first impression. If you had made a less-than-stellar first impression, expectations for your second meeting will be pretty low—and easy to exceed. If your first impression was good, expectations will be high for the second. If you meet them, you'll have established a reputation. If you don't, you'll have to start thinking about third impressions.

Building Relationships

If I had to come up with another synonym for "soft skills" besides "emotional intelligence," I'd probably go with "building relationships."

Everything we've talked about in this chapter has to do with connecting with other people. On one hand, there's connecting with customers and others outside your organization. People want to do business with others they know and trust. Ronisha Goodwin, College Recruiting Manager at the Hyatt Hotels Corporation, summed it up nicely: "Our managers have to be able to connect with both our guests and our employees. It's great that they are skilled at their jobs, but we need individuals who can speak to the 'human needs' of both our employees and our guests ensuring that they both feel understood and respected." Katherine Larner, an Account Executive at Pandora, adds, "Sales is incredibly focused on relationship building since people don't want to buy things from someone they don't get along with or trust (also, they tend to spend more money with people they like to work with and trust!). It's the same as when you tip a good waitress more than the usual 15 percent—that's because you liked their soft skills. It's not the *only* reason someone will buy from me, but it helps to get that extra 'tip' when you are an attentive and easy person to work with and continue to show genuine, personal interest in people."

On the other hand, there are the people you work with and for. And building relationships with them is equally important. A recent Harvard study found that only 15 percent of the reason people advance in the workplace is related to taught skills and job knowledge.[3] The other 85 percent has to do with people skills. And by *people skills* I mean *being liked*. "From month one, I did everything that I could to weave myself into the fabric of the company—whether it was joining the events committee, volunteering to help with a new program, playing on the company softball team, writing cards at Christmas, planning a good-natured prank on a coworker, or happily offering up my time for candidate interviews," says Ginger Lennon, a young Marketing Manager with Digital Influence Group, a marketing services firm in Boston. "I quickly found that it was much easier to get colleagues to not only like you, but to help you out and do great work for you when you are generous with your time and committed to building a fun, positive, and friendly work environment and company culture."

A majority of managers admit that before a formal promotion process gets under way, they've already identified the person they want to tap, according to a study done at Georgetown University by Jonathan Gardner and Berland Associates. They found that 56 percent of large employers that had more than one person in line for a promotion already had a favorite—and the criteria for being a favorite had nothing to do with skills; it was all about likability. Ninety-six percent of the time, the favorite got the job. What that means is that even if you aren't the most technically qualified for a job, you've still got a fighting chance for a promotion—if your boss likes you.

Keep in mind, though, that being liked all by itself isn't always enough. There has to be some substance there too. Melanie Mitchell, Senior Vice President, Search Marketing Strategy at Digitas, told me a great story that illustrates this point nicely. "I worked with a young man who was great at making his peers and the team laugh, but he hardly ever pitched in to do extra work when help was needed. He mostly did the bare minimum to get by. Nothing more. He typically came in at 9 and was out by 5:30 every day. One day a few people caught him sleeping at his desk, which did not go over well with management. Eventually, he left the company on his own terms to pursue another job. But about eight months later he reached back out to us. He heard we had a position open and said that he still had fond memories of the people, culture, and working with us. When we connected with the team that was hiring—the same team he'd worked with before—the short answer was "no thanks." Not because he wasn't a nice guy or funny, but because they needed someone to pitch in and truly be part of the team. And based on what they knew about him from before, he clearly wasn't that guy."

Becoming a Leader in Your Organization

Becoming a leader will help you build your brand and get ahead faster. Of course, for that to happen, managers have to see you as leadership material. What does that mean? Managers are looking for people who have vision, who see possibilities where others see dead ends; individuals with courage who are willing to take calculated risks to achieve results; individuals who set the bar higher than most others and who jump at the chance to exceed expectations; individuals who inspire trust and confidence in their coworkers, excel at resolving conflict, and work well on teams.

Developing leadership qualities is definitely possible—and since you're now working on your soft skills, you're well on your way. Now it's just a question of getting practice. And the best way to do that—and to demonstrate your leadership potential—is to take on leadership roles wherever and whenever possible. But don't sit back and wait for the offers to pour in. You'll need to go out there and find them.

What Makes a Leader?

Being a leader is incredibly important: In our study, 78 percent of managers and 84 percent of employees say that leadership skills are either "very important" or "the most important." Below you'll find twenty leadership traits that I heard from the dozens of manager we interviewed for this book:

1. Be a team builder (86 percent of managers and 82 percent of employees say this is very important or most important)

2. Have relationship-building skills (75 percent of managers and 79 percent of employees put this at or near the top of their lists)
3. Have character, energy, passion, charisma
4. Be dedicated to accomplishing tasks, goals, missions, objectives
5. Be open, honest, straightforward
6. Think creatively
7. Be fair—give everyone a shot and give everyone credit
8. Be well organized and have the ability to delegate tasks
9. Deal well with others—understand conflict resolution and be sensitive to the emotions of others
10. Have the confidence to take risks
11. Work well under stress
12. Recognize new opportunities as they arise
13. Be able to craft and articulate messages to an audience
14. Have a relentless work ethic and a never-give-up mentality
15. Inspire greatness in others
16. Be competent—to understand everyone else's role and still be an expert in your own
17. Be able to ask the right questions, find the right answers, and make good decisions
18. Be humble—don't take credit for everything
19. Take personal accountability for the success of your team
20. Have good communication skills

I often find that looking at a list isn't as effective as a good, real-world example. And because everyone defines *leadership* a little differently, I want to give you an opportunity to hear from managers themselves what they're looking for. Megan Cherry, a College Relations Recruiter at Tyson Foods, is looking for young people who are "very professional, very mature, very good at delegation, but very good about knowing where your breaking point is and giving praise where praise is due." Brian Pototo, Director of Global Talent Acquisition at Brocade, told me, "I have three Millennials on my team who impress me on a regular basis with their enthusiasm, dedication, and commitment to their work and our team." And PepsiCo's Paul Marchand says, "We look for leaders who have integrity, are collaborative, and are constantly curious and challenging. Those who see new opportunities, who are adaptable, and who show flexibility will see many doors open throughout their careers." And James Wisdom, Second Vice President of Integrated Marketing at insurance giant Aflac, looks for "willingness and the energy to embrace the unknown and solve a puzzle, organized thinking, and the capability and pluck to ask the right questions to deconstruct what may appear impenetrable."

As I said earlier, becoming a leader is a great way to build your brand and accelerate your upward path through your company. Good managers know that good leaders are the future of the organization, and they've always got their eyes open for talent. Develop the skills that are most in demand and you'll get noticed more. And you'll never get anywhere if you don't get noticed.

The Difference Between Leaders and Managers

As we discussed in the previous chapter, workers in older generations were often promoted based on seniority and number of years spent at the company. But in today's workplace, where everything has to be learned and everyone is expendable, seniority-based promotions are pretty much a thing of the past. Respecting your boss, however, is definitely *not* a thing of the past. He or she has experience and juice within the company—both of which can help *you* advance your career.

At the same time, while the words *manager* and *leader* were once used interchangeably, the definitions have changed. Not all managers are good leaders and not all leaders are good managers. In general, mangers are more operations- and goals-based—making sure the trains run on time, that things go according to plan, that targets get met and budgets don't get blown. Leaders are more forward-thinking and innovative, asking "Where do we go from here?" or "Who else do we need on our team to be able to get to the next level?"

How to Lead Your Team Members So They'll Support You

Want to be a great leader? Want to accomplish great things quickly and efficiently? Of course you do. Well, it all starts with your team. The better you know them, the easier it will be to motivate them. And the more motivated they are, the more they'll accomplish. It all starts with paying attention: What kind of people are they? What motivates them? What doesn't? What are they oversensitive about? Knowing this will save you a huge amount of time and energy.

Next, you need to set clear goals and milestones and get buy-in from everyone. Good leaders stay organized and always know what's going on, where, and who's working on it. Then, every chance they get, they give the people on their team proper credit. You need to do the same. You'd be amazed at how many people don't give others credit—and then wonder why they can't get their team motivated.

Good leaders also have open-door policies and go out of their way to make their team members feel comfortable working with them. They make their team members feel like they're part of something bigger than themselves. It's up to you to make sure your team members know about the company's goals and agenda and to show your team how the projects they're working on affect the whole company.

Making Tough Conversations Easy

So far we've talked about a lot of different ways to communicate with the people you work with, and how being an effective communicator is a very in-demand leadership skill. But there are two more aspects of communication that we need to cover: How do you deal with conflict (between you and someone else as well as between two other people)? And how do you deal with criticism (receiving and giving)? No one wants to deal with unpleasant situations, and people who can handle tough communication challenges are a rare breed. If you learn how, you'll definitely set yourself apart from your peers and position yourself as a true leader.

ACCEPT CRITICISM...   When people give you feedback, you have to be willing to hear it without having it ruin your day or give you a bad attitude. Being able to handle criticism shows that you're interested in improving yourself and that you want to be part of the team. As devastating as criticism is, and for quite a few people it can be, try not to let it get the best of you. I know it's easy to get defensive when someone says something negative about you—especially if the criticism is unwarranted or less than constructive. But before you take a mental swipe at the person who critiqued you, consider whether there might be a grain of truth in there somewhere. If you need to, you can get a second opinion from someone you trust.

...AND LEARN FROM CRITICISM   If there *is* a grain (or a ton) of truth in the criticism you receive (and there almost always is), think about how you can learn from it. Honestly, what could you have done or said differently? If you suddenly found yourself in the same situation again, would you do the same thing? Being able to learn from criticism is not an easy thing. But it's something that will definitely get you noticed by your manager and others.

AND LEARN TO CRITICIZE. As you move your way up through an organization it's inevitable that you'll have to do some critiquing. Some people love to jump down people's throats. They actually look forward to being able to knock people down a peg or two and aren't above reducing someone to tears. They're insensitive jerks. Don't be one of them. Find a way to get your message across in a way that doesn't do any harm and that actually makes the person you're speaking to want to improve. The best way to do this is to start the conversation on a pleasant note: find something to compliment the person on, something she does especially well. Then move on to the main event and return to something positive before finishing up the discussion.

Project Management: Where Hard and Soft Skills Collide

There are a few areas where hard skills and soft skills go hand in hand. One of the most pivotal is project management—the process of taking an idea from conception through to completion. To be a good project manager, you'll need to be extremely organized, have the ability to prioritize, create to-do lists, assign ownership of various elements of the project, and track milestones and deadlines—all hard skills.

But the project managers who truly excel are the ones who can keep their team on track, help them work through obstacles and stay focused when they run into them, encourage their teams when they feel discouraged, and motivate them to work together to accomplish things they might not have thought they could accomplish—all soft skills. The secret here is to break things down into digestible chunks. Say you've allotted three weeks for your team to finish a project. Figure out what needs to happen in week one and which people can best get the job done. Then think about weeks two and three. Throughout, check in regularly with the team to see how they're doing and what additional resources they might need.

Building a strong network and becoming a leader are mutually re-inforcing. When your colleagues respect you and your manager trusts you, it's much easier to take charge of a project. Promote yourself into leadership roles rather than waiting around for someone else to give you more responsibility. Let people know that you want to be in charge, while assuring them that they'll be integral to the success of the project. Prove yourself with the first project, and you'll solidify your position as a leader and you'll get trusted with bigger projects. As you manage larger projects, you will become more visible, with more responsibilities, and you will gain new experiences and relationships that you can leverage in the future.

Soft Skills Are Life Skills

One of the greatest things about soft skills is that they don't just apply to your work life. Soft skills that might seem work-related can help you in your personal life and vice versa. A friend of mine, Bill Connolly, was petrified of talking in front of others. But after taking an improv class, he was able to eliminate his fear of public speaking, which helped out at work but also helped improve his dating life. Adam LoDolce, an-other friend, had always been shy and awkward around women, so he forced himself to take a class on dating. It worked, and the skills he learned in that class—starting conversations, showing interest in other people, coming across as confident—also helped him attract more customers to his business. As you go through your day, think about the skills you're learning on the job and try to figure out how to apply them in other areas of your life.

If you're fortunate enough to work at Google, you should definitely sign up for their "Search Inside Yourself" program. In a *New York Times* interview, Karen May, Google's Vice President for Leadership and Talent, said, "We have great people. Now how do we keep them? Teaching employees with terrific technical abilities also means helping them to develop presentation skills and communication skills, helping them to understand their impact on other people, their ability to collaborate across groups, and cultivate a mentality from which great motivation can spring." So far, over 1,000 employees have been through the course, which teaches attention training, listening skills, self-knowledge and self-mastery, developing useful mental habits, and dealing with failure.

Of course, Google's program is a pretty rare case. Plenty of people struggle with acquiring and polishing their soft skills. As we've discussed, there are a lot of ways to do that. But the most successful one (which is also the hardest) is to jump into the mix and give it a shot. It might be tough the first few times (or few dozen), but the more you do it, the better you'll get.

Master Soft Skills to Become the Person Everyone Wants to Work With

If you're looking to move into a leadership position you need to be working on developing and improving your soft skills. Unless you're able to fit in with your company's culture, be a team player, and motivate others, you won't even make it to the short list of candidates.

So starting today, pay more attention to how other people see you. Try to get feedback from your manager about how your soft skills are today, and check back with her every six months or so to see how you're progressing—more often if she's identified something that is a serious problem.

Having strong soft skills opens up opportunities for you to become more social and build stronger relationships—relationships that can benefit you at work and in your personal life. Very few people are able to accomplish big things completely on their own—you're almost always working with a team. When you're known as someone who is good at developing strong, positive relationships with your team, and can rally them to tackle tough business problems, you'll become an even more valuable resource. That will help you grow your brand and will position you to move up in your organization.

5

Online Skills: Use Social Media to Your Advantage

Social Media, it turns out, isn't about aggregating audiences so you can yell at them about the junk you want to sell. Social Media, in fact, is a basic human need, revealed digitally online. We want to be connected, to make a difference, to matter, to be missed. We want to belong, and yes, we want to be led.

—SETH GODIN,
AUTHOR OF *THE ICARUS DECEPTION*

By becoming proficient in the most prominent social networks, like Facebook, Twitter, LinkedIn, and Google+, and by identifying and learning how to use ones that haven't been invented yet, you'll keep yourself ahead of the curve. You'll be able to build and grow a strong network of contacts you can call on in a variety of situations, whether it's to generate buzz and sales for your company's newest product, or to build your own personal brand. Having a strong personal brand will make you stand out at work, increase your visibility, and position you for promotions. Combine that with a strong social network and you've got the ultimate safety net for any economy.

I started using Facebook when I was a junior in college, and now everyone in the world is accessing it, and it's having a profound impact on our society. (Social media is so widespread that 92 percent of toddlers already have an online presence.[1]) We're connected to our friends, families, coworkers, and random people that we meet at events and through our daily travels. Even the few people I know who refused to open a Facebook account a few years ago are now actively using it because in today's world it's just about impossible for anyone to get along without it. In the past few years, Twitter has promoted the embarrassing antics of Charlie Sheen (#winning) and even played a role in the Egyptian uprising that marked the beginning of the Arab Spring of 2011.

Twitter is an incredibly powerful tool that can be used for good or bad. In 2012, people used Twitter to keep victims of Super Storm Sandy informed about where to find basic food and shelter and how to find lost friends and relatives. On the other hand, not everything you read on Twitter is true. Also during the storm, a Wall Street analyst sent out a series of completely made up tweets claiming that the New York Stock Exchange was under three feet of water and that all power to Manhattan had been cut off. He was fired from his job and there was even talk of prosecuting him.

Following the right sources is important, and following industry experts can help keep you up to date on the latest developments in your field and what the thought leaders are up to. These are people who are completely immersed in the topic, and because they (usually) enjoy sharing their knowledge, you can learn a ton from them.

Having a large social media presence and following can also add a lot of value to your career. From a purely personal perspective, your social media connections can help you improve your productivity by giving you access to information faster. From a getting-noticed-and-building-your-brand-at-work perspective, your social media connections can help you support your company in a variety of ways that are sure to attract attention from your manager and coworkers. For example, if your company has a major product announcement, you can promote it through your network to generate buzz and get extra attention for the release—and you might even land a new client. If a customer is complaining on Twitter and you stumble upon the tweet, you can let your PR department know, resolve your customer's issues, and come out looking like a hero. (If you let negative news go unchallenged it's only going to spread.) And when your company is looking to hire, you can source target candidates through your online profiles and maybe even make a few thousand dollars from your employee referral program.

Think of your social media profiles as assets that you'll be building on throughout your career. The networks you build can help you stay connected with people you know and build new connections with people you don't know. And, as we'll talk about in later chapters, the more people you know, the easier it becomes to open doors to new opportunities. Build and use your networks wisely now, and they'll pay big dividends later.

But watch out. If you aren't careful, you can get yourself into real trouble. You might have heard about the aides to Representative Rick Larsen, Democrat of Washington, who tweeted from their personal accounts about how cool it was to be sitting in the seat of power at midday, drinking Jack Daniel's, and watching Nirvana videos on the taxpayers' dime? You know who isn't sitting there anymore—from the seat of power to the hot seat in 140 characters.

You'd think people would know better, wouldn't you? *You* know better, right? Then again, how often have you hit Reply All on an e-mail when you meant to hit just Reply? It can be pretty embarrassing.

We all do it. Fifty-four percent of people under twenty-five and 32 percent of people over twenty-five[2] say they've posted something they later regretted. Those numbers seem too low to me. I believe that anyone who says they haven't done it, either hasn't noticed—or hasn't been caught . . . yet.

The fact is we live in a fast-paced world where the pressure to respond and to post is constant, and where it's all too easy to make mistakes. Unfortunately, there's often an inverse relationship between the time it takes to post a comment and the negative impact that post can have. In other words, the simplest mistakes can have the biggest—and longest-lasting—repercussions.

That's why a host of companies are now making money cleaning up people's online reputations. They know that, to a great extent, who you are *online* is who you *are,* period. People you'll never meet—across your company, across your industry, across the world—can read about you with their morning coffee, and to them, what they read is the absolute truth about who you are.

Do you think your managers and coworkers aren't looking? Do you think there's a firewall between your online and offline lives, or between work and personal time? Think again. Eighty-five percent of companies now use social media to research employees—for promotions as well as new hires. Sixty-three percent use Facebook and Twitter to unearth digital dirt. Seventy-one percent monitor employee social network use.[3] Oh, and if you were hoping things would get better, think again. A new study by Gartner found that 60 percent of companies plan to *increase* the amount of snooping they do on employees' social media by 2015. The moral of the story? Big Brother is here, so watch what you post!

Of course not *everyone* is looking over your shoulder. Steve Fogarty, Senior Manager, Strategic Programs at Adidas, doesn't do what young workers call "creeping" (aka spying) on employees' profiles. "As long as an employee is performing well on the job, then I'm not interested in what they do in their social life or on social media," says Fogarty. "Of course if they do something press-worthy or damage the brand in some way and others bring this to light, then of course this could have negative consequences." But managers like Chris Petranech, Sales Manager at PayPal, do it all the time. "I like to understand their interests and how they use social media to represent themselves online," he says. "Ultimately they are a reflection of my team within the organization." Others go even further and actually assess the quality of employee's social networks. "I connect with everyone I work with on Facebook, Twitter, and LinkedIn, if they're there," says Michael Brenner, Senior Director of Global Marketing at SAP. "And I secretly judge people who have very few connections on social channels."

Poor use of the Internet is as detrimental to your career as showing up late for a client meeting in your pajamas. Employers see your online reputation as a direct reflection of their brand. In other words, the who-you-are-online-is-who-you-are-period thing goes a step further and becomes who *you* are online is who *your employer* is online—whether it's on Facebook, Twitter, your personal blog, or the company Web site. A damaged rep online can be a firing offense, which means managing your online reputation is now an unwritten part of your job description.

But managing your reputation isn't just about not getting fired. Your online brand is how you position yourself in the company, how you demonstrate your expertise, how you define the way managers and coworkers see you. Managing your online brand is one of your most powerful tools for career advancement, and it's something you need to do thoughtfully, regularly, and proactively.

Building Your Online Brand

The best way to proactively build your online brand is by making deliberate postings that position you the way you want to be seen. That could be thoughtful comments on articles related to your job, relevant information you publish on Twitter and your personal blog, or videos you post showcasing your latest project. These and other postings together define you to your managers, your industry, and the world. They pop you up to the top of that Google search; they flesh out your profile on LinkedIn, and they define you in the corporate talent pool where promotion decisions are made.

It's all about creating, controlling, and managing your own reputation so it can help you build the career you want. If you aren't consistently posting to social media, you aren't linking to relevant blogs, you aren't leaving comments on other people's blogs and sharing information that's relevant to your job, and if you aren't networking through LinkedIn, updating your online résumé, or you don't know what *this week's* Google search will reveal about you, you're letting other people control your reputation—and that's a huge mistake.

Young employees often ask me why, if their goal is simply to rise to the top of their company, is it so important to build their brand in the "outside" world? My answer is this: Because becoming a recognized expert in your field increases your value to your company. If your blog is widely read, if people comment on it and pass it along, if your articles appear in online journals and you're invited to speak on panels, your company will perceive you as an expert; you'll be recruited for higher level jobs. And with good reason. You aren't just *acting* like an expert—all show and no substance—you'll *be* an expert. By regularly gathering and analyzing data and transforming it into your own Web content, you'll be developing insights that make you a valuable company resource. Your brand will be an accurate reflection of what you bring to the job.

"One of my first projects when I started my job was to create a recruiting blog that would tell Intel's story and connect with our target audience, job seekers," says Sejal Patel, a Social Media Strategist at Intel. "I joined several online forums and discussion groups. After my first online chat, I made a connection with a local recruiting professional who was writing a white paper on social media and recruitment.

She ended up interviewing my manager and me and included us in her paper. A few months after that, she invited me to be part of a panel discussing social media and recruitment at a well-known recruiting conference! That helped build my company's brand, but definitely helped me build my own as well."

Jason Duty, Director of Global Social Outreach Services at computer giant Dell, told me a story about how building a social media presence also built a young man's career. "I originally met him at a Dell event for social media practitioners. At the time, he actually had very little social media experience, not even a Twitter handle, and had just graduated college with an undergrad degree. During the event, it was very apparent that he was a total nut for technology, and you could see his interest piquing during the day as we got deeper and deeper into social media conversations. After the event, we kept in touch, primarily through social media. The following year, we hosted the same event and invited many of the original participants back, including this young fellow. I was amazed at how he had embraced social media—in just a year he had accumulated a lot of Twitter followers, but more importantly he had launched a blog with significant multimedia content and podcasts and had built his subscriber base up into the tens of thousands. He also completely wowed Michael Dell with his knowledge of technology and how it's used by various demographics. It just so happened that at the time I was creating a role on my team for a social media program manager, and I immediately thought this guy would be a great fit. Honestly, even without that role being created, I still would have found some way to hire him. He just joined a few months ago and is already having a significant impact on my org's capabilities in social media."

Your Blog: Good for You, Good for Your Company

Blogging doesn't just bring attention to you; it can also bring eyeballs to your company. According to a 2009 survey by Technorati,[4] 71 percent of bloggers surveyed said their blogs have increased visibility for their company, 63 percent converted prospects into purchasers through their blog, and 56 percent said their blogs bring recognition to their company as a thought leader in the industry. Can't hurt the annual review, can it?

Creating Your Online Identity

You already have an e-mail account—probably several. Facebook and Twitter accounts too. And you may be on LinkedIn or other social networks. But that's only the beginning. A critical component of your online brand is your online identity, and that goes well beyond just using e-mail and social media. The process actually starts with something as simple as your name, or, since we're talking about the Internet, your domain name. Here's how to create your online identity.

REGISTER YOUR DOMAIN NAME. Your domain name (*www.your-name.com*) is the central hub for your digital reputation. It's usually the first thing to come up when someone searches for you online, so the more control you have over it, the better. You don't want a cybersquatter registering it before you do and then charging you an arm and a leg for the rights to your own name. (Yes, it happens.)

Register your domain name even if you don't plan to create a personal Web site (although I'll tell you below why you should create one anyway). The cost is minimal—about $10 a year, possibly a little less if you register or renew for more than one year at a time. The easiest way to do it is at GoDaddy.com.

If possible, register your full name: BenSmith.com. If your name is taken, use your middle initial (BenRSmith.com), your full middle name (BenRickSmith.com), or your name with your industry association (BenSmithPR.com). This ensures that someone doesn't think a different Ben Smith is you. It's hard enough managing your own online brand; you don't want to worry about being confused with someone else! If all the .com's are taken, you can also register the .net and .me URLs.

CREATE PROFILES ON SELECTED SOCIAL NETWORKS. If you don't already have profiles on Facebook, LinkedIn, Twitter, and Google+, now's the time to create them. They're the easiest way to create your online identity and promote yourself to others. When establishing your social profiles, you want your online identity to be consistent, so use the same name, picture, and profile information for every account. Use the domain name you registered (even if it includes your middle name, initial, or professional association) to distinguish your profile from another with the same name.

Ideally, you want to register on the four biggest platforms: Facebook, Google+, Twitter, and LinkedIn, but (and this is a big but) be mindful of your time. Once you create a social media profile, you'll

---

Special note: I'm suggesting that you try to keep your profile names consistent across all the social networks you're on. Because there are so many, there's a good chance that the name you want may not be available on all platforms. You may want to use KnowEm.com, which matches your name against hundreds of social networks so you can see where it's available.

need to actively manage it. That means checking it *daily,* if possible, to create and respond to posts and see what others are saying about you. *So don't register for more networks than you can actively manage.*

FACEBOOK is the largest social network in the world. If it were a country, its more than one billion members would make it three times the size of the U.S. Half of all Facebook users log in every day.

If you're a Facebook power user, feel free to skip ahead to the next section. But because the most common question I get from people is "What's the best way to manage my personal and professional Facebook presence?" I want to spend a couple of minutes on exactly that.

I suggest that you use your Facebook profile as your personal page and create a Fan Page (or separate profile) for your professional image. A Fan Page acts just like a regular profile: You can post photos, videos, links, and everything else you need to promote your personal brand. If you then make your regular profile "Friends Only," everyone else who searches for you will find only your Fan Page. It's one solution for keeping your public and private selves safely apart. Facebook offers complete instructions for creating a Fan Page here: facebook.com/pages/create.php.

Although it's a little riskier, if you really want to, you can have a single profile for your combined personal and professional lives. You'll just need to be really careful to put your friends and business contacts in separate groups. Then when you post updates, you can select which group or groups you want to what you reach. Once you've made a Fan Page, be sure to make your regular profile private. To do this, go to your Privacy Settings and:

1. Make your Default Privacy setting "Friends" only. If you have already friended professional contacts, tell them about the change and give them your Fan Page link. Then unfriend them from your personal page.

2. Set "Who can look me up?" to "Friends" only and uncheck "Let other search engines link to your timeline." This will give you more control over who can find and view your profile.

3. Don't let people tag you in photos. Tagging opens you up to public viewing, and since you can't control what other people post or tag, why take a chance? To do this you'll need to go into Timeline and Tagging from the Privacy menu and set the checkbox so you can approve all tags before they're posted on your wall.

4. Turn off all platform apps, games, and Web sites. With few exceptions, which we'll talk about below, they look unprofessional.

5. Limit the Audience for Past Posts to "Friends." If you've already posted something your colleagues shouldn't see, this will minimize the damage. Another approach (albeit a pretty time-consuming one) is to change the Privacy settings on each individual status update that you, or someone else, has posted on your wall since you first started using Facebook. As a last resort, you can change the date on each status update, hide the status update altogether, or remove it from Facebook completely.

With Facebook Timeline profiles, it's more important than ever to proactively manage your privacy settings. If you don't, your updates may be viewed by your management, and they might think less of you based on all of those party pictures or political-bashing updates that you've published. When your timeline is visible, people can look back at what you've posted years ago too. I don't know about you, but I was the party chair for my fraternity in college, and I don't want clients seeing pictures or updates from my past. I spent three hours reviewing all of my updates from 2004 to 2006 in order to ensure everything was protected, and it was time well spent. Then, I turned on all moderation settings for posts and pictures tagged with my name and disabled the ability for others to write on my wall. This gives me full control of my profile.

Another question I hear often is, "Why should I build my brand on Facebook?" The answer is pretty simple. You do it because almost everyone you know or would want to know is there. That includes your friends and coworkers. But it also includes employers, recruiters, and potential business partners who use Facebook (often along with LinkedIn) to find great people for their organizations. Facebook is an extremely effective way to keep people you know up to date on what you're doing, and to let the rest of the world know how great you are. And here are some tips on how to boost your brand using your Facebook Timeline:

• Create a branded Timeline cover image. The dimensions of the cover are 840 pixels wide by 310 pixels tall. Use Photoshop, Paint, or another program, as well as professional pictures to create a Timeline that captures who you are and what you're interested in. You can also get creative by putting the URL of your Web site as part of the picture.

• Add applications to your Timeline by going to facebook.com /about/timeline/apps. These apps can notify your friends and viewers about your interests and hobbies. One of my favorites is the "Washington Post Social Reader," which allows you to share recent stories you're reading and will keep you up to date on news and developments in your industry.

• Feature specific status updates that you are most proud of by using the star feature. You can show your major accomplishments immediately when someone lands on your profile, which can help boost your brand.

And finally, before we move on to Google+, I encourage you to—at the very least—claim your Facebook user name (e.g., facebook.com /danschawbel) even if you aren't ready to commit to managing your

---

Do You Know How Many Coworkers Are Following You on Facebook?

Social media has kind of made the world into a small town, where everyone knows what everyone else is doing—even if it's private. So whatever you do, always keep in mind that someone else could see you, and, just as in a small town, that rumors spread incredibly quickly—and are impossible to control.

So before you scream at a waitress for messing up your order or you go out and get plastered with your friends, think about whether you really want pictures of that evening making the rounds on Facebook. And imagine what the president of your company would do if she happened to be sitting at the next table. There's no way that that couldn't affect their impression of you. No, of course it's not fair, and yes, you do have a right to a private life. But the reality is that we're in a 24/7/365 world and everything gets factored in. When was the last time you met a new person on Facebook and saw that you didn't have any mutual friends? It's been a loooong time for me.

I can't even keep track of all the horror stories I've heard—either from amazed managers who've fired someone for doing something stupid outside the workplace or from embarrassed young people who got caught and suffered the consequences. There was the guy who called in sick on October 31, then went to a wild Halloween party dressed as a fairy and decided to post pictures on Facebook. Guess who saw them? And there was the young woman who posted on her Facebook page that she hated the company she worked for and despised her boss. It wasn't until she saw her

---

boss's comment on her status: "You're fired," that she realized she'd forgotten she'd friended him. Oops.

Of course, the small-town nature of social media has its advantages. If you're involved in charity or volunteer work, you've written a brilliant article on some topic, you have a lead role in a community theater production, or you do anything else that's cool, it's easy to let people know about it.

---

profile at this time. You can check availability at http://facebook.com/usernames. This prevents someone else from claiming it in your stead, makes it easier for someone to find you, and looks more professional when you advertise your profile on other Web sites

My company analyzed four million Facebook profiles and over fifty million data points from Identified.com, and we found that the average young worker is connected to sixteen coworkers on Facebook and has nearly 700 friends. Yet only 36 percent list a job entry, meaning that most of them are using Facebook for personal postings but sharing that information at work. Hmmm. Probably time for a little work life/private life separation!

We also found that the average young worker leaves his or her first job in just over two years. This means that your friends could become your coworkers at some point in your life. That's exactly what happened to Alex Leo, who's just starting her career as the Director of Web Product at Thompson Reuters Digital. "I knew several of the people I'd end up working with at Reuters beforehand because of social media. A few of them have a fabulous presence online and we communicated a lot, especially on Twitter. This made coming on board at the company exceptionally easy because I already had people I knew and liked there."

GOOGLE+.   Google's social media platform, Google+, makes it easy to keep work and play separate. It prompts you to create Circles—

groups of contacts—and then lets you control which Circles see which content. Create one for family, one for hiking buddies, one for professional contacts, and so on, then design your content accordingly. Sign on at https://plus.google.com. Now that Google+ is fully integrated into Google's search engine and algorithm, it's important that you start using it if you want to become more visible. Here are some tips and things to keep in mind as you use Google+:

• The more followers you have (people having you in their Circles), the higher your status updates will rank when someone googles a topic you know about. And when people search for you on Google, your Google+ profile will rank high and may even come up when people start typing in your name if they're already connected with you.

• As with Facebook and Twitter, you can reshare other people's Google+ updates. You can also network with people in your industry by using the "+Name" tag, which will immediately notify that person that you've tagged them.

• Unlike Facebook, though, you can use the Google Hangout feature to set up a video conference with people in your network and get to know them better. This is especially useful if your contacts are in a different location, whether that's on the other side of town or the other side of the world.

• As with the other social media platforms, use Google+ with caution. The pitfalls of carelessly blurring the line between public and private are even more serious with Google+ than the others. Because it's part of Google, anything you post as Public will end up in Google searches where anyone can find it.

Have You Got Klout?

Your Klout score (klout.com) is a measure of your online influence: how many people follow you online and how many share your content. Your Identified score (identified.com) measures how attractive you are to employers based on your education, experience, and network. Employers are starting to use these scores, in addition to performance reviews, when deciding whom to hire and promote. The best way to improve your scores is to consistently create good content that other people want to share and respond to.

LINKEDIN. LinkedIn is *the* source for professional networking. It's not just a matter of whom *you* know anymore; it's whom *they* know and whom *they* know. LinkedIn is your tool for reaching all those contacts. Once you've posted your profile you'll be invited to "connect" with people you know and from there you'll have access to those people's connections as well. You'll be able to search for individuals you'd like to meet and see whether you share a common contact who might be able to make an introduction. At the same time, because LinkedIn is probably the most popular business social network, other professionals will be able to find and connect with you.

Just as you did on Facebook, claim your LinkedIn username (linkedin.com/in/danschawbel). Go to Edit Profile, scroll down to Public Profile, and click Edit. On the right side of the page you'll be able to Customize Your Public Profile URL. Use your domain name if at all possible. While you're there, copy and paste the fields from your résumé and make sure your Public Profile features you correctly. Your Public Profile is a short version of your profile that people see if they are not "connected" to you. It doesn't show your connections, nor does it permit people to contact you other than through LinkedIn's InMail system, a paid account feature. Here are some tips and things to keep in mind as you use LinkedIn:

• Think of your LinkedIn profile as a living, breathing résumé, something that will keep you relevant as long as you keep it current. Won an award or earned a promotion? Post it! Wrote an insightful article on a business-related topic or read a great article by someone else? Post it too! The more you contribute, the more people will get to know you.

• Use LinkedIn as a professional directory to find out more information about the people you work with, people you meet at events, and leaders in your industry. It will help you have more talking points with them and you'll look like you care and/or are interested in them.

• Review the LinkedIn Today newsroom by going to linkedin.com/today. I find it to be the best and most underutilized page on LinkedIn because it crowdsources all the most important topics that you care about and gives you access to the most shared on LinkedIn.

• Join as many LinkedIn groups that are related to your field or industry as possible. There is a fifty-group limit, but the more you join, the more profiles you'll potentially have access to and the more people you can connect with. When you join the group, be sure to participate in the group's discussions. Answer questions, share you knowledge, and increase your visibility. You never know who else is in a group and might be wowed by your expertise.

- One thing a lot of people overlook is getting recommendations and endorsements from previous bosses and other people you've worked with in some capacity. These help establish you as a high-performing, high-value employee. And that's important whether you're planning on staying in your current job or making a change. These recommendations are generally a paragraph or two long. LinkedIn also has a feature that allows members to endorse others for specific skills. It's kind of like the Facebook "Like" button. No lengthy explanations, just a simple click. These quick endorsements are very effective in building personal brands, because the more you have, the more visible you'll be when people search for professionals with your skills. The number of endorsements you have for each skill is an indicator of you're perceived talents. If one isn't showing up much, do a better job at displaying them at work and online. You can also click on a skill to see how in demand it is. If your skills aren't in demand, start focusing on others.

TWITTER is a microblogging platform that allows you to send messages—called tweets—that are 140 or fewer characters. It's yet another way of connecting with people. And because *everyone* is on Twitter, it's also an excellent way to keep up to date on what industry influencers and thought leaders are up to. If you don't already have a Twitter account, you can set one up at twitter.com in about five minutes. Once you're up and running, you can search for other users by topic or company name and start following them, meaning you'll receive their tweets, which might be stand-alone messages or could contain links to other blog posts and other content. Twitter will also help you connect with others in your industry. By tweeting out useful information, resources, facts, quotes, and links to your blog, you will attract followers who will start to see you as a resource. Limit your tweets to your area of expertise so you become known as an expert in that area. People who tweet indiscriminately tend to be ignored. As with the other social media platforms, use your full name and a professional picture so people know they're connecting with you and not someone else. Here are some tips and things to keep in mind as you use Twitter:

• Create a custom Twitter background that has more information about who you are and what you do. You can also include a larger picture of yourself and possibly your company's logo, if you get permission and they consent to you owning the profile.

• Use Twellow.com to search for specific people in your industry to follow. Try and avoid everyone else because it will get way too cluttered if you're following hundreds or thousands of people. Focus your energy on the few people that you're most interested in. You can also use tools such as TweetBeep.com and Hoot-Suite.com to manage all your social networks in one console. You can use them to track conversations that mention you, your industry, or anything else you specify, as well as to manage status updates on multiple social networks simultaneously.

• Interact with your followers and the people you follow whenever possible, instead of pushing random pieces of content with no context.

• Search Twitter to find—and participate in—interesting discussions. You do this by using a hashtag (the # character) followed by the topic you're looking for. Searching for #millennials, for example, will bring up all sorts of conversations. Read the discussion threads and jump in. If you're searching for something that's currently in the news, you can actually follow the discussion in real time. It's a very cool feature.

If you feel you can stay on top of them, you may also want to create profiles on other social networks. ZoomInfo.com is a simple professional database; YouTube is the top video-sharing site in the world. Use it to post professional videos and even a video résumé; Quora.com is a social network that connects you with people with similar interests and industry-specific networks; Instagram allows you to share and edit photos instantly on your phone and share them with family and friends on other social networks; Pinterest is essentially a giant bulletin board where you can "pin" different images, video, and other content on your own pinboard and on those of people who follow you; Foursquare allows you to use your smartphone to see whether there's anyone you know wherever you are.

But remember: You're creating a *professional* profile, one designed to help you advance your career. That means thinking carefully about what you post.

- *Do* post:
  - your skills
  - your relevant work experience
  - your major accomplishments
  - links to your professional Web site, blog, and videos
  - links to any content you've uploaded (articles, commentaries, blog posts, etc.)
  - testimonials, recommendations, and references (if approved by the writers)
- *Do not* post:
  - personal photos and videos
  - personal anecdotes
  - personal status updates
  - anything that doesn't enhance your professional image. (That means no party pictures and no updates on how many beers you just drank!)

What's in *Your* Tagged Photos?

If you say you wouldn't post beer pictures online, you're smarter than most. According to a 2011 survey by MyMemory.com, the average British Facebook user is under the influence of alcohol in three quarters of his or her tagged photos. Fifty-six percent of respondents admit they have "drunk photos" they wouldn't want coworkers to see.[5] What do you have online that *your* coworkers shouldn't see?

Develop Your Own Web site

As I mentioned before, once you've got a domain name, you should definitely create your own Web site. More than anything else, your site will define your professional self. It will most likely be the first thing to come up in a Google search for your name, which gives you the premier platform for describing yourself to the world. It's where you'll advertise your achievements and promote your expertise; where you'll post awards, testimonials, or recommendations; where you'll link to any YouTube videos you've posted, your blog if you have one, and any online content you've created. It can include information on your company and links to relevant parts of your company's Web site. And of course, it will link to your Facebook, Twitter, and other social network profiles. All together, this information will define your personal brand.

If you're worried about price, don't be. You can create a Web site absolutely free. WordPress.com, About.me.com, Tumblr.com, Sites. Google.com, and others offer free templates and hosting that will enable you to create a basic, functional Web site. The downside to the free options is that they're cookie-cutter and won't help you stand out from the crowd. So I recommend that you use a free site as a placeholder until you're ready to invest in a custom one. Designing a custom site could cost $600 or more (unless you've got the skills and software to design your own). You'll also have to pay a Web hosting service to host your site (I recommend GoDaddy.com and Bluehost.com, which cost $50 to $100 a year). But the costs are well worth it: You're making a major investment in your career. Your Web site could be the first thing a prospective employer sees about you. And as we talked about in Chapter 3, you've got to make that first impression count.

Once your site is up and running, you've got to keep it up to date. A Web site doesn't require daily management the way social media accounts do, but it's a good idea to check it at least weekly to make sure it always has your latest projects and information. If you use Google Analytics (available for free), you'll be able to see who is visiting your site, how they found it in the first place (for example, the search term they used in Google), what pages they're viewing, and how long they're staying there. Knowing that will help you tweak the site to make it even more compelling. If you don't have a huge amount of time to update your site, there are a number of free or inexpensive options you can install that will pull the most recent posts from any or all of your social media accounts.

The Basics of SEO—Search Engine Optimization

If you want to be known as an expert, you're going to have to come up in searches for your area of expertise—not just searches for your name. In order to rank higher, you have to optimize your site through a process called search engine optimization (SEO). Because Google's, Bing's, Yahoo!'s, and other engines' algorithms are so complicated, a whole industry has developed to try to essentially manipulate the search engines' results. There are entire books on SEO, and we can't go into that much detail, but here are some of the basics to get you started. As you become a social media power user, you can get into the finer points of SEO.

DOMAIN NAME

By using keywords, such as your full name or a topic you want to cover, as your domain name, you will help increase your search engine rank, which brings your site up closer to the top of the results page when people search for those words (and, by extension, for your site).

KEYWORDS

Choose two to five keywords that you want to rank high in search engines and use those keywords all over your Web site, including the title and within blog posts. In order to see what keywords have the most monthly searches and how competitive they are, go to https://adwords.google.com/select/KeywordToolExternal.

BACKLINKS

The more Web sites that link to your site, the higher your rank will be in search engines. You should aim for both quantity and quality with the sites that link back to your site if possible. If you have good content on your site, then other sites will link back to it. Of course, if you're asking others to link to you, be prepared to reciprocate.

RELEVANCY AND AUTHORITY

Links from popular high-traffic Web sites that have content that's related to you are especially good. For instance, if *The New York Times* linked to your blog, it would propel your ranking much more than a random site.

WEB AND SOCIAL MEDIA TRAFFIC

The more popular your content is and the more you market it, the more traffic you will get. Traffic usually comes from search engines and social networks.

Again, the points above are just an overview of how to optimize your online presence. The more of them you can implement, the higher your Web site will rank. People can't read your content or engage you in conversation if they don't know you exist.

Develop Your Own Blog

Once you've got your Web site, it's easy to add a blog. Go to WordPress .org and download and install their Web hosting software. Simple instructions are available on the site. This will enable you to develop a custom-designed blog that will sit on your Web site. If you've decided not to create your own Web site, you can create a free blog using one of the templates at WordPress.com or use Tumblr.com for a simple blog format. But I recommend that you make the investment and get a custom blog design so you can stand out. Thousands of other blogs will be using the same free template (called *themes* in WordPress parlance). Do you want yours to look just like theirs? For under $100, you should be able to get a much more unique theme that you can customize to suit your needs. What to write about? Focus on a single topic that you feel strongly about or want to master, and stick to that. People will read you because they share your passion for that subject, value your insights, and trust that when they open your blog you'll deliver in that specific area. If you've built your expertise in inside sales, don't suddenly blog about PR. Not much of a writer? Here's a tip: *"Talk" it, don't write it.* Forget all that stuff from high school English (sorry, Mrs. Richardson) about full sentences, topic sentences, and not starting sentences with "and." Pretend you're talking to a friend and just tell him what you want him to know. Successful blogs aren't honors papers; they're written in the blogger's true voice. That's what conveys the blogger's enthusiasm and energy and what makes blogs fun to read. Of course you will want to pay attention to spelling and grammar because what you write represents your brand and you may be judged harshly. The point is that you don't want to sound like a textbook. You need a voice and blogs are more casual than regular articles or essays.

Of course, even the best, most readable blog is only readable if people find it. Which means you can't just write it and put it out there. You need to create pathways to it. And that means finding blogs and Web sites that will post links to yours. Are you blogging about trends in Human Resources? Try to get the best-read HR blogs to link to yours. Writing about your experience with Linux? Pursue links in the IT world. Set your sights high and go for links to the biggest blogs and Web sites; they get more traffic themselves and will lift you higher in Google rankings. How to pursue those links? I don't recommend groveling (*"Please, pretty please, link to my site . . ."*). It isn't effective and can turn people off. Instead, create good content that other bloggers and journalists in your industry will want to link to. Send your material to them; post relevant comments on their articles and blogs; let them see what you have to offer. As they pick up your material, initiate a relationship. Once they know you and your work, they'll be more apt to offer a link.

You never know where your blog—and your passion—will lead. Brian Stelter started a blog tracking cable news coverage of the Iraq War when he was a college freshman. The blog got so much traction that it caught the eye of a media networking company, Mediabistro. com, which hired him to expand the blog under their umbrella. Stelter says, "Passion is the most important trait I bring to my blog. I am motivated to blog every single day."[6] Today, Stelter has continued to follow his passion as a media reporter for *The New York Times*.

A word of caution before you create your blog: Blogs are driven by passion. They're only as good as the host's *frequent*, passion-fueled postings. Nothing's less interesting than a blog that was last updated six months ago. So don't start one if you won't truly enjoy writing it *at least once a week.*

Become a Content Producer

The key to maximizing your online brand is getting to the top of search engines with links that showcase your assets. And the key to rising in search engines is putting material out there for people to find. That means producing a lot of content. What kind of content should you produce? Blog posts, comments on other people's blogs, articles and comments in online publications, and even YouTube videos. Any professional content that appropriately shows off your skills will help your career. Don't know what to write or post about? Well, everyone's an expert in *something*. You just have to find out what your something is. Customer relations? Marketing? Excel spreadsheets? Do you have ideas about how to streamline a process? Or thoughts about a trend you're seeing? What insights have you gained that might be of interest to others in your field? Keep your writing general: Don't reveal company secrets. But try thinking of yourself as an expert in your field and see what content possibilities come to mind. (Following what others in your field are posting will also give you ideas.) Perhaps you're an expert in something outside of work that's nonetheless relevant to the workplace. I was working in product marketing at EMC when I began posting about my outside passion, social media. I was publishing about twelve posts a week, posting videos I'd filmed for Personal Branding TV, and writing articles for blogs and online magazines. My work caught the attention of *Fast Company*, which profiled me as an expert in the field, and the next thing I knew, managers at EMC noticed and approached me to co-create the company's first "social media specialist" position. Perhaps you too have a skill or interest outside of work that might be relevant to your company. Are you an excellent public speaker? A skilled negotiator? Fluent in a foreign language? Using the Web to promote your expertise is a way of demonstrating it to your employer. If you're a public speaker, post videos of yourself in action with a list of venues at which you've spoken. If negotiating is your forte, post a short article on your Web site about negotiations you've successfully completed. If you're fluent in a foreign language, post a video of yourself conversing in a businesslike setting, along with a list of your language-related skills (can you do simultaneous translation? written translation? cultural training for overseas travelers?). Post these to your Web site and social media profiles, then use your contacts and corporate intranet to search for opportunities in your company where these skills might add value. One surefire way to create content is to review and comment on other people's material. Comment regularly on your favorite blogs. Post comments on articles relevant to your field. Review work-related books on Amazon.com where you can create a profile as a reviewer, bringing you to the attention of others with similar interests. Just make sure your comments are thoughtful and add to the conversation. You want to be seen as a resource, not an opinionated crank.

Posting comments is also a way to start writing for other people's blogs and magazines—an excellent way to be seen as an expert in your field. Pinpoint a few small sites you'd like to write for and start posting. After a few weeks, reach out to the site owners and ask if you can do a guest article or blog post. Once you've been published a few times, pitch the owners of larger sites and include links to your published postings. Gradually work your way up the ladder to bigger and bigger media platforms. If you're still unsure of what to post about, think *current*. The world is constantly changing and managers want workers who can update them on the latest trends, events, and opinions. Online tools can help you stay current so you can pass on the latest news.

- Subscribe to industry blogs and newsfeeds. One of the best ways to do this is with Google Alerts, a handy service that will send you e-mails or RSS feels whenever content matching your search parameters shows up just about anywhere.

• Use OneNote, or another note-taking software, to organize your finds. Then use that news to create and update your online content.

• Manage Twitter and the rest of your social networks. Tools like TweetBeep and HootSuite make this pretty easy by putting all your social media together in one place.

• SocialMention.com allows you to see what people are saying about you and topics you care about in real time.

The goal of producing all this content is to get more visibility in search engines. The more content you post, the higher you'll be in search engine rankings and the quicker you'll appear when people search for your name or the topics that you're commenting on. But you can't just create content and put it out there. You have to drive people to it because clicks also raise rankings. The more people click open your content, the quicker you'll show up in searches. So every time you post new content, use all your platforms—your Web site, blog, social media accounts, and so on—to send people to it.

Staying Current:
Update, Update, Update!

Up until now, we've been talking about *creating* content. But creating content is just the beginning. Equally important is *managing* it, because your content is only as good as it is current. And in the online world, where news spreads like wildfire, content is constantly changing, and new experts are constantly demanding your eyeballs, current means *an hour ago, today, yesterday,* or at the very latest last week. If you're posting information about what you did four years ago, if you haven't updated your blog and profiles *this week,* you're a dinosaur and you'll lose visitors. And search engines will reflect that. When you refresh your pages and include the latest information, Web crawlers will notice and your sites will rise in the rankings. Search engine results typically include the date the post was written. Some people have a cutoff—they'll skip over anything that's more than a week, or a month, or a year old. Others don't care. As a result, it's getting kind of trendy these days to leave off the date from posts. The main reason is that it gives the impression that what you're writing is more recent than it is. This is something to consider if your content truly is evergreen and you aren't able to update your site with new content very often. But be careful because having a post that looks like it's hot news but refers to past events in the present tense can really reduce your credibility.

Every morning I wake up and go through online feeds. I spend one to two hours reviewing a thousand news feeds looking for information about my world. The time I spend pays me back in spades. Every day I have loads of information to offer the people following me online—and they appreciate my daily tips. I update my presentations minutes before I give them because otherwise they're obsolete. New data will have surfaced since the last time I gave a talk. I walk into meetings and can speak with authority about the latest trends in my industry. My colleagues know they can rely on me for current data. And because I organize the data as soon as I find it, I can find it again quickly—saving me time later when I need it for creating content.

So I recommend that you do something similar. Get up an hour earlier and scour the news feeds in your industry. Can't give it an hour? Then do a half hour. Whatever works for you. But the more time you invest, the more info you'll find that will help you stay current. Here are a few more recommendations that will help keep you and your content fresh and relevant:

• Make sure that all the information posted about you is up to date. It should reflect your latest project and your latest thinking, not what you were doing and thinking six months ago. For instance, as you progress in your career, ensure that your LinkedIn profile and blog bio remain updated and consistent with your new position and accomplishments.

• Make sure your keywords and tags are current. Trends change, ideas sizzle and die. Make sure your content and keywords reflect the latest thinking in your field so that people can find you when they search.

• Develop a schedule with monthly update reminders. Use a paper calendar, mobile calendar, Google Calendar, or any other tool that works for you. The most important thing to do is to actually do it.

The Net Is for Networking

It may not be your parents' workplace anymore but some things haven't changed. And one of them is this: *It's not what you know, it's who you know.* Today, as much as ever, it's people—more than résumés—that open doors.

What *has* changed is the number of people you have access to. Thanks to the Internet, you can now network with tons of people who can help you locate opportunities, connect you with the people hiring, write references, and put in a good word. It's truly a global village when it comes to career advancement. Companies are looking worldwide for talent and they're using the Web to do it, which means that even to advance inside your company, you're competing against global talent. You need to use the Net to do it.

Your online content will help show that you're the best person for the job. Your online networking will get that content in front of the people who count.

CREATE AN ONLINE RÉSUMÉ. High-potential employees are always looking for the next opportunity—the next challenge in the company that's a perfect match with their skill sets and experience. That means you need to have a résumé ready at all times—a résumé that's dynamic, full of links that show your expertise, and absolutely up to date. Say good-bye to that static Microsoft Word document you used in the past. Today's compelling résumés are online. In fact, your LinkedIn profile with its links to your multimedia content is exactly the résumé you need.

S o now go back through your LinkedIn profile and make sure to:

• Brand yourself as an expert, not merely an employee. Don't just post your job description; describe your experience and expertise. What are you really good at? What have you accomplished? What benefits do you offer your employer?

• Ask current and former managers, team members, and clients for testimonials, along with permission to post them online. Be clear with them about the purpose of the posting. If your current manager and coworkers think you're trolling for a new job, they may not want to advertise you to their competitors. Let them know your goals and how your profile will help you achieve them, and why having their comments is an asset. If they're at all uncomfortable, let it go.

• Link to your Web site, blog, YouTube videos, and any other professional content so you create a dynamic, three-dimensional portrait.

WITH WHOM SHOULD YOU NETWORK? START INSIDE YOUR COMPANY. Managers are always looking to recruit, even if there aren't jobs open. So use online networks and your company intranet to connect with people in other departments (two thirds of major companies now use internal Web 2.0 tools such as blogs and social networks). Those connections can help you learn about jobs before they're open and keep you top of mind when managers are hiring. Ask yourself, "Who in my company can help me advance?" Then look for links to those people. Have you heard about a project you'd like to work on? Use your network to connect with the manager in charge. Hope to work in another department? Ask a mutual contact to introduce you on LinkedIn and include links to relevant content you've created.

Before you reach out this way, though, speak to your own manager. The last thing you want is to go behind their back. Instant bad karma! Instead, talk to them about your goals. If you haven't already discussed your personal development plan with them, do it now. Tell them what you hope to achieve at your company and ask for advice on how to achieve it. Ideally, they can help you plot a path through the organization by defining projects and departments that will give you the experience and credentials you need. They can also help you with networking. Once they know your goals, they can connect you with relevant people and give you advice on the best ways to approach them. Why would your manager offer this support—especially if you're a valuable employee? If they're a good manager, they'll support your quest because it supports their own goals. For their own advancement they need to grow talent and grow the company, so when you shine, they shine too. That's why—if you've got a good manager—they can be your best ally for advancement. Of course, as we discussed in Chapter 1, not all managers are that open-minded. Some are threatened by their employees' growth, or fear losing their top talent. They won't facilitate your development plan and won't offer networking support. If you have this kind of manager, then you'll have to limit what you share. Talk only about your goals within the department. Do very little networking so your manager doesn't think you're looking for another job. Meanwhile, look for another manager or department you'd like to work for. You can't advance if you've got a manager who's holding you back.

EXTERNAL NETWORKING: BUILDING YOUR EXPERTISE. Even if your goal is to rise to the top of your current company, you should be networking outside the organization. For one thing, you never know where a lead will come from. Someone outside the organization may hear of a project or opportunity in another department of your company before you do. More importantly, networking isn't just about opportunity shopping. It's about building your skills and knowledge. The world is full of people who know more about your area than you do, who can be teachers or mentors and help you grow. So seek them out. When you find blogs or articles you like, see if you and the authors have any network contacts in common; see if you can arrange an introduction. Then ask them questions about the articles they've posted. Ask if you can run an idea by them or if they'd be willing to critique an article of yours before you post it. It may seem intimidating to approach an expert this way, but the fact is, most people enjoy mentoring others who show genuine interest. If you're gracious, appreciative, and respectful of their time, the experts you contact may be pleased you've made the effort, and you may be on your way to finding a professional mentor.

LinkedIn: Your Chief Network Builder

Once you've imported your own contacts into the application, check out Network Statistics under the Contacts tab in the upper toolbar. You'll probably see that you have access to over a million other people through your contacts' contacts! If you want that number to grow even more, you can search for colleagues, college classmates, and anyone else you think you'd like to connect with. And take a look through the LinkedIn-generated People You May Know suggestions. Every person you add to your network has a network of people who may be helpful as you advance your career.

Also add to your LinkedIn database by asking your previous and current managers for recommendations and introductions, and by joining industry groups listed under the Groups tab. If you have an iPhone, download the LinkedIn CardMunch app. It automatically turns a photo of a business card into a LinkedIn contact. Use it whenever you attend an event or grab a new person's card.

KNOW WHEN TO GO FACE-TO-FACE. Online connections are great, but there are times when face time is necessary and preferred. If your boss is more comfortable in the handshake world than online, ask in person if it's okay to connect on LinkedIn. When you discuss your development plan with your boss, and when you ask for an intro to another manager, do it in person so you can fully discuss your reasons. If a person you hope to meet is a bit old-school, ask your introducer to arrange a face-to-face meeting rather than a LinkedIn introduction. The Internet provides a host of tools for making connections but they're not always the most appropriate ones for the job.

CULTIVATE YOUR INFLUENCE. Online networking isn't just about meeting people. It's also about influence, about how you impact the people you meet, and what happens as a result. Yes, you want people following your tweets and blog posts; but even more you want them forwarding those posts to others. Yes, you want people reading your comments and articles; but more than that you want them quoting you in their conversations. You want them thinking of you as a valuable source of ideas and information, as an expert. Acquiring that kind of influence takes years, not days. It means committing to producing and monitoring content frequently and long-term. But the payoff is huge. The more people value your output, the larger your network grows, the more opportunities will open up. The more you'll take control of your career.

Use Video to Promote Your Expertise

Even if the idea of standing in front of a camera makes you stressed out, don't write off YouTube as a way to build your brand. You can put your *ideas* front and center and bring them to life. Have you finished a successful project at work? Are you a whiz at CRM? Do you frequently get compliments on your PowerPoints? Use your own or company photos, PowerPoint slides, clip art, and Web images (get permission for anything that's not yours), and edit them together using one of the free video editing programs available. Add a two- to three-minute script (that's all most people will watch) and you'll have a promo video ready for YouTube without your own blushing presence.

Keep in mind that you don't have to be in *front* of the camera to use video to build your brand. Brian Halligan, CEO of HubSpot, told me a great story about a woman who used video to turn a summer internship into a full-time job. "We hired Rebecca as a summer intern after her junior year at BU. Her task was to create our first viral video. She took a very unusual approach by taking an Alanis Morissette song and turned it into an inbound marketing song that ended up tipping on YouTube. The video did so well, we hired her after she graduated."

To Do and Not to Do

No matter which social media platform you're using, there are certain do's and don'ts you should observe. Some are pretty obvious, but you'd be surprised at how many otherwise smart people make stupid, damaging mistakes. So as you foray into the world of social media, here are some do's and don'ts to keep in mind:

• **Don't badmouth your company, your boss, or your colleagues.** Common sense, right? You leave a comment on someone's blog calling your company's annual bonus policy a "pathetic operation" and someone from the company is going to see it. Guaranteed. An intern at the fashion firm Marc Jacobs International waited until his last day on the job to tweet about his boss: "Good luck! I pray for you all. . . . I'm out of here. Robert's a tyrant!" Did it get back to his boss? Of course it did. So much for a reference from that employer. But that's not all. The intern's tweet was widely retweeted, and that made it harder for him to land his next job.

• **Don't share classified information about your company.** This includes:
- unposted job openings
- company salaries (including your own)
- news of acquisitions or mergers. Your little tweet can spread through social media like a virus and end up in the mainstream news—with you identified. Guess who won't be working for that new merged company?
- office secrets, gossip, or rumors
- stories where you don't have all the information. Remember Ashton Kutcher and the sex abuse scandal at Penn

State? Kutcher tweeted his support for coach Joe Paterno before he learned the facts—that Paterno had covered up longtime sex abuse by his assistant coach. Kutcher backpedaled when followers exploded in anger, but with each recant he put his foot in a little deeper. "Fully recant previous tweet! Didn't have full story." "As of immediately I will stop tweeting . . ." "Won't happen again." At least he hopes not.

• **Don't post anything you wouldn't want to see on a bulletin board in the cafeteria—or in court.** Everything can get forwarded—even your *personal* e-mails, so don't take a chance. That snarky e-mail about your coworker that you're about to send your closest friend? Save it for over dinner where

---

The Five Taboos: Politics, Class, Race, Gender, and Religion

Avoid them like the plague. They'll only get you in trouble. Believe me, I learned this lesson the hard way. Several years ago, I read something I liked about Ron Paul, the presidential candidate, and shared it on my Fan Page profile. Within minutes I started getting comments. "Why are you sharing this?!" "Since when are you a political guru?" "I find Ron Paul and your support of him offensive." I'd unwittingly given people a reason to dislike me! Readers expected me to write about personal branding, not politics—and they were right. My expertise is advice for the workplace, not the voting booth. So I quickly learned to keep my personal opinions on my private Facebook page—or to myself.

---

your words will disappear. And yeah, you may look great in a swimsuit and sexy holding a drink in your hand, but this is your professional image, remember?

• **Do add to the conversation.** Don't blog and comment just to read your own writing. People will tune you out. And don't write thin little comments that are nothing but excuses to slip in a reference to your name and Web site. That turns people off. We're all carving minutes out of busy days to catch up online, so make our time with you worthwhile.

• **Do offer great advice and free insights.** The more you give away, the more people will ask you for advice. And the more people come to rely on you for advice, the more valuable you become to your employer (current or future).

• **Do review everything you write to make sure it represents you in the best light.** That means (yes, Mrs. Richardson) use good spelling, punctuation, and grammar. If these are not your strong suits, ask a friend to look things over before you post.

• **Do promote your company.** Has your company got a great promotion going? Have you just released some excellent news? Post it on your Web site and spread it to your social networks. First, though, check with your manager; make sure your promotion is appropriate.

• **Do promote other people.** No one achieves success in the workplace alone. Most people are part of a team to which numerous people contribute, and even solopreneurs rely on others such as researchers who provide or analyze data, assistants who provide administrative support, and managers who clear obstacles out of the way. Make a point to acknowledge these supporting players when you promote your own work. Don't be phony—or Academy Awardish ("I'd like to thank my great-aunt Bertha, and my second cousin Neville, and my third grade teacher . . ."). That's as bad as hogging all the glory to yourself. But genuinely sharing credit when appropriate will make you look as good as the people you're recognizing.

• *Do ask for help.* Thanks to social media, you no longer need to know it all—or interrupt your boss with stupid questions. When you hit a stumbling block, use the Internet. I learned this back in my EMC days when I was stumped on a project. Rather than interrupt my boss I tweeted my question (I made it general so I didn't reveal sensitive information) and within an hour I got hundreds of responses. Doing that saved me a lot of time and helped my reputation. I didn't waste time guessing, researching, and underperforming, and my boss admired my "creativity." A word of caution, though: Don't overuse this tactic. After all, it's *your* job and you're the one expected to do it.

• *Do share your story with the media.* Don't be shy: One of the best ways to get noticed and to rise in search engine rankings is to get covered in the media. So *after you get approval and support from your manager and PR department* (see below), figure out which media outlets are the best match for your expertise and intended audience and pitch them. Which magazines or journals does your audience read? What blogs do they follow? What do *you* read, and where would you like to see yourself in print? Once you've targeted specific outlets, read through back issues to get a feel for their preferred content. Are they heavy on technology stories? Try to tweak your article in that direction. Is their tone casual or formal? Try to adjust your writing to their style. Many magazines (print and online) have Guidelines for Writers sections on their Web site that tell you how to prepare and submit articles. Follow those guidelines. If your target publications don't provide that info, locate contact info on their Web site and call or e-mail to find out how to submit your article. Your pubs may prefer a query to a completed article. If so, prepare a brief summary of your article along with a list of key points and a grabby headline. Pitch smaller publications first to practice. Then, once you're published, include links to those articles when you pitch larger outlets.

Hold On to That Post . . .

Seventy-three percent of people think employees overshare on social media. And they're right! Here's a cautionary tale for you. When I worked at EMC, a fellow employee started making HR videos outside of work, which he posted to YouTube. The videos were general—not about EMC—but one mentioned something the company felt was proprietary. A colleague saw it and sent it to HR—which sent it to Legal. The employee managed to retain his job, but it was a nail-biter. He and I both learned a lesson: Before you blog, comment, write, upload video, or create any kind of public content, make sure you know what's acceptable to your company—because what you *think* is perfectly safe may not appear that way to company managers and lawyers.

Here's how you can avoid overexposure:

REVIEW YOUR COMPANY'S POLICIES. Many companies have media and/or social media policies. The policy may be as simple as requiring you to put a disclaimer on all content that says something like, "The views and opinions expressed here are my own and not my company's."

Or it may be long paragraphs of legalese that spell out detailed restrictions. Know what is and isn't permitted before you open your mouth or click Send.

TALK TO YOUR BOSS ... *IN PERSON.* Describe what you'd like to do and get their okay. It's not only polite, it's smart politics. Ask: Is it okay to blog? To write articles? To post videos? Should my content be reviewed before posting? What are the company's sacred cows? What does the company consider safe? It's better to know the limits ahead of time than to ask forgiveness later.

KEEP IT GENERAL. Once you get clearance to write, keep your content general. Your postings can be relevant and useful without revealing confidential information. Discuss trends in your field, offer opinions on related topics, comment on industry news, offer advice to other professionals. But don't discuss what you do day-to-day. Remember, you're not an investigative journalist, you're a commentator. Feel free to analyze someone else's scoop—just don't deliver your own.

SAY NO IF YOU HAVE TO. You hate to turn down an interview request from *Time* magazine, but if your company says, "Sorry, a senior exec will do it," you have to back off.

When Personal Life and Work Life Conflict

One of my friends is a male model. Nothing risqué. He keeps his clothes on. He appears in fashion magazines. Nevertheless, it's not something he particularly wanted his boss and colleagues to know. At the same time, he wanted a Web site where prospective clients could find him. What to do? How to create a public platform that his coworkers wouldn't find? The answer I gave him was only partially satisfactory: use only your first name or nickname for any online modeling content. Anything else and your company will surely find out. Ultimately, he decided against the Web site because the risk seemed too high—and I think he was right. Unfortunately, there is no safe way to keep people from finding us online.

Given the potential risks, how do you handle conflicts between your work life and personal life?

DECIDE WHAT YOUR BOUNDARIES ARE.   Before you post anything—whether it's to your social network, Facebook Fan Page, or personal Facebook account—ask yourself if you're comfortable having your professional contacts see it. Because as careful as you are, chances are they *will*. When in doubt, don't post.

CREATE ALTERNATIVE PROFILES.   If you decide to post personal content that might show you in a less than professional light, use just your first name, a nickname, or a pseudonym. Omit identifying information (and pictures!) whenever possible to limit your visibility to professional contacts.

BE UP FRONT WITH YOUR MANAGER.   If your unprofessional content is already online, 'fess up with your boss. Better for her to hear about it from you than to find it herself or hear of it from someone else. The repercussions are apt to be less severe.

How to Fix a Bad Rep

In college, Ryan Miner started a Facebook group that opposed the formation of a Gay-Straight Alliance on campus; publicly he made insulting comments about homosexuals. After graduation, however, his views matured. "I could not have been more wrong," he says. "My words were unabashedly despicable. . . . I was in no position to cast such judgment, and I pray that I can be forgiven and learn from this awful experience." Unfortunately, the media storm that accompanied his college actions has made forgiveness elusive. Because of the attention he received, Ryan is now forever "attached to my mistake in the annals of Google. . . . I have been denied employment and was even fired from a great opportunity as a result of the incident. . . . each time I submit a new résumé, a sense of bleak fear overcomes me, wondering whether or not a company will Google my name only to toss my résumé in the trash. . . . If only I could relay to a potential employer that my beliefs have changed and I would never engage in that type of behavior in the future. But you reap what you sow, and I will continue to deal with the consequences of my mistake."[7]

Ouch. Makes you wonder whether Ryan will ever be able to recover his reputation. But more to the point, what can *you* do if something incriminating appears about you online? Here are a few strategies to help you minimize the damage:

PAY ATTENTION!   You can't just send something off into cyberspace and hope for the best. Whether it's an article, a blog comment, or a Facebook entry, you have to monitor everything you post—and everyone's reactions to it. Check in daily to see what the response has been and make sure it's okay. If it's not, take fast corrective action.

I speak from experience. When I was first starting out in my social media position at EMC, I was also doing personal tweeting about success in the workplace. I knew I couldn't tweet while at work, but I wanted my tweets to be frequent and current. So I prewrote them and scheduled them to appear every three hours. What I didn't count on was the perception these frequent tweets created. Coworkers at EMC tweeted back that I was tweeting all day at work! Fortunately, because I monitored the Twitter stream, I realized the problem and quickly explained that I had automated the postings. Within days, the flap died down. I was able to correct my mistake pretty easily. If your misposting is more significant, the fix may be tougher. But whatever the gaffe, the best policy is to address it head-on. Admit your mistake. Issue a correction or apology. Describe what you've learned from the situation. A well-handled correction can actually win you support.

ASK FOR CORRECTIONS. Sometimes the mistake is not yours; it's misinformation someone else has posted. Don't let it go! Periodically search for your name and act immediately to get erroneous information corrected or removed. Avoiding the situation will not make it go away; it will only increase the potential for damage. You may be surprised at how easy it is to get things corrected or removed. Most sites don't expect to hear from people they cover; sheer surprise may prompt them to remove the offending post. If not, fire off your own correction. Don't be belligerent or snarky; just correct the mistakes using as many facts and sources as possible and let the truth speak for itself. You'll not only correct the misperceptions; you'll gain the moral high ground.

CREATE A BARRIER. If you can't fix the negative postings about you, or there are simply too many to pursue, your best bet is to flood the Internet with positive references so the negative ones sink to the bottom of any search. Here's where all that content you've posted really comes in handy. The more you post, the lower the bad news stories will fall.

COME CLEAN WITH YOUR BOSS. As we said before, if there's dirt on you online, there's a good chance your boss will see it. So you're best off simply telling them what's there. Yes, it's embarrassing; yes, it feels dangerous. But it sure beats having them learn about it from someone else.

GET PROTECTION. Several sites now exist to help you protect yourself from Internet damage. Reputation.com, Secure.me, and others troll the Internet, alert you to damaging posts, and offer possible fixes.

Remember Anthony Weiner, the New York congressman who sent an (ahem) inappropriate photo to a follower on a social media site . . . and the fallout that followed as he tried to disown it? Did *anyone* believe he hadn't sent it? Did it even matter? The guy's going to be haunted by that scandal for the rest of his life. Thankfully for us Weiner made that mistake so we don't have to. We know better. We know how powerful the Web can be for creating and promoting our personal brand—and how ruinous it can be if we misuse it. So embrace the power of the Web. Explore the ever-growing number of tools it offers to burnish your professional image. But remember how quickly a thoughtless click can backfire. Love the Internet—and use it wisely.

Social Media and the Generation Gap

Chances are that your social media skills are a lot more developed than those of people a generation or so older than you. Chances also are that you either are now or soon will be working for some of those older people. And while there's a lot of talk about the technology gap between younger and older generations, I think that social media is the perfect way to bridge that gap. I had a chance to talk with Scott Simkin and Carlos Dominguez at Cisco. Scott is a young Mobility Solutions Manager and Carlos is a Senior Vice President in the Office of the Chairman and CEO. Scott was telling me about the way he had used social media to connect with clients. "Fifty to seventy-five percent of my job day-to-day is social media marketing, and I've built up a community of 100,000 people with Twitter, Facebook, Google+, Slide-

Share, all the typical communities. I'm out there talking to our customers, talking to our partners, getting in a room with ten bloggers and being able to showcase our product or connecting them with our technical experts. I can thank the guys at Twitter and Facebook for my raise and promotions!"

The one obstacle Scott had to overcome was some resistance to social media from people senior to him. Fortunately, he was able to get Carlos into his corner. "The majority of people my age, in their fifties, who are in leadership and in many cases senior leadership roles in organizations don't really use these technologies or they say it's stuff that their kids use," says Carlos. "The numbers in the last report I read still show that about a third of the Fortune 500 block social media sites from the corporate Internet. So on one hand you've got this great example of what Scott was able to do with social media, but on the other hand, there's a lot of fear from the people of the Wite-Out generation like I am who may be pushing back."

So although Scott had to convince his VP and directors, "just having that top-down acceptance of it is tremendous for someone in my position." He gave Carlos the last word: "The world and the rules have changed dramatically. And if it's just Gen Y people like Scott who are leveraging social media to help them move up the food chain, the senior execs who aren't embracing it, or at least supporting it, are going to become obsolete very, very quickly."

Using Social Media to Get Ahead— And Managing Your Online Presence Before Someone Else Does

The Internet has become the global talent pool, which means that a lot of the opportunities that will come to you in your career will happen within social networks instead of in "real life." Social media gives you access to people you wouldn't have access to in the past, and you can leverage that access to connect with even more people who can further your career. Besides making it possible for you to develop relationships with your coworkers and expand your network outside the office, the Internet and social media allow you to gain insights and learn skills from the leading experts in their fields. Where else can you follow Richard Branson, Steve Case, and others and interact with them? You don't need to navigate an entire organization trying to connect with them, they are already there.

The Internet also makes it a lot easier to solve problems and stay current on industry news and development. Got a question? Put the word out through your social networks and crowdsource some answers? Want to be part of important conversations that impact people's lives? All you have to do is follow thought leaders in those areas and the information will come straight to your smartphone.

The Internet is everywhere. Even if you're one of the very rare people who don't have some kind of social media presence, I'm betting you can find all sorts of stuff about yourself (some of which might actually be accurate) by googling your name. Whether you like it or not, your managers and coworkers are going to check you out online. So will people you're having a business meeting with, and so will anyone you're dating. There's so much pre-in-person googling that Google has become the new handshake—it's how most people first begin to learn about each other.

One of the big challenges around social media is to keep your personal life from spilling over into your professional life. There's no question that something that might seem perfectly innocuous in your personal life could sabotage your career. For that reason, you need to monitor your online brand monthly if not more frequently. If you're not controlling your story, someone else will be.

A lot of people I work with feel very uncomfortable doing many of the network-building and identity-building things I'm suggesting in this chapter because they feel that it's too self-promotional. I can't really argue with that: No question, building a brand is self-promotional. But that doesn't mean you have to look like a narcissist when you do it. It's possible to promote yourself in a way that is humble and non-self-congratulatory, a way that makes your experience and expertise apparent without shouting, "Look at me!" So don't be put off by the idea of self-marketing. And be sure to read the next chapter to find out how to gain visibility without being a self-promotional jerk; the chapter will help you find ways to market your skills without alienating your colleagues or looking utterly self-absorbed.

6

Gain Visibility Without Being Known as a Self-Promotional Jerk

Don't worry when you are not recognized but strive to be worthy of recognition.

—ABRAHAM LINCOLN

In the previous four chapters I've talked about how important it is in today's changing workplace to stand out by creating and managing your career, and how to get the hard, soft, and online skills you'll need to really stand out in the workplace. In this chapter, we're going to deal with a question that I hear a lot from young workers: How do I let everyone know how good I am without people thinking I'm a self-promoting jerk?

Before we start, we need to define two terms I'll be using a lot in this chapter. First, there's *self-promotion*, which is strategically letting people know what you can do, what your abilities are, and what you've accomplished—in a way that keeps the focus on how all of that benefits your team and your company. If you don't do at least some of it, you're screwed. You want to stand out, and it would be great if your accomplishments could speak for themselves, but most people you work with and for won't be aware of everything you bring to the table and you'll end up frustrated and angry when you don't get the credit you deserve and as you watch less talented, less competent coworkers get promoted ahead of you. Self-promotion is good—as long as it doesn't go too far.

Second, there's *bragging*, which is often used interchangeably with self-promotion. While there is some overlap, the two are actually very different. Again, self-promotion is more about the external: your skills and accomplishments in the context of how they benefit other people, your team, and your company. Bragging, however, is all about the *internal*: you, you, you—how great you are and how you're better than everyone else. Sometimes it's hard to see where self-promotion ends and bragging begins or when self-promotion goes from acceptable to obnoxious. But by the end of this chapter, you'll have a clear understanding and, more importantly, you'll know exactly how to stay on the right side of the line.

You Can't Promote Something Nobody Wants

Although no one likes a braggart, most people are okay with self-promotion—as long as it doesn't go overboard. But again, self-promotion is about your accomplishments. You may or may not be a fan of Justin Bieber, but there are millions of tween and teen girls who love him. And the way he got where he is was by doing a lot of self-promotion. In his case, it was putting videos on YouTube of himself singing. If no one had seen those videos, Bieber would be just another guy. But he got himself discovered. And while his looks contributed to his success, the fact is that he has talent. Talent is the only path to a sustainable, thriving career and Bieber is still around, so he has it. People were able to forgive the rather aggressive YouTube campaign because they enjoyed his singing.

Another singer, Lady Gaga, is almost as well known for her outrageous stage costumes as she is for her music. But the music—her accomplishments—came first. If she wasn't writing and performing songs that people were interested in, she could wear anything she wanted including a dress made out of raw meat and brag about what a great voice she has and no one would care. The same goes for athletes, actors, and any other kind of celebrity. It's all about the accomplishments. Michael Phelps doesn't have to tell people he's a great swimmer. All he has to do is get out there and swim. It's similar with you. (The difference is that Michael Phelps does his self-promotion at the Olympics, so everyone in the world knows exactly what his accomplishments are. You, on the other hand, will most likely have to *tell* people about what you've done.) If you have a weak personal brand and you haven't accomplished much, you can promote yourself all day long and no one will notice. The key is what we talked about back in the previous chapters: acquiring skills and using them to position yourself as an expert.

Promoting Yourself Online

Google recently did a study on how social media tools are used in businesses. They found that people who embrace those tools at work are more likely to get promoted than those who don't. The big problem with social media, however, is that more often than not it becomes a vehicle for self-promotion. Jean Twenge, a professor at San Diego State University, did a study of Gen Y and social media.[1] She found that 57 percent of young people believe that their generation uses social networking sites for promotion, narcissism, and attention seeking. In the same study, almost 40 percent of young people agreed that being a self-promoter or a narcissist would help them succeed in this highly competitive world. The 57 percent stat is undoubtedly true. But the 40 percent one is flat out wrong. Being a narcissist and excessive self-promoter will *not* help you succeed. In fact, the opposite is true.

The number one rule of networking—whether online or in person—is: Give before you receive. If you've got a Twitter feed and you're tweeting advice a few times a day, people will overlook occasional self-promotion as long as they're getting value. If I had to quantify it, I'd say that if 80 to 90 percent of your tweets have solid content, people will be fine with the other 10 to 20 percent being self-promotional because you've given so much more value. That goes for all of the other social media tools that are out there.

The online world allows people to opt in or out very easily. Provide good value and help others and people will opt in to whatever you're doing. Turn every tweet or status update or wall post into an advertisement, and you risk being ignored or blacklisted.

So think about the impression your social media presence is giving. Are you posting twenty status updates every day or sending hundreds of tweets, giving people a blow-by-blow description of everything you're doing in real time? Are you uploading dozens of pictures every week or changing your profile picture more than once every two or three months? If so, stop it. You may not think of it this way, but the fact is that you're well on your way to being seen as a self-promotional jerk. So slow down and remind yourself to give value before you promote yourself.

Six Rules of Self-Promotion

1. Make yourself worthy of being talked about. If you've got a strong personal brand, you're an expert in something and do top quality work, you get along with others, and you're a team player, people will naturally talk about you and what you've done.

2. Be well known for one specific thing. Again, this goes back to hard skills. When you're the one your coworkers can't do without when they need something done, you'll have more evangelists than you can count.

3. Take responsibility. Even if you're a top performer, you can't always count on other people to sing your praises. Vanessa Schneider, a young PR Manager at Eventbrite, put it quite nicely. "Be your own publicist," she told me. "That doesn't mean be a braggart or a jerk. But it does mean make sure that when you've had a big win, you invite others to share in your excitement. Of course, the way to do that is by getting them excited about the results, not about adding new points to your personal scorecard."

4. Find ways to expand your role. When you take on new responsibilities you're going to get noticed. And if you handle those responsibilities well, you'll get noticed even more. In an ideal world, you're giving people a live demonstration of how your talents and skills can benefit them and the company instead of having to tell them. But be prepared to tell them anyway—you can't just count on people seeing what you want them to see.

5. Make others look good—especially your manager. If you talk up others, they'll usually look for ways to do the same for you. When you help your manager succeed, that manager will put you on more projects, and that will increase your visibility. When that manager gets promoted and starts staffing their new team, they'll naturally want people who've proven themselves to be loyal and whom they can count on to continue to make them look good. So as they move up through the corporate ranks—whether with the current employer or a new one—they'll promote you right along with them. I've seen it happen over and over again.

6. Get some evangelists. What others say about you is more impactful than what you say about yourself. In the workplace, an endorsement from your supervisor or a high-profile coworker is so much more powerful than you saying the same thing.

Self-Promotion in Action: How to Craft Your Own Image at Work

In addition to my six rules, there are a number of other steps you can take to make yourself better known at work, keep your self-promotion effective, and prevent you from slipping into obnoxiousness.

Whenever you have the chance, seize the opportunity to show that you're excited about the work you're doing and the progress you're making on your latest project. Of course, you're only going to do this if it fits into the conversation. If you're in a meeting and everyone is talking about supply chain issues in China, don't bring up the fact that you got your latest sales project in under budget. Best case, you'll look awkward. Worst case, you'll look stupid. But if the project does come up, by all means, talk about it—but try to keep the focus off you. Enthusiastically telling people about a successful project you've been working on allows you to quietly self-promote *and* to bask in some of the glory earned by the project.

Be sure to take credit for what you do, but give plenty of credit to others who are doing great things. If you're presenting with three other people, make sure everyone has his or her name on the presentation and has a chance to share in the success—even if you're the leader. Acknowledging others' contributions in this way makes you look good without you having to say a word. It also makes others want to celebrate *you* when you have success. "You won't have to bring attention to yourself because others will do it for you," says Dean Lawyer, a B2B Director at T-Mobile. "Find out how your work can assist others in accomplishing their goals and make sure you are making a positive impact on others through your work." However, Dean warns: "Do not let others falsely take credit for your accomplishments."

Take every opportunity to become more visible. You can do that by signing up for classes, attending functions, and taking on additional responsibility. The more your name gets out there, the more it gets recognized. "I increase my visibility in my organization through excelling in my normal workload and getting my name associated with any extracurricular activities," Jeffrey Strassman, a young Audit Manager at Grant Thornton, a major accounting firm, told me. "In my office I'm a leader on the training committee, I am the 'champion' on certain office initiatives, I get involved in our sponsored social organizations, and so on." And as long as you're making yourself more visible, don't forget about meetings. Speak up. If you don't, you'll never get noticed.

And if you're not walking around getting to know your colleagues, team members, and folks from other departments, you're missing a great opportunity to let people know what you're doing, and to build relationships with potential supporters who can help you move your career forward. The more you have a chance to get to know people in person (and to have them get to know you), the better the chances that you'll impress them and that they'll promote you. If you're a remote worker and face-to-face meetings aren't possible, send regular e-mails with updates. You need to stay top of mind and continually remind people that you're out there and doing great work.

Before you open your mouth to say anything that might remotely be considered self-promoting, you need to know who's listening. Some people will love hearing about your accomplishments (assuming you do it subtly). But others may see your successes as a threat to their job or security. You'll want to tailor your message to avoid stepping on others' toes. It's especially true when it comes to your boss. Pay close attention to how they handle themselves, get feedback, run meetings, and talk about their own accomplishments. That should give you a hint as to how you should promote yourself to them.

It's also very important that you have an accurate view of how valuable you are in a workplace. That's sometimes hard to do. One way to assess this is by keeping track of the number of people who ask you for help or favors. If the number is pretty small, you either need to do a better job letting people know what you're capable of, or you need to acquire some hard and/or soft skills that your workplace demands.

Performance reviews are the perfect time to do a little self-promotion—after all, you're there to talk about you. But stay focused on the external. If you're being considered for a promotion, the people who are making the decision want to know what you've accomplished, challenges you've overcome, how well you work with your teammates, and how you're adding value to the company.

Finally, come up with a good elevator pitch. This is for the hypothetical scenario where you're unexpectedly sharing an express elevator with your boss and you only have between the lobby and the thirty-second floor to impress them. What one thing will you talk about? Trying to shoehorn a million ideas into a forty-five-second elevator ride will make you seem desperate and pompous. Keep it concise and stay focused on how you can help the company.

When Someone Takes Credit for Your Ideas

Unfortunately, not everyone you work with will have read this book, and they won't know how important it is to give credit where it's due. And believe me, having someone take credit for your ideas or your contributions is not an easy thing to deal with. At the very least, it's going to be frustrating. Then, your frustration will turn to anger. When that happens, you run the risk of doing or saying something you might regret. So what should you do if someone steals your thunder?

Step number one is to set up a meeting and talk to the thief privately. Mention that you were disappointed that you didn't get a shout-out and ask what his or her intention was. Your goal here is to get them to voluntarily correct their mistake and tell everyone who needs to know what your role was. Don't come out swinging or making accusations. It's possible that leaving you out was just an oversight. In that case, they'll probably be contrite and apologetic and will do whatever they have to do to put things right.

But what if the person who stole your idea brushes you off and refuses to correct the error? In this case, you'll set up a meeting with your manager. And without coming across as hostile, angry, or vindictive, lay out the facts. "I know my name didn't come up in the meeting, but I want to let you know that I was also on the team that did XYZ and I think I made a significant contribution to the project, and I just want to make sure that you were aware of that." The most important thing is to not come across as a whiner or complainer—even if you're right. Let your boss know that you're happy with the way the project turned out, that you enjoyed working on it, and that you look forward to working on more projects.

Striking a Balance: The Right Way to Answer, "What Do You Do?"

In the U.S., when you're introduced to someone, it's common that the first topic of discussion starts with a simple question: What do you do? (This is something that's actually peculiar to the U.S. In many other countries asking that question is considered rude.) Answering that question gives you a great opportunity for self-promotion. If you don't give enough information in response to that question, the other person may think you're not very interesting and won't be interested in continuing the conversation either. Too much and you'll be noticed, but people will think you're arrogant and obnoxious. So you need to find a level of self-promotion that's just right.

This is a lesson I learned the hard way. Everyone I know knows that I'm a big self-promoter. Once I was out with some buddies at a bar and caught the eye of an attractive female bartender. After bringing our drinks she asked me what I do. I launched into a long recitation of all the things I've accomplished professionally. When I was done she looked at me and said, "That was really unattractive."

That, ladies and gentlemen, is a great example of self-promotion run amuck. What I should have done—and what I recommend that you do whenever someone asks you what you do—is given a few highlights and then turned the spotlight on the person who asked the question.

Of course, in the workplace, things are a little different. To start with, people generally aren't going to ask that question—they'll assume that since you work at the same company you're doing something productive. But they will ask you what you've achieved. To answer that question properly, you'll need to adopt what I call the "proper self-promotion mind-set," which means continually reminding yourself of three things:

a. I'm in a team and I'm a team player.
b. My work is important and benefits the company.
c. My work isn't about me, it's about others.

If you maintain this mind-set, it's unlikely that you'll ever come across as bragging or a jerk. Imagine that you and your team absolutely nailed a presentation to a big client. But your boss wasn't there to see it. When he gets back from vacation or wherever, he's going to want to know how things went (of course he'll already know because the client called to tell him). Your conversation with your boss might go something like this:

"Hey Mike, too bad you couldn't have been there—what a meeting! Bill did a great job of laying out the facts, Muriel's PowerPoint kept them on the edge of their seats, Randy wowed 'em with a demo of the new product, and I answered their questions and wrapped everything up. They're coming in Tuesday to sign the contract!"

The Dangers of Excessive Self-Promotion

Taking self-promotion too far can produce some pretty negative side effects. At the very least, you run the risk of isolating yourself or alienating others from you. If people don't want to work with you, you'll be hurting your team, the projects you're working on, and the company as a whole. And your boss might think that you're running around taking credit for other people's accomplishments. If any of that happens, you could end up doing irreparable damage to your career. You'll have a tough time moving up. What management looks for when deciding whom to promote is someone who has presence in the workplace, someone others look up to and admire.

As you move up the food chain, you'll eventually have to manage others. And to do that effectively, it has to be less about you and more about the people you supervise who do things on your behalf.

The Tongue-in-Cheek "How-to-Tell-If-I'm-an-Obnoxious-Self-Promoter" Quiz

Read the following True or False statements:

1. I use the word "I" in conversations more than any other word or letter.
2. Instead of asking what others do, I immediately launch into what *I* do.
3. I frequently talk about myself in the third person.
4. I publish on Facebook or Tweet about useless things more than five times a day while at work.
5. When I talk I make sure my voice is louder than anyone else's in the room.
6. If I accomplish something at work I make sure all my coworkers and their mothers know about it.
7. When I do self-assessments, I never criticize anything I've done or not done.
8. I "borrow" creative ideas from coworkers and take credit for them.
9. When I take on a team leadership position, it's to build myself up, not to benefit the team.
10. I'm too busy playing Angry Birds on my iPhone to pay attention to what anyone else might be saying.
11. I namedrop constantly and talk about people I've never actually met as if they were my best buds.
12. I think I'm my manager's boss, not the other way around.

Now I want you to take this short quiz. If you have fewer than three Trues, you're not terribly obnoxious. If you've got three to five, you're moderately obnoxious, and if you've got six or more, you've got some serious obnoxiousness issues and you might want to fix that.

Visibility Creates Opportunities

Call it visibility, standing out, or getting noticed, they all create opportunities to get ahead in your career. If people don't know about you and what you've done, how will you ever get tapped for a promotion or get a performance bonus? A lot of people don't like to talk about their accomplishments—but then they get incredibly resentful when they get passed over for something they know they deserve. The only solution is to speak up. If you don't, there's a good chance that no one will ever find out. And if they don't know what you can do, they'll never think to turn to you when they need help and they'll never ask you to join a team that really needs someone with your talents and skills. The trick is to do it strategically, in a way that adds value to your team and supports the people around you. It's pretty rare for someone to accomplish great things without any outside help at all. And you'll never be able to perform at your full potential if your team doesn't support you.

7

What Managers Look for When They Decide Whom to Promote

*If you are going to achieve excellence in big things,
you develop the habit in little matters. Excellence is
not an exception, it is a prevailing attitude.*

—GENERAL COLIN POWELL

Remember back in college when you were getting ready for finals? Some profs were good about letting you know what the most important themes were. That helped you focus your studying on the topics that really mattered. But if you're like most people, you had at least a few instructors who said that *everything* you'd covered during the whole semester—every page of every book—would be on the test. Those exams were nearly impossible to prepare for—who could possibly master *everything*?

It's a similar situation when you're being considered for a promotion. Wouldn't it be nice to find out the qualities/skills/abilities/traits that are the most important to managers when they're looking for future leaders to promote?

I thought so, too. So my company surveyed 1,000 managers to find out what's most—and least—important to them when making hiring decisions. And, thinking that there might be a disconnect between what *is* important and what young workers *think* is important, we also surveyed 1,000 young workers (ages twenty-two to twenty-nine) to get their thoughts. Understanding both sides of the equation will be invaluable as you plan your career. At the very least, it will help you assess your current skills and may point out some areas that you need to develop or hone. When you know what your audience (managers) wants from you, it's much easier to sync with them and deliver exactly what they want—and more—by focusing on the traits you'll need to move up and get promoted faster. It will also help you target specific opportunities within your company to build your brand. On the other hand, if you *don't* know what your audience is looking for, how can you possibly meet their expectations? As a result, you'll spend too much time focusing on the skills that aren't as important to managers, and your weak points will prevent you from getting ahead.

Here's what we found out:

Soft Skills Rule

As we discussed in Chapter 3, soft skills are the most important skills to acquire. Hard skills—your technical abilities—are valuable, but not as valuable as soft skills. Given that, we weren't terribly surprised when managers put three soft skills at the top of their list of what they're looking for in the next generation of leaders. In order, they are:

1. Can prioritize work
2. Positive attitude
3. Teamwork

Of course, numbers on a spreadsheet can't always convey subtleties and they can't capture differences between organizations. For Mike Flores, VP of Global Strategy Alignment at McDonald's, critical thinking and teamwork skills are at the top of his list. "We're looking for somebody who is good at listening and absorbing information and being able to process it, who asks the right questions, and who is able to work well with other individuals in a team setting," he says. "Overall, if you come in with an open-minded curiosity, a certain instinct for working together, and the ability to solve problems you can shine pretty quickly here."

Still, some managers, including WWE's Jason Hoch, are focused on the bottom line: "It's important for the younger generation to be thinking in terms of 'How do I drive business? How do I drive revenue? How do I have a vision around what's next?' People who do that are the people that can go places." And Allan McKisson, VP of HR at Manpower Group, sums it up like this: "Do you make things better and help the people around you?" Ultimately, managers want people who can prioritize and achieve goals, are likable and are team players.

When employees understand what managers are looking for, they can get ahead faster. When surveying managers and employees, we found some interesting discrepancies between the traits managers say they value most and are required for advancement, and the ones young workers *think* are the most important.

On the following page is a list of the top twenty, as rated by both managers and employees. It's to see the similarities and differences between the two columns.

	MANAGERS	EMPLOYEES
1	Can prioritize work	Communication skills
2	Positive attitude	Leadership ability
3	Teamwork	Can prioritize work
4	Organizational skills	Positive attitude
5	Communication skills	Teamwork
6	Able to adapt to change	Goal-oriented
7	Strategic thinking and analytical skills	Industry knowledge
8	Leadership ability	Able to adapt to change
9	Goal-oriented	Organizational skills
10	Industry knowledge	Strategic thinking and analytical skills
11	Relationship-building skills	Relationship-building skills
12	Professional presence	Professional presence
13	Technical ability	Likable
14	Likable	Technical ability
15	Work virtually	Work virtually
16	Digital savvy	Years of experience
17	Cultural intelligence	Cultural intelligence
18	Years of experience	Digital savvy
19	Global perspective	Global perspective
20	Extracurricular activities	Extracurricular activities

But don't focus too much attention to the Employee column. As harsh as this sounds, when it comes to career advancement, it doesn't really matter what *you* think is important—it's what your *manager* thinks that carries the weight. If you're not focusing on the skills that managers value most, you're not spending your time the right way. Use this chart as a guideline—not every manager has exactly the same priorities so it's a good idea to ask yours for their own top ten or top twenty list. Then use that information to help you decide where to put your efforts. For example, take organizational skills. Managers put them at number 4, while employees put them at number 9.

The Hardest Skills to Find

Coming up with a list of ideal skills and qualities is one thing. Identifying people who have those skills and qualities is something else entirely. So we asked our panel of managers to go through that same list of twenty skills and tell us how easy they think it is to actually *find* people with those skills. Here's what they said (the number in the third column is the percentage of managers who said it was "hard" or "next to impossible" to find people with that particular skill).

How are you doing relative to what managers say is important? If you've been spending all your time developing your digital savvy, expanding your global perspective, or doing extracurricular activities (skills that employers feel are a dime a dozen), you might want to consider focusing instead on developing your strategic thinking, analytical, and communications skills, and on boosting your knowledge about your industry (the skills employers have the hardest time finding). Unless, of course, you're happy right where you are and have no interest in advancing your career. If you're reading this book, I have a feeling that isn't the case.

Just a quick note on why the top five are so important. First of all,

	MANAGERS	
1	Leadership ability	34%
2	Strategic thinking and analytical skills	32%
3	Communication skills	28%
4	Industry knowledge	28%
5	Relationship-building skills	27%
6	Professional presence	27%
7	Can prioritize work	26%
8	Organizational skills	26%
9	Able to adapt to change	26%
10	Years of experience	26%
11	Cultural intelligence	25%
12	Positive attitude	24%
13	Technical ability	23%
14	Teamwork	22%
15	Goal-oriented	22%
16	Likable	19%
17	Work virtually	19%
18	Digital savvy	19%
19	Global perspective	19%
20	Extracurricular activities	15%

leadership. Good managers are always looking for people who have either natural leadership ability or who have the ability to learn. But as you well know, that isn't always easy. I'm sure you've met your share of leaders who really have no leadership capabilities.

Next, we've got strategic thinking and analytical skills. In today's business world, words aren't enough—you have to back up almost everything you say with hard data. If you understand metrics, can work with numbers, and use them to sell your point of view, you're a hot commodity.

Communication skills are so important that we spent most of Chapter 3 talking about them, so refer to that chapter if you think this is an area you need to work on.

Industry knowledge is important because companies need to know

---

Two More Critical Skills

In addition to the skills on our list, there are two more that many employers feel are in short supply: follow-up and preparation.

People think by sending an e-mail, that's it," complains Andrew Goldman, VP, Program Planning and Scheduling at HBO/Cinemax. "Frankly, that's just the first step. You have got to follow up, to make sure the e-mail was received and understood." Goldman adds that young employees are often not adequately prepared in meetings—especially when they're interviewing for a promotion in his department. "I have interviewed tons of people for my groups and I can tell immediately if somebody has come in doing their homework or not. That to me is a big thing. With the Internet, you can do your homework while waiting in the lobby on your smartphone. I don't recommend it, but you have to go in with smart questions. To not come in prepared is the worst thing you can do."

how they're doing relative to the overall industry, what their competitors are up to, what their customers want but aren't getting, trends that might affect them in the short and long term, and so on. This supports my point about why it's more important to be a specialist than a generalist: The better you know your industry and your customers, the better you'll be able to serve them.

Finally, we've got relationship-building skills. In a world where information is only a few clicks away, being able to get answers isn't nearly as important as being able to work with others—often across multiple international borders, time zones, and languages—to create solutions.

You're Not Alone: Companies Have a Responsibility for Developing Talent Too

In addition to the soft and hard skills managers are looking for in their employees, there are some key factors that the companies themselves have to provide if they're going to be able to develop talent from within. One of the best—and cheapest—is mentors. It's harder to succeed if you don't know how to maneuver within the corporate system. That makes you less efficient, which ultimately costs the company money. Every organization has people who've been around awhile and who've accumulated wisdom that more junior people can benefit from. Even if your company doesn't offer an organized mentorship program, find one for yourself. And don't think mentorship is a one-way street. As a young person you have plenty of knowledge that can probably help make some of the more senior folks more efficient (social media, for one).

Smart companies will put training programs together to help employees develop their soft skills, which will eventually help them become better managers and leaders. In order for employees to learn soft skills, they have to be challenged and put in positions where they have to work in teams to accomplish business objectives. If your company doesn't offer this kind of in-house training, go back and review the sections in Chapters 2 and 3 on how to acquire soft and hard skills. There are many free and low-cost ways to learn anything you need to know.

Liam Brown, COO of Marriott International, summed it up nicely. "They need to know precisely what they are supposed to do, they need to have the tools to do the job, and they need to know that somebody cares about them," he told me. "If we have entry-level associates who demonstrate those capabilities and those abilities, they can rapidly grow into the leadership ranks." Marriott's promote-and-develop-talent-from-within system produces some great results. "Twenty-three years ago I was a general manager of a Courtyard by Marriott and to-day I oversee all of the select service and extended stay hotels in the United States," says Brown. "And we have lots of stories like that. A Regional Director who started off as a gatehouse attendant making $3.75 an hour at a Residence Inn and now oversees twenty hotels and has a senior role in the company, and we have a number of Vice Presidents who started off in hourly roles such as waiters, concierges, doormen, and so on."

Jeff Shuey, Director of Global Solutions at Eastman Kodak, goes a step further, putting a lot of the responsibility for employees' success on their managers' shoulders. "The most important factor for me when evaluating performance is tied directly to designing and aligning goals with realistic timelines and skill sets. These are set in conjunction with the employee. It is a dialogue, and in some senses a contract," he told me. "My role as a manager is to help people on my team succeed. Which means breaking down barriers, opening doors, and helping all of our efforts roll up into the bigger picture."

Companies that have high-potential programs in place, such as GE, Marriott, Raytheon, and EMC, have a better chance at retaining top talent long enough to breed them into the next generation of leaders.

Making Yourself Promotable

Managers consider a number of factors when making promotion decisions. Of course, each manager's decision-making process is unique, but just about everyone includes these in their top five: being able to prioritize your work and meet deadlines; having a positive attitude; working well with your team; and putting the team's best interest ahead of your own (don't worry: If the team benefits, you will too).

Having a solid understanding of what your manager is looking for will help you focus on acquiring—and promoting—the skills that will increase your visibility, build your brand, and open up career paths that will be closed to your peers who haven't got the insights you do. Oh, and don't forget about persistence and preparation. You'll never get ahead without them.

8

Develop Cross-Generational Relationships

The most important single ingredient in the formula of success is knowing how to get along with people.
—THEODORE ROOSEVELT

I n today's workplace, it's not unusual to find people from four different generations, each one with its own unique cultural and communications styles, values, needs, and wants. When intergenerational conflicts arise—and they always do—productivity and profitability suffer. Each generation has its own, unique communication preferences and ideas on how work should get done. If you understand these preferences and ideas, you'll be able to build relationships with those who can advance your career. Say you're in the habit of showing up for work late. Boomers are going to have a real problem with that because they're big on rules and believe that everyone should be on time every time. (I'm not saying that you make coming into the office late a habit, but if you're getting your work done at home, you're likely to ask yourself why being a few minutes late every once in a while is such a big deal.) Keep in mind that not everyone in a particular generation will react the same way in the same situation. There are plenty of individual differences. As you can imagine, managing a workforce with so many variables can be challenging, which is why there are so many resources out there aimed at managers and executives. In the previous chapter, we talked about the importance of developing skills that your audience wants. When it comes to dealing with older generations (Boomers and Gen X), the situation is similar. In both situations (and pretty much everywhere else in life), you can't give people what they want unless you know what that is. When you understand how different generations operate as well as their feelings and what motivates their behavior, you'll have a much easier time forming relationships with them. Failing to understand other generations could lead to unnecessary conflicts at work that can hurt your career. In this chapter we're going to focus on understanding what makes each generation tick and how to use that understanding to avoid the pitfalls most people fall into, promote yourself, and advance your career.

The Four Generations: Who Are These People, Anyway?

On page 157, there's a chart that summarizes the major differences between the four generations. But I want to take a few minutes to go into each one in a bit more detail.

Gen Y (born 1982–1993)

With about eighty million people (in the U.S.), this is the biggest generation. They grew up with parents who were actively involved in their lives, helping them make decisions, and in many ways acting as their chief advisors (these parents' constant hovering over their children has earned them the moniker "helicopter parents"). That may be why Gen Yers (also called Millennials) tend to always want to be connected with friends, family, and others around them. They're extremely tech-savvy and do a lot of that connecting on Facebook and Twitter, which they're using every day. And they're a growing economic force: As consumers, Gen Y will have more buying power than the Baby Boomers by 2017.[26] Most young workers in this generation are in their first job right out of college, although some have already moved on to second or third jobs and some may be in lower-level management positions. Gen Yers will account for 75 percent of the workforce by 2025, according to the Business and Professional Women's Foundation. (Some companies have already started ramping up their Gen Y hiring; at Ernst & Young, for example, the workforce is already 60 percent Gen Y.)

Some of the biggest differences between Gen Y and the other generations are in the workplace. Gen Y has largely rejected the attitudes of Gen X and the Baby Boomers (more on both below). Overall, this generation is a bit impatient. They don't think in terms of loyalty (the idea of having one job for life makes no sense to them). They don't want to wait five years to make an impression. They want to work their passions and do something meaningful right now. If they don't find meaning in their day job, they are quick to have a side project outside of work that gives them meaning. Seventy-five percent of Millennials say it's important to have a "side-hustle" that could turn into a career, reports MTV.[27] Workplace flexibility is a must. They don't understand the need for a traditional nine-to-five schedule—they want the freedom to work when they want and where they want, using any tools they want (and they resent it when companies block social media use). Flexibility is so important that they're willing to give up some salary to get it. Gen Yers want mentors and easy access to management and executives. They also want informal feedback between formal reviews and they want to be recognized constantly by the people around them (this is the generation of kids who grew up in a world where everyone gets a trophy, win or lose), which may explain why they thrive on collaboration and teamwork.

With many Boomers unable to retire because of finances, Gen Y's impatience can sometimes turn into frustration as they find themselves unable to advance as quickly as they'd like. One of the biggest problems I see with Gen Y workers is that they sometimes have a kind of workplace ADHD (attention deficit hyperactivity disorder)—if their needs aren't being met *right now,* they're ready to jump ship. If you're feeling antsy because your path upward is being blocked by an older worker who put off retirement for a few years, do yourself a favor and relax. Have patience, and show some loyalty. Your time will come. Trust me.

Gen X (born 1965–1981)

The 47 million people in this age group are independent, resourceful, and self-sufficient. They also place a high value on personal freedom and were the first generation to put themselves and their personal lives before their job and career. And, in my research, I found that Gen X is the generation that's most stressed about the economy. Today, they're mid- to high-level mangers. They value flexibility more than stability, but not quite as much as Gen Y does. They value family and personal relationships more than Boomers, but aren't quite as willing as Gen Y to trade a higher salary for more flexibility. They take more risks than Boomers but aren't as entrepreneurial as Gen Y. And, like Boomers, they work well independently, as opposed to Gen Y, which prefers teams. This raises an interesting problem because Gen X, for the most part, is in middle management positions, and the people they're managing are Gen Y. Unfortunately, a lot of them are having a tough time figuring out how to deal with a generation (Y) that seems to need constant attention. At the same time, Gen X is chomping at the bit, waiting for the Boomers to retire so they can move up in their organizations. They've put in a lot of years planning for succession, and feel they've earned those corner offices.

Baby Boomers (born 1945–1964)

Although this generation may seem kind of stodgy and old-fashioned to you, it's important to remember that they were known for rejecting and redefining traditional values. Boomers are by far the wealthiest generation in the workplace and they're typically pretty high up in the food chain. Because they can remember life before personal computers and touch screens, they tend not to be quite as technologically adept as Gens X and Y, preferring face-to-face interactions over most other forms of communication.

On the whole, Boomers are very work-centric. They believe that hard work pays off and they're motivated by perks, prestige, and titles. They often define themselves by what they've accomplished, aren't averse to coming into the office seven days a week, and strongly believe that younger generations need to pay their dues before advancing. They're competitive, confident, and self-reliant, but because of the current economic situation many are postponing retirement.

On the downside, Boomers tend to be uncomfortable with conflict and may be oversensitive to feedback. As they move closer to retirement, Boomers occupy most of the senior management positions and they like being in charge. Be nice to them: They control most of the wealth and right now they're picking their successors. Most will be from Gen X, but some may be from Gen Y.

Gen Z (born 1994–2010)

I saved Gen Z for last because this generation is only now hitting the workplace, and if they're working at all, they're probably interns or in an entry-level position. But look out. In a few years, you may be competing with Gen Z. Born into a highly competitive global world, they understand that they're living in an era when colleges are expensive and it's tough to get a job. As a result, Gen Z tends to be very entrepreneurial.

Gen Z is essentially Gen Y on steroids. Typically the children of Gen X, they don't know what life is like without the Internet. Twenty-three million strong and growing, they're sometimes called *digital natives* and are completely dependent on—and comfortable with—technology. They use it for everything from ordering a pizza and checking the weather to applying for jobs, connecting with friends, and dating. Gen Z also has a bit of an ego—at least in the eyes of the other generations—and they're used to putting their whole lives online, telling their friends and anyone else who will listen everything they're doing, from brushing their teeth to sitting in traffic to getting a promotion at work (don't believe me? Just check out the kind of information most people tweet about). As great as all this technology is, Gen Z is so plugged in that face-to-face communications are sometimes a challenge. Gen Z is definitely the one to watch. Before you know it, they're going to be in the workforce and gunning for your job.

Working with—and Learning from—Older Generations

It's always easier to work with people with whom you share a common culture and outlook. But in the workplace that's not always possible. And while we know that there are cultural differences between, say, Asians and Europeans, the cultural divide between older and younger generations is just as deep. And as with just about any conflict that comes up between cultures, a lot of the problems are rooted in stereotypes and preconceived notions.

In our study, for example, we found that while young workers generally have a pretty positive view of their managers and what they offer,

HOW GEN Y COMPARES TO OTHER GENERATIONS

	Gen Z	Gen Y	Gen X	Baby Boomers
Additional names	Generation M, Net Generation, Internet Generation	Millennials, Echo Boomers, Generation Next	Post-Boomers	
Born	1994–2010	1982–1993	1965–1981	1945–1964
Size	23 million	80 million	45 million	76 million
Core values and attributes	Tech-savvy, globally connected, flexible, tolerant of diverse cultures	Realism, confidence, diversity, morality, competitiveness, attention seekers	Skepticism, fun, informality, balance, education, pragmatism, adaptable, manager loyalty, independent	Optimism, involvement, antiwar, equal rights, work ethic
Education	Not worth it	An expense	A way to get there	A birthright
Communication	Social media, smart-phones, text messaging, complete transparency	Social media, smartphones, text messaging	Cell phones	Landline phones
Management style	Collaboration	Collaboration	Self-command	Command and control
Training	Will train themselves	Continuous learning	Training creates loyalty	Train them and they will leave
Job changing	Natural and no loyalty	Changing jobs is a usual routine	Changing jobs is necessary	Changing jobs puts you behind
Career goals	Work for yourself	Build multiple careers	Build a portable career	Build a single career
Work/life balance	Not expected	All about workplace flexibility	Need balance now	Need help with balance
Work ethic	Multitaskers, independent, working at light speed	Goal-oriented, looking for meaningful work, collaboration	Outcome-oriented, care less about advancement and more about money	Loyalty, process-oriented, value ambition and teamwork
Entitlement	Achievement	Contribution	Merit	Experience
Average tenure on the job before switching	n/a	2 years	5 years	7 years

Data for this chart was compiled by my company, as well as other sources.[3]

managers often have a negative view of their employees. For example, we found that employees feel that their managers have experience (59 percent), wisdom (41 percent), and are willing to mentor them (33 percent).

On the other hand, managers say that Gen Y employees have unrealistic salary/compensation expectations (51 percent), a poor work ethic (47 percent), and are easily distracted (46 percent). The most negative opinion that Gen Y employees had about their managers is that they don't give proper credit to them (26 percent). Managers view Gen-Y employees as having new perspectives and ideas (30 percent), creativity (27 percent), and being open-minded (23 percent).

Clearly, there are some pretty big disconnects between younger and older generations. The good news is that they're not insurmountable. The other news (it's not necessarily bad, just different) is that because there's a good chance that most of the older people you work with are senior to you, it's up to you to take the necessary steps to bridge the gap. Here's how:

Boomers sometimes value work over personal relationships. So make sure you do your job well, because that's ultimately what they're looking for first. They're also big on work ethic, so always bring your projects in on time and make sure they see the work you're doing. Physically being at the office is important too because it's easier for them to see what people are doing. When you respect their values, they'll notice you more and see you as a leader, which will help you get ahead.

As you may have seen in the chart, Boomers spend an average of seven years on the job before making a move, and many have worked for the same company for decades. For the most part, that kind of loyalty doesn't exist today, and while ten years may seem like an eternity for you, be respectful and don't bring up the fact that you don't expect to be there any more than a few years (the average for Gen Y). But again, the more effort you put in and the more loyal you are, the more you'll be rewarded with recognition and increased responsibilities.

Sixty-six percent of managers say they prefer face-to-face meetings over any other means of communicating. Fortunately, 62 percent of employees know that's their managers' preferred method and try to use it. Technology is hardly dead, though. The second most popular way of communicating between managers and employees is e-mail (26 percent of managers and 25 percent of employees say it's their preferred method). If you haven't already heard or you haven't already been told how your manager prefers to communicate, stop by the office and ask. Keep in mind, though, that it's possible to change things. You may be able to show your manager that for quick communications, texts and IMs are often more efficient than a phone call or an in-person meeting. Anytime you can improve efficiency, you'll be seen as someone who's adding real value to the organization.

Shared interests, activities, or even stories are a great way to develop relationships with people from other generations. Learn as much as you can from them. "I feel that older workers have a lot of wisdom. I listen to what they have to say and while there may be a generational gap, their advice is invaluable and still applies," says Laura Petti, Booker for Fox News's *Your World with Neil Cavuto*. Mallory McMorrow, a Senior Designer at Mattel, agrees: "They've seen projects fail and they know why. Hopefully I'm able to tap into their experience to avoid rookie mistakes, and help the group as a whole move forward."

But not everyone sees older workers that way. "My impression of older workers sometimes is that they are only in positions of higher authority because of the number of years under their belt," Ryan Brown, a young Sales Solutions employee at Twitter, told me. "Just because someone is younger doesn't mean they can't compete at a high level." While Ryan is right that being young doesn't mean you can't compete, the first part of his comment is exactly the kind of attitude that Boomers resent. And it's the kind of attitude that could cost you your job. So if thoughts like Ryan's are running through your head, stop now. You're the new kid and you're walking into an established company with established ways of doing things. Sure, you may be able to change things, but that'll take a while. In the meantime, drop that attitude and start paying more attention to your performance and making things happen for your company and yourself.

When you identify someone who has skills or experience you want to learn from, ask them to formally or informally mentor you. The best approach is a direct one, something like, "I want to learn the financial approach to business. Can you help me?" or, "Can you involve me in the brand management aspects of the company?" or, "Can you involve me more in the digital content of the company?" Believe me, this is an approach that works. And if you don't believe me, listen to Matthew Nordby, EVP, Chief Revenue Officer at Playboy Enterprises, Inc. "When people come to me with a very specific request and acknowledge that they have a deficiency or an area they would like to learn more about, I am more inclined to put them in a position to learn about that business and also be personally invested to see that they get the skills they need." Seeking out mentorship or guidance sends several powerful messages. First, that you respect the other person's wisdom and knowledge. Second, that you're committed to learning what it takes to make the company (and you) successful. As a result, you'll get more visibility, more responsibility, and you'll get ahead faster.

Be prepared to prove yourself. "When I first began, there were only a few other young people," said Amanda Healy, a Senior Channel Marketing Analyst at CA Technologies. "I was often asked if I was an intern, or worse, a daughter visiting her mother or father at the workplace. While initially frustrating, I slowly began to view my youth as an advantage. Carefully crafting my comments, questions, and suggestions to reflect my knowledge of the field and overall maturity, I was able to alter others' initial impressions. In also ensuring my form of dress was professional, I was able to demonstrate that while young, my commitment to my work and my level of skill was mature. After a while, I noticed at large meetings that when I raised my hand to speak or ask a question, people's ears tended to perk up. I think everyone was interested in what 'the kid' had to say." Nothing, as they say, succeeds like success. Show what you can do and you'll have more people interested in investing time and money in you.

Most companies recognize that not everyone has the same technical chops. "For the most part, the biggest difference I've seen is the technical savvy of the people entering the workforce today, which often far exceeds our current employees," says Marc Chini, VP Human Resources at GE. If you can make yourself a resource and help others improve their tech skills, they'll be in a better position to accomplish their goals. And when you've helped them, they'll almost always find a way to help you too. If you can't make something happen or you don't have an answer, you can still be a valued resource by finding the right person. The person you find will be in your debt and the person whose need you satisfied will see that you're a team player. And all of that builds visibility.

Identifying People Who Can Support Your Career

Your first step in strategic relationship building is to identify one or more mentors—individuals you think can help you get where you want to go. In some companies, there's a formal process where young employees are assigned a mentor when they first join the firm. Here's how Paul Marchand, Senior Vice President of Global Talent Acquisition at PepsiCo, describes his company's mentorship to me: "We have a resource group called Conn3ct which is focused on building a global network of young professionals within PepsiCo and creating a passionate and inspiring environment for the next generation of PepsiCo leaders. It's a vehicle whereby Millennials' voices are heard, energy is harnessed, and ideas are implemented, enabling members to receive critical executive exposure and sponsorship early on in their career."

Mentorship is a way for you to find out what you should be doing now, makes you more connected with execs who make decisions, and gets you to learn a lot from people who've already been there, done that.

Unfortunately, not every workplace is as progressive. For example, Steve Cadigan, VP of Talent at LinkedIn, told me about a former employer, where "there is 'Exec Row'—and you don't go up there unless you have permission." And that's really unfortunate, because mentoring pays some pretty significant dividends. Fifty-three percent of young workers in our study said that having a strong mentoring relationship would make them better, more productive contributors to the company, and 32 percent said it would get them to stay at their company longer. Managers were even more optimistic, with 62 percent saying mentoring would make young employees better and 36 percent saying it would decrease turnover.

If you're lucky enough to work at a place that has a formal mentorship program, congrats. Congrats are also in order if your employer has a more *informal* structure that encourages young employees and managers to connect. At LinkedIn, for example, there are regular "sit and learns" where employees have a chance to meet executives of all levels. But when thinking about a mentor, you need to start with an honest evaluation of the skills or experience you lack. If you don't know that, you can't possibly identify the right person.

Generally speaking, mentors are senior people in your organization. They know where the company is going, they know the system, and they can draw on their experience and wisdom to show you what you should be doing and when. "He's really focused on helping me build my career, directing me where to go, figuring out what I enjoy doing so I get on those projects," says Kristin Gonzalez, a young Tax Consultant at Deloitte. "With him I can talk about pretty much anything. If I'm having trouble working with any managers or partners or seniors or other staff, or if there's something I really want to work on and I'm not working on it I go to him and I can say,

'Hey I really want to get on this project, is there any way you could make that happen?' That's what he's there for, he's a career mentor."

Mentors can come from a variety of sources. Ideally, your manager will mentor you, at the very least giving you good-quality feedback on what you're doing well, not so well, and how to improve. Your manager is also the perfect person to introduce you to her manager, who may be a mentor to you as well. If your manager is *not* mentoring you, or seems uninterested in you and your career progression, you need to either get transferred to another department or team or start thinking about finding another job soon.

You may also seek out a manager or exec from other departments within your company—one, for example, that you're interested in transferring to. In this case, your mentor would be able to help you get the skills you need to make the transition.

Finally, identify people outside your company you trust and admire. These mentors can give you a less biased, bigger-picture view of the industry than you're likely to get from within. Mentors in this category could be prominent industry bloggers, executives you heard speak at a conference, and so on. We'll talk about how to reach out to these people below.

Mentoring: Not Only a One-Way Street

When most people talk about mentoring, they're usually thinking of a senior person taking a junior person under his or her wing. And while that's important, a lot of people overlook the value in reverse mentoring—where you, the junior person, help someone more senior. A classic reverse mentoring situation is when the younger worker helps an older worker with social media or new technologies. Why would you want to do be a reverse mentor? Because it's good for your career.

Mentoring is about building relationships with people who can help you. The time you spend teaching an older executive how to post to the company blog and send a tweet at the same time is definitely helping him acquire new skills. At the same time, you're probably going to be learning more about the company's vision and direction and how you might fit in at various levels. You're also increasing your visibility and gaining access to someone higher up in your organization, someone who may be able to guide you in your career and help you make good choices as you move up, someone who will either help you directly or use his contacts to open doors in other areas.

There's one more important piece to the mentorship puzzle that most people forget about: Mentorship is an ongoing relationship and it's essential that you keep your mentor up to date on what you're doing. Your mentor may be pretty high up in the organization, but chances are he or she still has a boss. And everything you do—the results you achieve, the promotions you get—reflects on your mentor. Make your mentor look good and they'll keep helping you. Let them down and you could find yourself without a strong supporter.

While there's definitely a lot you can learn from older workers, the flow of information doesn't just run in one direction. While plenty of Boomer and Gen Xers are as tech-smart as you are, many are not. So help them learn how to stay up to date with traditional social media and tech platforms (Facebook, LinkedIn, Twitter, etc.) and how to use the new social media tools that have cropped up in the last twenty minutes. Your emphasis should be on using technology for business and career, but if someone asks you to help set up personal accounts go ahead (as long as you do it on your own time). "Let's say you're working with a boss who is not as adept, to say the least, as you are. What a great way and opportunity to show him a skill that you have and expose him to something that you are really into and teach them something at the same time," says Eden Pontz, an Executive Producer at CNN. Of course not everyone will come right out and ask you for help, which means you might have to take the first step. Pontz suggests an approach like this: "You identify a couple of people in the office who you noticed aren't using social media to the fullest and offer your services, saying, 'Hey, this is something I really enjoy doing, let me know if you ever have any questions, I'd be happy to help out and if I don't know the answer I'd be happy to go find you the answer.'" In other words, know your value, what you can do, and what you're good at. See situations where you can provide people with what they need and you'll be seen as a helpful, valuable resource. That's the kind of stuff that gets people promoted.

As we've discussed, older generations often see changing jobs as something negative or disloyal. But in today's market, the most successful people are the ones who have had multiple job experiences at a variety of companies.

While there's no question that Boomers and Gen Xers have done plenty of innovating and risk taking, on average, younger generations are even more innovative and entrepreneurial. With you, it's less about corporate hierarchies and more about doing things that are new or cool. Remember: Entrepreneurship doesn't always mean starting a new company. There's often a lot of room to innovate and be creative within your company.

Finally, because a lot of Boomers have put work first for most (if not all) of their careers, they can use some help balancing work, family, friends, and community. So once in a while take a few Boomers out for a drink after work. You can benefit from the stories they'll tell you, and they can benefit from being subtly reminded that everyone needs to have a life.

Quiz: You Know You Fit the Gen Y Stereotype When . . .

- You're in your manager's office more than in your own cubicle.
- You recently went outside the chain of command to pitch an idea to an executive instead of your own boss.
- At lunch, you daydream of sitting in the CEO's chair.
- You wear headphones and blast music, hoping and praying that no one bothers you.
- You make excuses to work from home and often end up taking the day off.
- You expect managers to sing your praises.
- You're using your work computer to IM your friends about making plans for the evening.
- You think about starting your own company because yours "just doesn't get it."
- You wonder why you haven't been promoted yet.

Understanding Generational Needs in Order to Get Noticed

Building relationships with older generations is critical to getting ahead, and the best way to do that is to understand them. Mastering the art of working and building relationships with people from other generations (and by that I actually mean "people from older generations") is critical to developing your career and getting ahead at work, at the very least because they decide who gets raises and titles. It all comes down to what I call workplace mentality. That means that regardless of your age or position, you and the people you work with and for can learn from each other. "The younger generations don't have all the answers, and the older generations don't have all the answers either, says Kathy Mandato, Senior Vice President of HR at NBC Entertainment. "We can all learn from each other—and we need to just be really open to that."

Appreciate the wisdom and experience that older generations bring to the table. But make sure you show them what *you* bring to the table and the value *you* add to your company. That way, you can bond over shared values and interests. Too many young professionals don't take the time to understand how generations differ and they fall into traps, such as choosing the wrong form of communication (phone instead of texting, for example). If you want to get ahead and build a successful career, you need to pay attention to these differences and have them in mind as you confront different generations at work.

At the same time, regardless of generation, everyone's job is to make the company more successful. By understanding how older generations operate in the workplace, you can better cater to their needs and build stronger relationships. It's up to you to find out what the corporation's goals are and to figure out how you're going to add value. It's also up to you to keep your expectations reasonable. For example, no matter what anyone tells you, there's no such thing as a dream job—there will always be aspects of it that you won't enjoy or even like. There will be responsibilities that you'll have to master before you can move on or up. And don't go in expecting a high starting salary. You'll have to earn it. Same goes for promotions. Oh, and if you want respect, you'll have to earn that too—by showing respect to others.

9

Build Your Network
at Work and Beyond

The currency of real networking is not greed but generosity.

—KEITH FERRAZZI,
AUTHOR OF *NEVER EAT ALONE*

n real estate, they say that the key to success is "location, location, location." In business, it's "relationships, relationships, relationships." Whom you know and how those people perceive you will determine your path to the top. That means that you're going to have to start looking at professional relationships in a whole new way. No matter how good your soft skills are, it's not enough to interact solely with people in your department. You need to strategically seek out relationships that can help you get ahead.

Networking is the easiest form of self-promotion because it involves creating relationships based on shared values, interests, and goals—the kind of relationships that you'll be able to rely on throughout your career. As a result, other people will become aware of your talents in a way that won't come off as self-promotional.

No matter where you are, there are networking opportunities. In many ways, networking is simply meeting new people and exchanging value. In the beginning, it's all about generosity: The more you give, the more people will want to network with you. Help others achieve their goals and they'll (usually) help you achieve yours. Don't worry if the person you're networking with isn't in a position to help you now. People change jobs so much these days that you never know when that help might come. At work, networking usually happens through projects. Working on lots of different projects—especially those that are high-profile and cross-functional—will naturally expand your network. But don't stop there. Network outside work too. The more people you network with, the more visible you'll be and the easier it will be to meet new people. People will introduce you to more people and your network will grow organically, which will open up more doors and allow you to promote yourself faster than you can imagine.

The Five Rules of Relationship Building

Building business relationships is, in a way, kind of like dating. Here are five rules you absolutely must follow if you want your relationship to succeed (and yes, you can use these rules in your dating life as well):

1. Targeting. You may have 2,000 Facebook fans, 500 LinkedIn connections, and 300 Twitter followers, but how many of those people can actually help you advance your career? You need to be specific about the people you build relationships with. At the very least, you should have something in common, have some shared interests, or at least look up to and admire your "target" for her professional accomplishments.

Think about the 80/20 rule in business. Businesses derive 80 percent of their revenues from 20 percent of their customers.

It's similar with building relationships. Not everyone is in a situation where they can support your career and there will be some you just don't like or you have nothing in common with. You obviously can't invest the same amount of time and energy in every relationship, so try to focus on the ones you click with right away and whose company you enjoy. Otherwise, you'll be spreading yourself too thin.

2. Mutualism. The people you want to get to know have to get at least as much out of the relationship as you do. If they get less, they'll feel cheated and will be much less likely to offer to help in the future. By creating a win-win, there will be a relationship instead of a one-night stand.

3. Giving. The trick with networking is to reach out— sincerely—to help others without asking anything in return. When you do that, people will naturally want to help you. This is a strategy that many of the most successful people online have used to build their following: They give people free content and resources *before* they ask for something. Years ago I contacted a *New York Times* journalist. On the phone she was prepared for me to ask her to quote me in an article. Journalists constantly feel used by people who are looking for free press. But instead of asking for promotional support, I asked her how I could help her with a story I knew she was working on. She was stunned by this gesture. Now we have a relationship and she's more than willing to support me.

4. Being authentic. If you don't mean it, don't say it. You may think you're fooling someone, but eventually they'll find you out.

5. Reconnecting. Building a relationship is one thing. Maintaining it is another. I often get e-mail or LinkedIn invites from people I knew back in high school but haven't heard from in fifteen years. Sometimes it's just to reconnect. Other times it's to ask for a favor. After fifteen years? Come on. Staying in touch means taking advantage of your boss's open-door policy to drop in and say hi, having lunch with colleagues every month or so, and at the very least e-mailing, calling, or texting. Your goal is to stay top of mind or close to it. Another way to keep in touch with people you work with or used to work with is to ask them for LinkedIn recommendations. But do this only

Friends in the Workplace

Typically, you don't think of your friends as mentors. But having friends at work can be incredibly valuable to your career—and more. One reason is that besides being there and supporting each other, you and your friends can be more open (and, in many cases, more honest) with each other than in a mentor-mentee relationship. In addition, a Gallup study found that people who have best friends at work are seven times more likely to feel engaged in their job than those without friends. They also found that those with three friends are 96 percent more likely to be satisfied with life than those who have fewer friends at work.

There's another reason to maintain workplace friendships: The world is becoming smaller by the minute—experts say that with social networking there are now only four degrees of separation between you and just about anyone else on the planet. You could end up managing or being managed by a friend, or a virtual friend could become an in-the-flesh coworker.

after you've moved on to a new position. If you ask for a recommendation while you're still employed, they may think it's because you're getting ready to move on. No sense dropping that bit of information until you're 100 percent ready.

Tips for Networking

As easy as it sounds—hey, just get out there and meet some people—I've found that networking is actually not all that intuitive. So here are some tips I've put together that should make what can sometimes be a pretty daunting task a little easier:

- **Listen.** It may seem painfully obvious, but it's the most important step.

- **Be genuinely interested in others.** Questions to ask anytime you're making a good business contact: What projects are you currently working on? Where did you go to college? How long have you been here? Is this your first job after college? What do you like most about the organization? How did you get into the field? Things to commit to memory when meeting someone (take notes if you have to): name (you'd be surprised how many people forget this one), position in the company, location they work at, a project he's been working on, and something personal (but not too personal). Remembering a manager's birthday or the names of his kids sends a very powerful message that you care and that you're paying attention.

- **Network everywhere, not just at work.** For most people, the easiest places to network are also the most relaxed and least structured: casual get-togethers, chance meetings, and even informal networking events. For Natalie Nauman, a Production Assistant at ESPN, networking opportunities are everywhere. "From the gym to the café, I try to network daily because you never know who you're going to meet that can one day help you move further in your career. I network by simply saying hello, starting small talk, and eventually, usually, you get to know the person. Then the more you see them, the more you get to know about them and that is how a connection is made."

• **Be proactive.** If you wait around for interesting (and potentially helpful) people to introduce themselves to you, you could be waiting a very long time. So be a little aggressive. "We all know that networking is crucial to career development but, for Gen Y, the most important thing to remember is that though members of senior management might seem intimidating, they're people too," says Alison Kubinski, then a Senior Assurance Professional at Ernst & Young. "They want to help younger generations grow and succeed—but you have to be willing to ask for what you want."

• **Focus on your current network first.** Most marketing and salespeople will tell you that it costs a lot less to develop new business from current customers than to find new customers. It's the same with networking: It's going to be a lot easier to strengthen and deepen the network you have now than it will be to build a new one from scratch.

• **Use your current connections to help you expand your network.** Add new contacts to your social networks. But be conservative. Adding someone to LinkedIn is pretty safe. But think long and hard before you make someone a Facebook friend or follow them on Twitter.

• **Use common interests or settings to kick off conversations.** It's a lot easier to bond with people when you have something in common, whether that's working in the same department, having gone to the same college, or even eating in the same restaurant or following the same sports teams.

• **Don't be a snob.** Yes, it would be great to hobnob with all the top execs, but that's not always possible. "You never know who knows who. And that admin or analyst you met might have someone's attention much higher up the food chain that can help you," Dan Guyton, a Corporate Analysis Manager at TJX, told me. "Admins are *key*, especially in big companies. They're the gatekeepers to the people you want to get to."

• **Become a connector.** If you aren't able to help someone but you know a third party who can, make the introduction. If they end up benefiting from each other, you'll look like a hero.

How NOT to Network

Over the years I've been consulting on workplace issues, I've heard hundreds of stories of well-meaning attempts to network gone very, very wrong. Here are some of the valuable lessons my clients learned the hard way.

To start with, don't be sneaky about your agenda. If you come across as being dishonest or disingenuous, people will shut you out. Don't ask for a lot and give nothing back. Don't make a networking encounter feel like a business transaction (I'll do this for you if you do that for me . . .), and please don't pass out business cards to everyone in the room. Trying to meet everyone will ensure that you aren't able to spend enough time with anyone to actually get to know who they are. So focus on one or two of the best prospects.

Once you do start making connections, be careful that you don't move too far too quickly (is this sounding like dating advice again?). That means never badmouth your employer, or spread office gossip. The world is a small place these days and there's a really good chance that anything negative you say will get right back to the people you'll wish later hadn't heard it. It's also important to wait until you develop a genuine friendship with someone before you start opening up about your deepest, darkest secrets. Too much personal info too soon can make

Dealing with Adversaries

Very few people ever think about how they'd handle a fellow employee who is so focused on their own career that they'd think nothing of sabotaging their teammates if it meant they'd get a promotion or more recognition. Hopefully, this will never happen to you, but just in case, it's good to be prepared.

Always take the high road and never give in to the temptation to retaliate. If possible, ask the other person what the problem is and whether you might have done something to offend them. If you did, apologize. If the problem continues, tell the other person that you see what's going on and that you want to figure out a way to work together in a less adversarial way.

It's also important—to the extent possible—to ignore the negativity. Instead, surround yourself with friends and supporters and do what you can to bring more people into your camp. If all that fails, you'll need to talk to your boss about what's happening and ask for her help in resolving the issue.

people feel uncomfortable—especially if they don't feel close enough to you to reciprocate.

Finally, keep your phone in your pocket. No texting, no e-mail checking. Don't even answer the phone unless your wife is in labor.

Using Projects to Develop Relationships Across Your Company

As we've discussed, working on projects is a great way to strengthen relationships with your teammates. In addition, because projects often involve more than one team, they're a great way to meet new people, learn new skills, and gain some valuable visibility outside your team. So keep your eyes open for opportunities to work on projects—especially ones that are cross-functional, meaning they involve two or more departments. For example, Operations and Marketing, or HR and Accounting.

Use your company's internal social networks or intranet to find projects. Ideally, you'd like to get on projects that have strong executive backing. Those will give you the most visibility. But as a junior person, that may not always be possible. So also keep your eye out for projects that other people won't do or have failed at.

Before you jump into a project that's outside your regular work responsibilities, make sure you get your manager's approval. If you aren't doing what you're being paid to do, he won't support you in your quest to venture into other areas.

At every step along the way, make sure you're a team player and a top performer. When you make other people look good by helping them achieve their goals, there's a good chance that they'll invite you to work with them on more—and more important—projects. It's always easier to network with people you worked with, so the more projects you're on the greater the networking possibilities.

Get Involved with Activities
Outside the Office

Do you remember the old nine-to-five workplace? If you do, enjoy the memory, because there's no such thing as a nine-to-five job anymore. Sure, you may physically be in the office only eight or nine hours a day, but the line between your personal and professional lives has pretty much disappeared. That means it's not enough for you to shine only at the office. If you want to move your career forward, you're going to have to use your nonoffice time too.

The bad news about the blurred private/job line is that you're under the microscope 24/7. There's nowhere to hide, so you have to constantly be aware of your image and how you're being perceived by others. One snide comment about your boss, a few too many drinks when you're out with friends, being rude to the barista at Starbucks, or an ugly breakup of a romantic relationship with a coworker could come back to haunt you at work. But there's good news too. You now have hundreds of opportunities to build your brand, expand your network, and develop relationships with people who can help you further your career.

Keep in mind that not every single activity you do outside work has to be meaningful. Sometimes there are people you don't seem to click with on a work level but you might on a more personal level. Activities outside work can bridge the work-personal gap. For example, playing on a company softball team or serving meals at a homeless shelter with people from other departments might let you see their other side—and show you that you've got more in common than you'd thought.

I know this may sound like a lot of work, but chances are you're already doing it. Think back to when you were applying to college. Yes, you needed decent grades, good SAT scores, and a few glowing recommendations from teachers. But to make yourself into an especially attractive candidate, you needed to mention the clubs you were in, the work you did in your community, and a lot of other things you did outside high school. It was the same when you put together the résumé to land the job you have right now: You talked about your academic accomplishments and about any job experience you might have had. But most likely you also included at least a few lines about the social or professional groups you were in and maybe even your hobbies and interests.

A lot of young people are especially interested in social justice or charity projects. What's important to you? The economy? Education? Global warming? Animal rights? Whatever it is, it's definitely possible to save the world and get ahead. In other words, to do things that have a positive impact on the world and make you look good at the same time. When you're interested in things besides work, you become a more interesting person.

Why Do It?

There are a number of really good reasons to get involved in extracurricular activities:

- **It makes you a well-rounded person.** And that's never a bad thing.

- **It makes you a happier person.** Who wouldn't want a little more happy in their lives?

- **It helps you build your network.** Being involved in extracurricular activities helps you meet more people. "I am part of the Full Circle Fund, a group that helps social entrepreneurs succeed. I had been involved for two years, fighting to improve the educational system and making contacts," says Aaron Mc-

Daniel, Senior Director of Global Strategy & Business Development at AT&T. "Then at work I was part of a team that was tasked with developing our firm's education market strategy. The relationships and background helped me an incredible amount."

• **It can increase your visibility at work.** "I began volunteering for the Worldwide Employee Benefits Network (WEB) during my job search," Carrie Hirst, Regional Marketing Coordinator at Allstate, told me. "I am now on the steering committee of that organization. My involvement in WEB has helped me stand out on the job. It also gives me some credibility when reaching out to more seasoned professionals in my industry." A recent CNNMoney survey confirms Carrie's experience when it found that workers who help others organize social activities and who make an effort to become friends with their coworkers have a 40 percent greater chance of getting a promotion.

• **It might help you when you're looking to change jobs** (or help you get one in the first place if you're ever unemployed). This is exactly what happened to Shane Dunn, Assistant Director of Student Engagement, Alumni Relations and Annual Giving, MIT Sloan School of Management. "I served on the Operations Committee of the Council for the Advancement and Support of Education (CASE)—the professional organization that supports and promotes the work of educational fundraisers and alumni relations professionals. During the three days of the conference, I spent a considerable amount of time getting to know the other volunteer committee members—after all, alumni relations and fundraising are in the 'relationship business' so it's natural to do so. Six months later, a woman who served on the Operations Committee with me called me in her new role as Director of Alumni Relations and Annual Giving at the MIT Sloan School of Management. She told me she had recently created a new position in the office and she wanted me to take the job. She asked me to interview with her team, which I ultimately did. Without a formal offer in hand, she offered me the job on the spot."

• **It will help you develop new skills that can help you do your job better.** Susan Gambardella, VP of Global Account Team at Coca-Cola, told me this story. "I had a young employee who would spend her vacation days volunteering at a high-security jail counseling inmates on how to develop career plans and business plans for when they are released. This young woman, as a result of these experiences with various felons, is not scared of any customer and is effective in very difficult negotiations."

• **It gets you thinking about things in a different way.** I often find that I have my best business ideas in the middle of a vacation (or even the middle of a shower) when my mind is as far from work as it can possibly be. I'm sure you've had the same experience. Giving your brain a break from work may very well help you come up with new ideas for how you can get noticed and get ahead when you finally do get back to the office.

• **It can allow you to see other ways to use your strengths at work.** Here's how Rachel Handler, a young Editor at Groupon, described it to me. "I occasionally volunteer with 826CHI, helping local kids to improve their writing skills. Working with children and trying to explain the principles of writing to them allows me to look at words with fresher eyes—after I spend time with them, I feel a bit more creative and more in tune with the way I write."

• **It's just plain refreshing.** Giving yourself opportunities to shine (or do something meaningful) outside the office will make you feel better about yourself. And that sense of confidence almost always follows you to work.

Finding Outside-the-Office Activities

The best employees (and by "best" I mean the ones most likely to get promoted and move up in their careers) are very strategic in the ways they use their time outside the office. Let's talk about how that works.

The easiest place to start is with professional, company-, or industry-related activities that take place outside the office. This could be taking classes and doing the kind of soft skill and hard skill building that we talked about in previous chapters. Being around people with similar interests is a great way to build your network. Ditto for going to conferences. The time after the keynotes or between breakout sessions can be invaluable. Everyone else there has something in common with you, and that's a great jumping-off point. Consider becoming a member of whatever group is putting on the conference (if you're in marketing, for example, that might be the American Marketing Association). Then, over time, gradually increase your level of involvement. Volunteer to work on a subcommittee, join the planning group, and maybe even run for a board position. I talk to a lot of managers and executives and I guarantee you that they notice employees who show this kind of interest in their profession. "Professional networking groups that directly relate to our profession would be a great way for employees to further their knowledge and skills and gain an edge in the workplace," says Travis Kessel, Vice President, Recruitment at Edelman Digital.

There are other work-related activities you can do on your own time. For example, you could start an industry-related blog, do some guest posts for other blogs, or become an active member of industry forums. You could also write articles for your local newspaper or relevant trade magazines. And you could pursue speaking opportunities. You could start by giving a talk at your alma mater about your company or your job. Once you get comfortable, you can apply to speak at industry conferences or even run workshops. As long as what you're doing complements what you're doing at work, the net result of all of this is that you're building your brand and boosting your visibility inside and outside your company.

Another easy place to build your outside-the-office profile is through non-work-related social activities you do with coworkers or colleagues. This might be joining your company softball team, getting a group together to enter a diabetes fundraising half-marathon. It could also be something more informal, such as going to retirement or birthday parties. Because activities like these often attract a lot of managers, this is an excellent way to get noticed.

Then there are philanthropic activities you might do on your own, things like becoming a Big Brother or Big Sister, volunteering at a local soup kitchen, or spending a weekend with Habitat for Humanity building homes for the homeless in your community. There is one small drawback to doing activities alone: All the great work you're doing may go unnoticed. That means you may have to do a little horn tooting at the office. When people are hanging out in the lunchroom talking about their weekend, you can always drop in something about what you did. But be very careful. It's critical that whatever you do, you do it sincerely. If people (especially managers) get the idea that you're doing some charitable work only because you want to build yourself up, you'll do yourself more harm than good. As the old saying goes, "Integrity is what you do when no one's watching."

Having Trouble Finding the Right Activity?

Sometimes finding the right activities is a bit of a challenge. You can jump start your search by asking your manger what sorts of opportunities there are, what the best groups are, the best organizations to volunteer for, and so on. Don't forget to ask for an inside contact—it's always easier to get involved if you know someone. You can also get a lot of ideas by joining some LinkedIn groups and/or other industry forums. And while you're online, do some online research:

- For associations, check out Job-hunt.org/associations.shtml
- For philanthropic groups, try Foundationcenter.org/findfunders

---

When a Rifle Is Better Than a Shotgun

According to Job-hunt.org, seven in ten people belong to at least one organization. That's great. However, 25 percent of people belong to four or more. That could be a problem. In general, it's better to do a few things well than a lot of things poorly.

The issue here is perception: People need to see that you're fully invested in what you're doing. And if you're involved in thirty different things, you can't possibly do all of them (or, for that matter, any of them) well.

- For volunteer opportunities, try Volunteermatch.org
- For events, try Meetup.com, where you can search for events in just about any imaginable category. Then go to some of the meetups. Another great source is Eventbrite.com, where you can search for events—local, regional, or national—that are relevant to what you want to do.

How to Maximize the Career Benefits of Outside Activities

I mentioned above how important it is to be sincere when getting involved in extracurricular activities, especially philanthropic ones. At the same time, though, we're talking about using those activities to further your career, so it's important to know how to get the most career benefit from the great stuff you're doing.

When you join an association or get involved in a charitable cause, put it on your LinkedIn profile. If appropriate, put it on your Facebook page too (I'm always surprised at how many people overlook this simple but effective step). At work, share insights you've learned from your outside activity with your coworkers. Comments like, "Oh, we were just talking about that at last night's meeting of the Widget Association," are a perfectly acceptable way of subtly promoting yourself that shows you're constantly trying to learn about your field and adds value to your team and your company.

If you give a speech, record it and put it on your Web site, your social media pages, or even your company's Web site. Ditto if you wrote an article or particularly insightful blog post. If possible, get an endorsement from the person who gave you the speaking opportunity, from people in the audience, or people who read your article. All of this shows that you're respected in your field and increases your visibility, your credibility, your network, and your value to your company.

Networking for Life

Always network before you need to. If you wait until you need some business contacts, it could take you weeks or months to make them. Networking, whether you do it at work or outside the office, allows you to better adapt, opens up new opportunities, and protects you against forces you can't control at work. When you're networking, you're putting together a team of people who will be able to help you get ahead faster. Remember, though, it's all about mutualism. Add value and you'll get value back, but never take more than you give. Don't look at networking as a chore or as something you have to do temporarily in order to advance: Networking is life. Never stop networking, whether it's inside your core group, in other departments, at networking events, when traveling, and online through social media. Be selective so you don't waste anyone's time, and figure out how your skills or connections can benefit other people so they'll return the favor and help you as you progress in your career.

It's a 24/7 world and just because your work hours are over doesn't mean you can stop learning, developing yourself, and making new connections. There are hundreds of nonworkplace opportunities that you can take advantage of and use to strengthen your brand. Select the more appropriate outside activities, such as joining an industry association that will help you achieve your goals. Be sure the activities you do add value to you and your employer. Don't try to do too many activities at once because you'll burn yourself out and you won't be able to give 100 percent to each one. It's better to focus your energy on a few that you can do really well than several that you can do a so-so job at. These activities will make you more aware of what else there is out there, help you test your skills in different environments, and give you plenty of great opportunities to meet new people outside your day job.

Your network is your net worth and your greatest career asset. It's worth more than what you know, your job title, and even your salary. What makes networking such a powerful tool is the same thing that makes public relations more effective than advertising. You can talk yourself up all day long, but the publicity you get from having other people talk you up is priceless. As you grow your career, you should be growing your network too. A strong network can promote you without you actually having to be in the room. They can advocate for you when negative things are said about you and sing your praises to people who can open doors for you, and in many cases they can even open doors for you themselves.

10

Turn Your Passion into a New Position

Choose a job you love and you will never have to work a day in your life.

CONFUCIUS

Businesses are always looking for ways to find top talent and keep their costs down. However, given today's economic situation, the two often seem mutually exclusive—in other words, you can either have top talent or cut costs, but not both. A growing number of smart employers, though, have figured out a way to have their cake and eat it too: hire from within. Let me give you a few quick examples.

Novelis, the world's largest manufacturer of rolled aluminum products with 11,600 employees in eleven countries, used to rely on external hires to fill talent needs. But over the past two years, 41 percent of new hires have come from within. And the company has reduced its recruiting costs by over $2 million during that time. Booz Allen Hamilton's internal recruiting system called "Inside First" filled 30 percent of the company's open positions with new hires in 2011—an increase of 10 percent from 2010. Enterprise Holdings made approximately 10,000 internal hires in their fiscal year 2012, up from 8,700 in FY

2011. These and many other companies are changing their focus from external to internal hiring for four reasons:

- **It's cheaper.** Recruiting costs go down, as do travel and relocation costs, advertising expenses, and training. It costs companies an average of $8,676 to hire someone internally, but $15,008 to hire externally—that's nearly double—according to Saratoga Institute's Human Capital Report.

- **It's quicker.** Typically, filling a position from outside can take anywhere from six weeks to six months (or longer). With internal hiring, the process usually takes just a few weeks.

- **It works out better.** It's easier for employees to succeed at a new job in the same company because they already have connections and knowledge about how work gets done. Forty to 60 percent of external hires are "unsuccessful," compared to only about 25 percent of internal hires, according to Human Resources Executive Online (hreonline.com).

- **It's good for morale.** "Promoting internally encourages employees and shows them that they have a future at the company, therefore serving as a retention tool," says Allison Cohen, Director of External Communications at Hill + Knowlton Strategies. Cisco found that its internal career program called "Talent Connection" has increased their employees' career satisfaction by 20 percent.

So what does this mean for you? Well, a lot of people have jobs that they don't particularly like but, because of the current economic situation, they're afraid to make a change. So they keep doing the same thing over and over and they get more miserable by the day. This is not the way life should be—and it's definitely not the way it *has* to be.

Here's one of the most important pieces of advice I can give you: If you don't wake up in the morning excited about what you're going to do at work, you'll never be able to progress in your career and you'll never succeed in life. Think about it. You probably spend more time at work than you do anywhere else. If you're happy there, you'll be happier in everything you do.

The trick is to turn your passions into your job. It's not always easy, but it is possible. I did it, dozens of young people I've worked with have done it, and you can too. When you're genuinely passionate about what you do, work becomes a hobby. And that passion becomes a beacon, attracting positive attention from your manager and coworkers. When you're passionate about your job, you'll naturally work harder, put in longer hours, and do it all with a smile on your face. That's good for your manager, it's good for your team, and it's great for your company. If everyone had a job they loved at your company, the business results would show. Genuine passion is almost always obvious—people will be able to see it in your eyes. When you're passionate about your job and your career, that passion is almost palpable. The positive energy you produce has a way of flowing outward to the people around you, who get inspired and want to work with you. Managers can't help but see passionate workers as people who will do successful things and should be put in positions where they can make those successes a reality.

But you're going to need some strategies to make that happen. And that's exactly what you're going to learn in this chapter.

Should You Make a Move? A Checklist

Before we get too far into this, let's take a few minutes to figure out whether making a move is (a) in your best interests, and (b) going to be possible at all. I want you to start by asking yourself the following questions:

- What are my passions? Another way to look at this is to track how you spend your free time. If you find that you're reading twenty articles a day on a particular topic, that's a pretty big hint.
- Am I using all my talents in my current job?
- What do I like most and least about my current job?
- Is there anything I can do in my current job to make it more enjoyable? (If so, you should explore these options before changing positions.)
- What is it about the job I'm thinking of moving to that interests me?
- Are there any aspects of the new job that I think I'd hate?
- What are the highest-growth areas in my current company? And what are the roles that are most in demand?
- I've got my eye on a new position, but am I really passionate about it?
- I've got my eye on a new position but I'm not qualified. What skills do I need to learn? How will I learn them? Do I need to take classes or shadow someone who's already working in that job?
- Have I honestly assessed all the different opportunities there are within my company?

A lot of people are afraid of trying to pursue their passions at work. They worry they'll get turned down, that it will complicate things at work, or that it could even end up hurting their career. I have two responses to that. First, managers actually like people who make lateral moves. It shows they know how to work in different types of organizations.

Second, if you ever want to be able to have a chance of enjoying your work life, you really don't have a choice.

Leveraging "Passion Projects" into a Full-Time Job

Sometimes your passions will come from outside of work—a hobby or activity you love to do but aren't getting paid to do it. Other times, you may have a passion for something that is being done (or could be) within your company. I want to give you two very different examples of people who were able to turn their passions into full-time jobs—without leaving their employers. The first one is my personal story.

On October 4, 2006—while still working at EMC—I started my first blog called Driven-to-Succeed, which was a career development guide for college students. It was my way of sharing what I'd learned in the recruitment process so others could prepare for the real world. The problem was that no one commented on the blog and very few people would answer my e-mails because no one had heard of me. Then, on March 14, 2007, my entire world changed. That was the day I read Tom Peters' famous article "The Brand Called You." Peters' words really hit home and I realized immediately that I could become the Gen Y spokesperson for personal branding because that's exactly what I'd been living all along. That night, after an EMC training session, I raced home and started my blog, PersonalBrandingBlog.com, and have never looked back.

That same day—exactly ten years from the day Tom Peters' article came out on the cover of *Fast Company*—the magazine wrote about my six-month-long personal branding journey. After reading the profile, Google invited me to speak (what a lesson in the power of publicity!).

Until then, EMC had no idea what I had been doing outside of work, and I didn't feel that they needed to because I considered it a hobby. But EMC's public relations people caught wind of the article and sent it directly to a Vice President who was starting a team to manage EMC's social media program. I got an e-mail the next morning from the VP, and we met. Through what I had been doing online, he saw how passionate I was about social media and personal branding. And by the time I met him, I was excited about the prospect of doing the same thing for the company. A few meetings later, I had created the first ever social media position at EMC—a Fortune 500 company—without ever having to fill out a single application. They were coming after me because they'd seen that something I was passionate about could benefit the company. And that's how I ended up making money doing what I loved.

Now, to give you an idea of how this looks from the managers' side, here's a story told to me by Brian Halligan, the CEO of HubSpot. "Pete Caputa was a young employee who joined our sales organization. Every month we gave him about 200 leads to work and he perpetually ignored them. It turns out that Pete's goal was to start a reseller channel for HubSpot. So instead of bringing in customers himself, he was signing up partners to do the job. Initially, he got plenty of pushback for his idea, but we eventually saw the numbers and 'fired' him from his job in direct sales and made his reseller project his new day job. Today, Pete has about forty people on his team and accounts for about 40 percent of HubSpot's new revenue."

If you learn just one thing from my story and Pete's, it's that you should keep doing the things you're passionate about and let others see that passion in action. If they don't know about it and never see it, how can they possibly support you? Having you work on projects you're passionate about is not only good for you, it's good for the company too. You'll put in longer hours, do a better job, and be a more committed, dedicated employee.

How to Do It

Unfortunately, because every situation is unique, I can't give you a series of steps that are guaranteed to take you from where you are to where you want to be. Sometimes where you want to be may be a lateral move, meaning a new job at your current company without a new title or a raise. Don't be afraid of lateral moves—people make them all the time. You might make a lateral move to acquire new skills and/or knowledge in other areas that are important to your career and the company you work for. Or you might do it because you see an area of your company that plays more to your strengths and interests than the one you're currently in.

Making a lateral move in a small company is often easier than in a big company (but not always). Sometimes all it takes to make a change is to raise the idea with your manager. Other times you may have to overcome significant resistance. Sometimes the transition can take a week, other times, six months or longer. Sometimes a manager in another department will recruit you, other times you'll have to make the first step. Despite the uncertainty, there are a few guidelines that will help speed up the process:

1. **Find out what's available.** But be careful—you don't want to give away that you're thinking about moving until you're actually ready to make your move. One easy, low-key (and under-the-radar) way to find out about opportunities is to use your company's internal social networks and job boards. If you need more information, ask around, but keep your conversations as informal as possible.

2. **Make sure you know what you're getting yourself into.** Speak to people who are doing what you want to do.

Network with them so you know exactly what their job entails before you jump. Really analyze the opportunity. What problems does the organization you want to join have? What openings do they have? How do you see your strengths helping your target organization solve its problems? And be sure you've really looked into what life would be like in your new position. What kinds of projects are they working on? Is the manager someone you can work for? Are your prospective teammates people you can work with? Will the new job truly allow you to use more of your talents and skills than you are using in your current job? Making a switch before you've answered these questions could turn out to be a disaster.

3. Build a name for yourself. We've talked about this in previous chapters, but it's worth touching on again. It's essential that you continually demonstrate that you're someone who has high-value solutions. That means putting yourself in positions where you can demonstrate your skills. If, for example, you're interested in transitioning to a Web position within your company, start by doing a critique of the company's Web site focusing not so much on what's wrong, but on what you would do to make it better. The same goes for anything else you see that your company could improve on. Do you see trends in your industry that no one else does? If so, start a blog and brand yourself as the expert.

How to Balance Passion-Driven Projects with Your Current Job

Sometimes making a lateral move is as easy as checking a box on a form. And some companies, such as Google, will allow you to spend a certain percentage of your workday (at Google, it's 20 percent) on projects that are outside your current job description but that benefit the company. Most of the time, though, you'll have to pursue your passion on your own time. Between your regular job, taking classes to improve your skills, networking with people you hope to work with soon, and all the hours you'd ordinarily spend pursuing your passion, you could end up putting in the equivalent of two full-time jobs. Consider it a sacrifice you're making today so you'll have a better tomorrow.

If you're lucky, you'll be able to do most of that extra work on the weekends, during lunch, or before and after work. But regardless of your schedule, your goal is the same: to impress your prospective manager so much that he wants to bring you in full-time. The most important thing to remember about balancing a passion-driven project with your current job is that the current job comes first. Always. You were hired to do a job, so do it. And do it well. If you let your current workload (or work quality) slip, no one will have the confidence that you'll be able to perform in your new job.

Getting Your Boss in Your Corner

As mentioned above, getting your boss behind you is essential if you're going to be able to make a successful transition to a new, more passion-driven position in your company. At the very least, he or she may be able to help you open doors and get access to people you couldn't reach on your own. Not keeping your manager in the loop could make you seem disloyal and might undermine your security in your current job. Plus, getting the reputation as someone who sneaks around behind managers' backs will keep you from moving to any other job. In our study, 73 percent of the managers we interviewed said they would be willing or extremely willing to support an employee who wants to move to a different position at work. Oddly, though, only 48 percent of young workers said they would be interested in actually making a move. I suspect that number would be a lot higher if those workers knew their managers would be supportive.

So how do you get your boss on board? It starts with letting him know what you're interested in—he can't support you if you keep your aspirations to yourself. The perfect time is during or right after a performance evaluation (I'm assuming you got rave reviews). You could simply say something along the lines of, "I know I'm really good at ____. Do you see any opportunities for me to use those skills on this team?" Hopefully, your manager will say yes. But at the very least, a good manager should say, "That's great. Next time there's a project that can use those skills, I'll keep you in mind."

Before you approach your boss, be sure to do some research. If you can show your boss that you've looked into specific departments and what their needs are, that you've investigated what positions are open and what the qualifications are, and you can articulate how your skills can benefit the company, it will be very hard for your boss not to support you.

And keep things positive. You'll have a lot more success if you talk with your manager about the things you love about your job and how you'd like to build on your skills, instead of talking about what you hate about your job.

Ryan Benevides, a young Senior Valuation & Financial Analyst at GE, told me a great story about how he landed his dream job—in part by getting his boss behind him. Ryan had been with GE for four years and decided that he wanted to move into underwriting and investment analysis. His managers supported him, but the company had a hiring freeze, and there were no positions available. Of course, he was discouraged. But he had a feeling that the hiring freeze wouldn't last forever. So he started calling all the managers in the department he was hoping to work in and asked each one a single question: "What is something that's important to your business but you're not able to execute because of HR issues?" After a week of interviews he combed through all the feedback and wrote a plan that ended up driving his career in the direction he wanted to go—and would benefit the department he wanted to move to.

Next, he set up a meeting with his manager and presented the plan. Here's how he describes what happened next. "During this meeting I made sure to point out that I would still be able to do my current job, plus I would be able to help meet the needs of an office with resource issues. I hoped that would allow them to create a new role—which, of course, I would be the one to fill. My manager was really supportive, and at the end of the meeting he helped get the proposal up through the appropriate channels to get approved. The result was a four-week resource-sharing initiative where I worked tirelessly to maintain the output of my current job and, at the same time, to help fill the most important gap in the target office's business. About three weeks into the initiative I was offered a job as a permanent member of the target office—in the exact function I wanted. I appreciate that sometimes doors need to be pushed before they can be unlocked and opened."

He was successful in creating a brand-new position for himself based on his interests, passions, and desired expertise. He saw the opportunity, got his manager to buy into it, and expanded his role temporarily in order to reposition himself for a job he really wanted. You can do the same.

One way to ease into this is to get involved in a few projects that involve the department you think you might want to move to. This will allow you to test the waters and your prospective new team to get a taste of the skills you bring to the table and the kinds of results you're capable of producing. This is going to involve putting in some extra hours, say five to ten per week in addition to the forty you're already working on your original job (if you're okay skipping lunches, you might not even notice much difference). Anything less than five hours you'll have a hard time getting a feel for what working in the new department would actually be like. Much more than ten and you may be too exhausted to do a good job.

If You're Passionate About Your Job, You'll Perform Better and Get Ahead Faster

I can't stress enough how important it is to focus on your strengths and passions in the workplace. If you aren't excited about what you're doing, you're not going to put in the necessary effort and you could end up slacking off, getting bored, or not feeling fulfilled. Once you know what you really want to do, start looking for a place within your company where you can do it—someplace you know you can really add value.

Before you commit yourself to making a change, make sure you're completely confident that the position you'd like to move into will actually enable you to put your passions and strengths to work. Next, get your boss on board. Having them behind you will make it easier to transition to a new position when the time is right. Finally, start doing additional work outside your current job to build visibility and show that you can produce results and be successful in the position you'd like to move to. Good companies—and good managers—that see their talent as their greatest asset will want to support you because it's good for you and for the company.

One quick caution: Remember, your current job comes first. Do not rush into this without first proving yourself. If you let your performance slip and you aren't doing what you were originally hired to do, no one will be interested in having you join their team.

Keep in mind: You don't have to move up and get a raise to get ahead in your career. Sometimes a lateral move is just what you need to get into a position where you can learn new skills, gain a better understanding of how your company works, and establish new connections. After you've been at your job long enough to have mastered it—and come to the conclusion that it's not the best use of your strengths and passions, start looking around inside your company for ways to better leverage them. If there's a role that seems a better fit than what you're currently doing, or there's a project that excites the hell out of you, go for it! Getting that new position will make it easier to get noticed and promote yourself because you will be happier (have a better attitude), work harder, and perform better. When you're doing something you enjoy, you naturally will want to be good at it and eventually master it. This will help you get ahead at work and become more successful.

11

Start Your Own Business
While on the Job

Virgin could never have grown into the group of
more than 200 companies it is now, were it not for a
steady stream of intrapreneurs who looked for and
developed opportunities, often leading efforts that
went against the grain.

—RICHARD BRANSON

Over the past few years, I've noticed two new trends in the corporate world. First, instead of buying start-ups in order to acquire the targets' technology, corporations are beginning to invest in start-ups in exchange for an equity stake. Second, realizing that they have to constantly innovate in order to stay competitive, companies are increasingly turning to their own employees for new ideas—and they're funding these employee-generated projects. In this chapter, I'll show you how you can take advantage of both of these related trends by becoming an *intrapreneur*—someone who acts like an entrepreneur but operates within a large company.

Everything we've touched on in previous chapters—from hard and soft skills to networking—is part of the solid foundation you're building at work. But becoming an intrapreneur is a real game changer. In fact, you'd be hard pressed to find a better way to stand out at work and promote yourself than to come up with an idea that moves your company forward. When you make a name for yourself as a forward-thinking person who's committed to the company's success and who's helping drive the bottom line in a new way, you'll get ahead a lot faster than your peers. Instead of waiting for a manager to retire or get promoted so you can move into his office, why not create your own role in your company? Becoming an intrapreneur allows you to position yourself as a leader, an innovative thinker and problem solver, and a real mover and shaker. Succeed as an intrapreneur and you'll become so valuable to your company that everyone will want to work with you. At that point, there's no limit to how far you can go in your career.

Of course, creating a new business at work and becoming an intrapreneur isn't going to be easy, but hey, there's no true reward without risk. I actually think it's risky to *not* take risks at work. The downside of taking a risk is that you crash and burn. But most smart managers respect someone who's tried and failed more than someone who's never even tried. And the upside is that people can't help but notice you if you're going above and beyond your job description. They'll want to work with you (and possibly, for you). And that's how careers are made.

Intrapreneurship Might Not Be New, but It's Becoming a Big Deal in Corporate America

Although the word *intrapreneurship* isn't used nearly as often as its cousin, entrepreneurship, the concept has been around for a long time. One of the first examples was Lockheed Martin's Skunk Works (more formally referred to as the Advanced Development Programs, ADP), which got its start in 1943. Skunk Works is credited with developing a number of revolutionary products, including the U-2, the SR 71 Blackbird, and the F-22 Raptor. The project was headed by Kelly Johnson, and according to Lockheed, "what allowed Kelly to operate the Skunk Works so effectively and efficiently was his unconventional organizational approach. He broke the rules, challenging the current bureaucratic system that stifled innovation and hindered progress."

Today, seventy years later, Skunk Works still exists at Lockheed, and hundreds of other companies have launched similar initiatives (sometimes even referred to as Skunk Works projects). Knowing they need to think entrepreneurially if they're going to survive and thrive, they've found that intrapreneurship programs help them attract top talent, fuel innovation, and build competitive advantage. As Ingrid Vanderveldt, Entrepreneur in Residence at Dell, told me, "Companies are under pressure more than ever before to be innovative and they know entrepreneurs are creative, innovative people who make big things happen on limited resources."

And companies are definitely walking the walk (instead of just talking about it), implementing corporate intrapreneurship contests, Entrepreneur in Residence (EIR) programs, and more. Overall, 30 percent of large companies now provide seed funds to finance intrapreneurial efforts, according to management consultant Gifford Pinchot. Let me give you a few examples:

- At Google, employees can spend 20 percent of their time on projects that are outside their job description—as long as they benefit Google customers. Google says that half of their original products were developed in these 20 percent programs. These include Gmail, Google News, and AdSense.

- Facebook has a nontraditional intrapreneurship program called the Hackathon, which promotes product innovation by encouraging engineering teams to collaborate on software projects. The famous Like button was a Hackathon product.

• PwC (a large consulting firm) has the PwC PowerPitch that encourages innovation by offering $100,000 to the team that comes up with the best service offering. PowerPitch winners have created new analytic centers and new innovations in cloud computing. The company estimates that 60 percent of its global workforce of 30,000 are engaged in the program.

• At DreamWorks, top execs—including the Chief Creative Officer and the CEO—are willing to listen to anyone who has an idea for a movie. DreamWorks is so serious about this that they teach their employees how to pitch—something hundreds of people have taken advantage of.

• Entrepreneurs in Residence at Dell meet with intrapreneurs and provide mentorship and guidance. The company also supports a MSTC (Master of Science in Technology Commercialization) program at the University of Texas to help intrapreneurs evaluate new ideas and possibly go out and start their own companies. The Dell Innovators Credit Fund will be making partial scholarships available to Dell employees.

There's no question that corporations are taking intrapreneurship seriously, supporting and embracing it—and they should get plenty of credit for that. However, it's important to recognize that a lot of it is being fueled by young workers, people with great ideas that they don't have the resources to develop on their own, young people who aren't afraid to take risks and to do something outside their current job description.

Before I get into how to become an intrapreneur, I want to spend a few minutes talking about *why* you might want to do it in the first place, and some of the challenges you may face. Let's start with the good stuff:

• **It's a great way to better align who you are with what you do.** If your job isn't everything you want it to be, you can change it by pursuing and developing pet projects you're passionate about.

• **Intrapreneurship allows you to create new positions and advance in your career faster than you might have been able to on the regular track.** The connections you'll make and the supporters you'll have behind you will allow you to potentially skip entire layers of the corporate hierarchy.

• **Intrapreneurship gives you unique experiences that differentiate you from your peers.** We've talked a lot in previous chapters about how important it is to stand out, to be seen as an expert or go-to person. Nothing will highlight you more than building your own business inside your company. Intrapreneurship is also a fun, challenging way to learn and make changes.

• **Intrapreneurship is less risky than being an entrepreneur because you'll have the corporation's resources available.** If you're an entrepreneur, you could be financing your idea with credit cards or borrowing from friends and family. If the idea goes belly-up, you could be out a lot of money and relationships could get strained.

• **Intrapreneurship can be a bridge to becoming a full-on entrepreneur later on.** By starting your own business on the job—on your employer's dime and time—you're gaining the skills, understanding of the process, and the confidence you'll need to run a business without your company's help in the future.

As you can tell, I'm pretty passionate about intrapreneurship. But there can be a few challenges because you're trying to do something that hasn't been done before or improving something that *has* already been done. With change comes resistance and you have to be ready for it. As we talked about in the previous chapter, your primary responsibility is to keep doing your current job in an exemplary manner. If you aren't impressing the hell out of everyone around you, you'll never get them to support your efforts to do something else. So at least in the beginning, you'll need to juggle (brilliantly) your day-to-day job along with your intrapreneurial goals.

Another challenge you might face is your fear of failure and that's natural so don't think you're alone. You may be afraid that you won't get the management buy-in you'd need to succeed or that you'll be fired if you fail. There's also a possibility that you'll bump up against a kind of reverse ageism: Since you're young, a lot of people will automatically think you're inexperienced, that you need to prove yourself, and that you might not be capable of starting a business. Your job is to prove them wrong through hard work, persistence, and creative ideas. All entrepreneurs know what rejection feels like and have the scars to prove it. Pushing through these obstacles will make it that much more satisfying when your project is a success.

Is Intrapreneurship Right for You?

Intrapreneurship isn't right for everyone. But if half or more of the following statements are true for you, you should definitely consider pursuing it.

1. You've got a passion for something your company isn't doing right now.
2. You see opportunities that others don't.
3. You're creative and innovative in your thinking.
4. You're willing to take risks.
5. You're a great networker and can build cross-functional relationships.
6. You're a natural salesperson.
7. You're good at working on teams and collaborating.
8. You're politically savvy and understand how your company operates.

I want to tell you about a friend of mine, Ken Pickard, an Advisory Senior at Ernst & Young, who definitely could have answered yes to most of the statements above. Ken had—and still has—a real knack for social media (1, passion). During Ken's second year with the firm, a senior manager in the Advisory practice asked him if he would be interested in joining her team for an internal competition, the Innovation Challenge (4, willing to take risks). The goal of the competition was to challenge employees to come up with new service offerings for Ernst & Young clients. After a brainstorming meeting, Ken suggested that his team, which consisted of several staff members senior to Ken, explore social media risk. "I questioned what, as a firm, we were doing to address the risks associated with businesses adopting the new technology," he said (2, seeing opportunities, and 3, creative, innovative thinking). During the first meeting, Ken convinced his colleagues that "the risks were real, that companies were investing in the technology, and that the global Ernst & Young organization hadn't developed a publicized offering to address the issues" (6, natural salesperson). Ken's team made it through the first few rounds of the competition and made it to the finals.

To make sure his team's product was the best it could be, Ken reached out to a team based in Switzerland that had been developing, and actually delivering, a similar service offering, and found ways to collaborate (7, good working in teams). At the same time, Ken formed an alliance with a competitor from one of the other finalists, a guy who had some knowledge in social media that Ken was lacking (5, networking and building relationships). He also took me out to lunch a few times and peppered me with questions about how he could use social media to empower his brand.

In the end, Ken's team won the Innovation Challenge, which really paid off in terms of building his own brand within the firm as an innovator, a leader, and subject matter resource. "Because of the experience and my ties to social media, I'm often sought by others to contribute to potential social media projects and I'm seen as a real thought leader. It's also made me a resident expert of our enterprise 2.0 platforms where I've held several presentations on how groups can utilize the software to work smarter and deliver better client service."

Okay, Ready to Learn How to Become an Intrapreneur?

Becoming an intrapreneur isn't something people typically fall into. If you want it to happen, you're going to have to get out there and make it happen. And to do that, you'll need a plan.

Item number one on your list is to master your job. This is actually a two-parter. First, become an expert in your current role. Second, you'll need to hit certain milestones if you want to pull this off. The first one is being at your job long enough for you to learn your role and feel that you could teach everything you do to another person. You need to prove your worth and demonstrate that you can handle the responsibilities you were hired to do. You'll also want to build in enough time on the job to make your boss look like a rock star and gain his trust before you venture outside your role. Otherwise, you're going to have a really tough time getting him to buy into and support your ideas (and to support you in your desire to expand your role in the company). In my experience, it usually takes six months to get to this point. Of course, if you can do it in less time, great! But don't rush things. It's better to take a little more time than to try to make a move when you're really not ready.

That said, depending on how you frame things, it is *sometimes* possible to become an intrapreneur when you're just starting out. Marie Artim, Vice President, Talent Acquisition at Enterprise Holdings Inc., told me about a young man who, while still a trainee, had some concerns about what was being communicated to new hires and whether it was consistent with what they had been promised during their initial hiring and orientation. "He built and implemented a New Hire Survey that he sent to new hires to find out what was working and what wasn't," Marie told me. "We saw immediate improvements in new hires retention and retention in first-level management. Those things are all really important to our business, made a huge impact on our business, and actually became the driving force behind rolling out a formal mentoring program."

Passion, persistence, and commitment are key to seeing your ideas come to life. "Every employee who wants to excel should look at taking on projects that push them to do better, contribute more," Dell's Ingrid Vanderveldt told me. "Thinking like an entrepreneur enables employees to think creatively and cost effectively about solutions that have the potential to make a big difference."

Throughout this process—and throughout your entire career—it's important to think in terms of how you can best leverage your strengths and weaknesses to help your company succeed. What are some things your company does really well? What does it do less well? What *should* it be doing to improve? How can your strengths and intrapreneurship goals get your company where it needs to go? With that in the back of your mind, you'll be better able to articulate to your manager how your intrapreneurial idea will benefit the company.

You'll also need to be able to clearly define your objectives and metrics. In other words, what does success look like and how can you measure it? Be absolutely sure that your project aligns with the corporation's mission and values.

In most cases your project will be directly tied to what your company already does. However, there are times when a project that, at first glance, doesn't seem quite right turns out to be so good that an employer will fund it anyway—as long as you can show how it will benefit the company. Jonathan Mildenhall, VP of Global Advertising Strategy and Creative Excellence at the Coca-Cola Company, told me a great story about a young man who worked for Coke and who wanted to start a jeans company with his wife—not something you'd typically associate with a soft drink company. But there was a connection. "We understand that he has this thing that he wants to do and we give him the financial security that he needs because he's part of the big corporation," said Jonathan. "Yet at the same time, we actually benefit because he's meeting with people in the fashion industry that we could potentially work with. He has this entrepreneurial spirit and that is enabling his corporate existence and his own business experience to exist side by side."

Dan Satterthwaite, Head of HR at DreamWorks, told me a similar story, about an employee who had an idea for linking social media networks together in a unique way. "We're now investing millions of dollars in developing something that has nothing to do with actual filmmaking, but takes the core competency of storytelling and high-speed graphics rendering into an entirely new business model for us," Dan said. "That's a pretty big deal for us because it didn't come from the mind of the senior most creative guy in the company, it came from somebody who's on the ground really working on making movies, but had a really cool idea."

As great as these two projects were, they would never have gotten off the ground if they hadn't had some pretty heavy hitters behind them. And if you want your company to support your idea, you'll need the same. Start with your manager. Sit down with them and talk about the potential opportunity you see. They've worked at the company longer than you have and they know the path to making a project successful, including how to assemble a team and how to get decision makers to buy in. Have a presentation that describes the opportunity, how it benefits your company, and what resources you'll need to execute (people, materials, funding). Once your manager is solidly backing you, ask for their help in lining up a senior exec or major decision maker inside your company to put his or her name on the project. That will help you get the resources you'll need to give you the greatest chance of succeeding.

Remember, this is your project, and you want to be the center of attention, right? But don't try to do everything—you're going to need help. In addition, trying to do it all makes you seem either like you can't get others to work with you, you can't delegate, or you're trying to hog all the glory. Instead, surround yourself with people who have skills you don't but who can make your idea even better. Look for people who are passionate about the idea you want to develop. Some will come from inside your organization, but others may come from outside.

Optimism and self-confidence are great qualities for intrapreneurs and entrepreneurs alike. But they can easily turn into naïveté if you don't have a backup plan. Having a great idea, a great team, strong backing, and deep resources significantly increase your chances of success. But even with all that, sometimes things don't work out the way you'd hoped. Life can be awfully unpredictable, and it doesn't pay to be overconfident. There are too many factors beyond your control, such as your company's health, management changes, and corporate mergers. So you'll want to have a backup plan—at the very least so you can salvage the work you've done and have something to show for it. Not having a contingency plan is just plain foolish (and it'll be interpreted by people you're trying to turn into allies as amateurish and immature).

You also want to have a contingency plan because intrapreneurship, just like entrepreneurship—and everything else in life, for that matter—is risky. You could get laid off tomorrow. You could get hit by a bus on the way into the office. Likewise, there's no guarantee of success in business—most ideas fail.

Taking risks is what builds successful careers. Those who don't, get stuck (in fact, I'd argue that not taking risks at work will be more harmful to your career than failure, because your company needs new ideas in order to grow. So if you're holding back on proposing a new internal business opportunity, don't. In our study, we found that 58 percent of managers are either "very willing" or "extremely willing" to support an employee who wants to capitalize on a new business opportunity. But only 40 percent of young workers are actually willing to take the plunge. And keep in mind that you could benefit even if your project doesn't get funded. Matt McDonald, a marketing manager for Aflac, participated in a company-sponsored competition to develop a mobile app that would benefit employees, agents, or customers. Out of 500 entries, Matt's team made it to the final eight. "We had an opportunity to present our idea to top executives at our World Wide Headquarters in Columbus, Georgia," he told me. "It was a truly engaging and rewarding experience—even though we didn't win the competition."

Two final things and then we'll move on. First: As you go through the process, check in with your team to learn what's working and what isn't, what you'd need to do to improve. How could you prevent mistakes in the future and repeat your success? Intrapreneurship is all about experimenting/testing ideas, measuring the results, and improving on them. It can sometimes take a few tries to figure out whether or not something is right for your company. Finally, as soon as your project is up and running, start thinking about your next one and what kinds of people, backing, and resources you'll need to build it out.

Making the Pitch—And Winning Support

In order to make your project successful, you need a well-defined plan and the resources needed to ensure the best possible chance of success. Your plan should include a summary of the idea, a list of resources you will need and the cost associated with them, an idea of what the potential market opportunity is, the potential increase of revenue or decrease in cost that could result, and a step-by-step program (including milestones) on how you're going to pull it off.

Do not just make things up. Chances are that you'll be pitching to people who have a lot more experience in your business sector than you do, and if they sniff any BS, you're dead in the water. You'll also need accurate estimates of how much developing your project will cost your organization in terms of hard dollars and opportunity cost. And you'll need to know who else you'll want on your team and what each person's role will be, including yours.

Once you have your plan locked down, it's time to win the support you'll need in order to bring the project to life. You will want to make a formal presentation to your manager first, then your coworkers and potentially other groups based on your project requirements. This way, when you present to your coworkers, you can already say that your manager knows about it and is supporting it, which will make them pay closer attention to what you have to say.

Overcoming Your Fears

Deciding to pursue an intrapreneurial project can be a little intimidating—maybe even frightening. Fortunately, there are a few different ways to boost your self-confidence. The most important way is to believe in yourself, because if you don't no one else will. In order to do this, you need to pursue only the projects where you can best leverage your strengths and personality. We naturally have more confidence in areas where we are strong. Aside from looking inside yourself, you should look for the support of the team that already surrounds you. If you can get others to feel as passionately as you do about something, you'll feel a lot better, you'll be able to be more productive and accomplish more. Aside from having a strong team, it's even more important that your manager is behind you. If you can win their support, then the team will more likely join you. Managers can open doors for you and give you honest feedback that will help build your self-esteem and prevent you from quitting early—before your idea might actually take off. When all else fails, it's critical that you have something to fall back on. If you create a backup plan before you pursue your idea, you'll be more likely to take the risks associated with being an intrapreneur.

You and Your Manager: Supporting Each Other Through the Process

As we've talked about, your intrapreneurial efforts have to benefit your company. And, of course, they'll benefit you too. But there are also other winners in this win-win scenario, the biggest one being your manager.

Most ambitious bosses want to build their organizations and develop their employees because the better their team does, the more visibility and influence the managers will have. The promotions, salary bumps, and bonuses don't hurt either. That means that your ability to create new opportunities will position your manager as a real mover and shaker in the company.

Your manager can support you by linking you to the right resources, allowing you to spend part of your workday focused on the project you're developing, coaching and mentoring you, and protecting you from politics. At the same time, you support your manager by being honest with them, letting them know what's going on and the obstacles you're running into, and making sure their name gets on the project along with yours so they can reap some of the rewards if it's a success.

In my experience, most bosses are more than happy to support their employees' intrapreneurial projects. But every once in a while a boss won't support a project or will actively undermine it. If you're unlucky enough to have a boss like this, be absolutely sure that you're doing everything you possibly can to make your manager successful at their job. The more the boss can see the benefit to them personally, the more likely they'll be to get on board. In addition, be prepared to work harder for your manager in order to earn their trust. To do this, focus on delivering results before they'll even think of letting you "be more than your job description" and take on an intrapreneurial project. If you can't consistently get your current work done, this won't work for you. If you don't feel that you've contributed enough with your current responsibilities, then wait until you do so you can be more confident and have an easier time selling the idea.

If you don't see your manager ever supporting your ambitions, then it might be time to make a job or company change. Your goal should be to work for a boss and a company that allows employees to thrive by being intrapreneurial. If your current situation won't let you do it, look for one (either inside your company or outside it) that will.

When Things Don't Go as Planned

No one wants to fail, but sooner or later we all do (in my view, if you haven't failed at something at some point, you haven't taken enough risks). So what do you do if a project of yours goes south?

Well, the first thing is to *not* give into the temptation to allocate blame. Before you blame everyone else—or take it all on your own shoulders—look at things realistically and objectively. What went wrong? What went right? Could you have predicted whatever it was that caused the problems? What would you have had to do in advance to head off the obstacles you faced? What resources (again, people, material, finances) would you have needed to make the project a success?

The goal is to change your attitude about failure—and to brand yourself as someone who can make a mistake or take criticism and learn from it. Don't get frustrated or resent someone who gives you feedback because we can all become better workers. In order for you to promote yourself, you have to realize that you're always a student and that there's always room for improvement. None of us will ever be so good that we can't learn from our mistakes. You should also be willing to give feedback to your coworkers in a respectful way. This is one way to earn trust in the workplace and be seen as someone of great value. Believe me, that's a rare skill and your manager *will* take notice.

Hey, Who Owns This Thing, Anyway?

One of the big differences between entrepreneurs and intrapreneurs is that entrepreneurs generally own what they invent and develop—and the profits are divided among shareholders and investors. With intrapreneurs, things are a little less clear-cut. If, for example, you create a brand-new product that needs to be patented, the patent itself may be in your name, but chances are that your employer will own it—along with the profits and royalties it generates. Doesn't seem completely fair, does it? After all, the idea was yours. But in the company's view, they paid your salary, funded the project, picked up the tab for the patent attorneys, and handled all the marketing.

Of course, your employer may choose to give you a bonus or assign you a share of the royalties, but they're under no obligation. The official policy on this may be outlined in your employee handbook.

Something to think about as you're putting together your plan: If you've got a billion-dollar idea that will completely revolutionize your industry, you might want to consider getting the patent done on your own. That way you can *license* it to your employer instead of signing all the rights over. But be careful. Taking an overly aggressive stance (such as bringing your attorney into the pitch meeting) could kill the entire deal and maybe even your job.

Intrapreneurs Make the Biggest Impact and Get Ahead Faster

Intrapreneurship is the wave of the future, and it's how companies will remain competitive, innovative, and attractive to young workers. And with good reason. As an intrapreneur, you'll be able to almost literally create something from nothing—something that can have a measurable impact on your company's performance (imagine having "created a new division at XYZ Company that increased corporate profits 20 percent in twelve months" on your résumé instead of "was promoted to Senior Marketing Specialist"). Intrapreneurship differentiates you like nothing else. Your reputation will soar, everyone will know who you are, and you'll definitely be seen (and talked about) as leadership material. And because you're still an employee, you'll also have access to resources—financial and talent—that entrepreneurs usually don't.

That said, if you want to become an intrapreneur, you must—and I really mean *must*—focus on your current responsibilities first. While you're developing your idea into a project, think about how it will benefit the company and what resources you will need, including people, material, and financial backing. Once you have your current job taken care of, get your manager, or someone else with decision-making power, to buy into your idea. Since it's pretty unlikely that you'll be able to execute your idea alone, put together a top-notch team. But keep in mind that this is a step-by-step process and that if you don't have a well-thought-out idea in place *before* you start going after backing, no one will invest a nickel in you. Plus, by doing all the hard work before you make the pitch, you'll be more confident and better able to prove that your idea can help the company profit and get people interested in supporting you.

As with any new venture, it's always important to have a backup plan. Remember: You don't know what's possible until you just go for it! If you pull it off, it could change your career for the better and leave a lasting impression on the people you work with. Bottom line: It's risky to not take calculated risks in your career. The workplace is always evolving and if you keep doing what you did yesterday, you'll never advance. You'll never get the rewards you're looking for (major promotions, salary raises, and so on) if you don't take risks.

Intrapreneurship is an extraordinary learning experience and can help you see your potential and get you noticed by the right people. Opportunities to be an intrapreneur are everywhere, but you'll need to seize them or you're going to miss out.

●●●

12

Moving Up, Moving Sideways, or Moving On?

Think of your career as a series of experiences.
Don't expect it to be with one institution or linear.

—LENNY MENDONCA,
DIRECTOR AND A
PUBLIC SECTOR
PRACTICE LEADER,
McKINSEY & COMPANY

Once upon a time, people who wanted to advance in their careers looked for a new *job*. Today they need to look for *opportunities*. What's the difference? Instead of seeing themselves as a narrow set of job-related skills, high-potential employees need to see themselves as a broad collection of skills that can be applied to many different challenges. Instead of plotting their path up a linear corporate ladder, they need to look *across* their company for the next challenge; that is, the next job or project that will grow their brand. A study by CareerBuilder shows that nearly seven in ten workers search for opportunities on a routine basis.[1] This is an entirely new way of thinking that uproots everything you've learned about how to advance your career. Your parents and grandparents had one-company-and-career-for-life mind-set, whereas the only way to get ahead today is to gain new perspectives and new experiences by moving around.

In a way, this chapter will answer a question I hear a lot from young people: "What do I do if I feel stuck in my job?" We'll talk about the importance of keeping your eyes open for your next opportunity and I'll show you when—and how—to make your move. Because, regardless of your position, you need to always be fully using your skills, challenging yourself, learning, and growing. And you need a supportive environment where you can showcase the value you add, and people who care and who can help you advance will notice. If over time it becomes clear that your current situation and your longer-term career plans aren't aligned, the best way to increase your visibility and get ahead in your career may be to move to another company where you can make better use of your talents to build your brand—and your new employer's. Feeling stuck in your career is horrible, and if you want to get unstuck, you'll need to take charge of your life and not wait around for others to pull you out. It's up to you.

Before we get into the specifics, I want to give you a few pieces of general advice that will serve you well. First, always be open to new opportunities. And when I say "always," I really do mean *always*. Taking your job for granted is a major mistake—your division or your entire company could get acquired or could go out of business and you could find yourself on the street with little or no warning. That's why I strongly suggest that from day one of your new job, you start thinking about the future.

Second, consider all your options. Most people, when thinking about their future, either imagine moving up in their organization or moving to a new company. But, as the title of this chapter suggests, those are not the only ways to get ahead. If you make a lateral move and wind up in a position with a similar title and pay grade, that's fine. You can still be noticed, get people to invest in you, and have a chance at making a huge impact—all of which will lead to a better title and a bigger salary. The more experiences you have, the more attractive you'll be as a candidate for a leadership role. Lateral moves can always open your eyes to new responsibilities (and opportunities) that may play more to your strengths and interests than your current job. Lateral moves may help position you for major promotions later. Remember that every situation is different, so you need to review all of your options and speak to a mentor or two before you make a final decision. The decisions you make now can have a major impact on where you'll end up down the road.

Regardless of the decision you make (or where you end up) you will gain new experiences. Keep a positive attitude and outlook and take advantage of the opportunities you get—and the ones you chase after as well. Careers can be highly unpredictable, so you need to be able to adapt to new situations, not get down on yourself if something doesn't go as planned, and always maintain relationships and build your network. You never know when you'll need a helping hand.

Itchy Feet: Finding the Right Time to Make a Move

After a year in your position/job, it's time to assess your situation. Are you getting a raise or promotion based on your annual review? Have you spoken to your manager about career opportunities and whether you're on the right track? You should always talk with your manager about your goals and get their input on what you need to do in order to achieve them. That will give you a much better chance of actually reaching those goals than just guessing and possibly coming up short. My rule of thumb is to wait a year or so before trying to change your position in your company. It usually takes most people at least six months to learn their role and another six to prove themselves in that role. After the first six months on the job, you'll have a pretty good feel for things. You'll know whether you can see yourself working there long-term and whether there's a true cultural fit, and you'll have a pretty good sense of what other possibilities might be available for you at your company. If you aren't happy, it's not a good fit and there aren't any career opportunities or long-term potential, it's probably time to search elsewhere. If there are opportunities and you enjoy the work and still feel challenged, then it's time to coordinate with you manager to establish goals and take on more responsibilities.

"You need to make a commitment to the company and the cause," Matthew Nordby, Executive Vice President and Chief Revenue Officer at *Playboy*, told me. "But once that commitment is fulfilled, you have a duty and an obligation to pursue your career to the fullest. So, that means taking a risk on a start-up or using your skill sets to move the economy in different ways. At the same time, I would be concerned about someone who stayed at a company too long. If you can't come and make an impact in five years and learn the business and be able to go out and monetize those skill sets and help move the economy then it's a bit counterproductive." If you aren't moving the needle for both yourself and your company, there's a problem, and you need to do something about it. If you aren't feeling challenged, you aren't growing or developing yourself, that can seriously hurt your career. If you want to promote yourself and get ahead you have to keep challenging yourself. That's the best way to accumulate the experience and connections you'll need.

Of course there are a lot of other factors that can affect your timing. For example, as mentioned above, if you're not feeling challenged anymore and you aren't learning or growing, it's time to make a change. The same goes if you don't see a clear career path forward at your company. But before you jump ship, be absolutely sure you've really pursued every possibility. When I spoke with Cynthia Trudell, Executive Vice President and Chief Human Resources Officer of Pepsi Co, she said, "One reason young people might leave the company is that they believe their career isn't moving fast enough or they feel that the company hasn't provided the set of experiences that they may want. But I always get disappointed if an employee wanted to do something and we never knew about it. So it's super-important that you make sure that all company data about you, including your career ambitions, is up to date so there's no possibility that we don't know what you want to do and how you want to grow."

Another reason to move on is if you no longer (or never did) enjoy what you're doing and you want to reposition yourself to do something that's more in line with your passions. That may sound a little petty, but it's a hard truth that affects a lot of people. Eric Schechter, Social Media Manager at Carnival Cruise Lines, put it quite nicely when he told me, "It's time to move on when your job feels like work. Life is too short to live every day in misery and not love and be extremely passionate about what you do for a living. If you're working just to pay your bills and put food on the table, I think it's more than reasonable to start looking for another opportunity."

Making Change from Within: How to Talk to Your Boss About Your Desire for Change

When it comes to changing jobs within your company—whether that's taking on more responsibility or moving to a completely different department—your boss can be your biggest ally—or your biggest stumbling block. Since most managers are happy to support high-value employees (if nothing else, it makes them look good to *their* bosses), I'm going to assume that yours is safely in the ally category.

Even if you know that your boss will support you, it's important that you prepare yourself before you have the actual face-to-face meeting in which you tell them your plans and ask for that support. There are two things your boss will want to know (and that you'll *need* to know).

First, what specific openings exist and in what departments? You can find this out by spending some time going through the company's job board. If you don't have a job board, put some informal feelers out—but be cool about it. Second, who's going to replace you? I'm always a little surprised at how few people think about this. But when you do, it makes a lot of sense. After all, your company hired you to do a job, right? If you move to a different department, that job won't be getting done. So even though you want to be seen as irreplaceable, you need to find someone who can move into your cubicle and keep your soon-to-be-former team running as smoothly as you did (of course, no one could do the job as well as you, but you know what I mean).

Keeping these things in mind makes life a lot easier for your manager by eliminating any worry that your job might not get done. That, in turn, will solidify your relationship with your soon-to-be-former manager and gives them even more reasons to support you.

Changing Terms: When to Ask for a Promotion and How to Negotiate a Salary Bump

At some point in our career, most of us feel that we aren't being adequately compensated for the work we're doing. Maybe it's someone who got hired more recently and got a big signing bonus, or maybe it's that you think your boss didn't notice the great job you did on your last project.

Whatever the reason, once you've decided that a conversation needs to take place, you can't chicken out. But first, you need to get clear in your own mind what your goals are. If you want a raise, how much? If you want more responsibilities, what would they be? If you want a better title, what is it? And think about less obvious things. Would a private office with a river view do it for you? How about being able to work from home three days per week?

Most people dread these conversations, and it's tempting to IM or e-mail your manger. Don't. This is important and warrants an in-person meeting. The best way to make "the talk" with the boss less unpleasant is to anticipate the questions they might ask and have solid answers to back you up. Here's what you need to do to prepare:

- **Gather plenty of evidence that you're worth more than your firm is currently paying you.** You need to walk into your meeting ready to wow, and well armed with quantifiable examples of how you have contributed to the company. Try to put a dollar value on your accomplishments.

- **Know how much you're worth.** Find out what people with similar experience are making within your firm as well as what people doing jobs similar to yours at other companies are making. But be subtle about this. Asking people directly how much money they make can be misinterpreted in a lot of ways, so unless you feel completely comfortable with the people whose salaries you want to know, start your research on the Internet. One good site to look into is PayScale.com

- **Know how much your manager depends on you.** The more indispensable you are, the better.

• **Know your floor and ceiling.** What is the least you'd be satisfied with? What's the most you could possibly hope for?

• **Be prepared to keep the conversation focused on your performance, value, and accomplishments.** The fact that you want to buy a new car or want to take an extended vacation to climb Mt. Everest is (or at least should be) irrelevant.

• **Time it right.** In a best-case scenario, you'd be in and out of your boss's office in five minutes. But sometimes these discussions can go on for hours. Take that into consideration when thinking about scheduling.

If you've had the talk and it's clear that you're not going to get what you want at your current company, it's time to consider other opportunities. Otherwise, you'll feel unfulfilled and resentful, you won't work as hard, and you'll have a poor attitude. Deciding to quit your job takes a lot of maturity. It's also a critical step. If you want to keep your brand strong and get ahead in your career, you'll need to be proactive.

Should I Stay or Should I Go? Aligning Your Personal and Corporate Brands

Not every job turns out to be exactly as advertised (or hoped for). So after you've been with your employer for six months or so, I recommend that you do a quick audit by asking yourself these questions:

- Does my brand and my company's still match up?
- Am I happy with where the company is going and how they're getting there?

- Is the company giving back to the community in the way I expected they would?
- Do I fit in with my coworkers, my boss, and the corporate culture?
- How satisfied am I with the dress code, workplace flexibility, salary, and benefits?

If you've gone through this brief audit and have decided that you'd be better off working somewhere else, it's time to start your search. In the next section, we'll talk about exactly how.

The Search Begins: Scouting Out Your Next Opportunity Outside Your Company

In the Brad Pitt–Edward Norton movie *Fight Club*, the first rule is: "Do not talk about Fight Club." Same goes for when you start investigating new opportunities. The main reason is that if your employer finds out, your job could be in jeopardy. And since it's always easier to get a new job when you already have one, getting laid off can only hurt you by making you look desperate and subject you to job seeker discrimination.

So in the early stages of your search, be very subtle and stay as much under the radar as you can. Start by making sure your online presence is updated to reflect your current skills and experience. There is absolutely nothing wrong with (or suspicious about) doing this. Then do some passive searching on LinkedIn, job hunting Web sites, and checking internal job boards. "Passive searching" means looking at listings but not sending out messages to your network letting them know you're looking—and not posting your résumé online *anywhere*. It's scary how easy it is to find information online (almost all companies have either people or automated systems that look for mentions of their company), and it's even scarier that some employers who find out that an employee is looking will retaliate by laying him or her off.

Then start using your social networks to connect with people in your industry or the industry you want to head into. If you haven't already built relationships, do it now so when you finally go public with your search, you'll already have your contacts in place. Chances are that you'll hear about job openings. And speaking of relationships, don't forget about headhunters and recruiters. These people usually have a very broad and deep understanding of what's going on in your industry, who the players are, where open positions are, how much they pay, and so on. If you've been contacted in the past by a recruiter but ignored the e-mail, it's time to start responding. Don't be afraid to ask a lot of questions. And don't be afraid to mention that you're considering a move. Headhunters' livelihood depends on maintaining clients' confidentiality, so your secret is normally safe with them.

A word of warning. When you start lining up interviews, make sure you schedule them around your current work hours. The last thing you want is for your boss to see you having lunch with a competitor in the middle of the workday. Most people in hiring positions understand that if they're interviewing someone who already has a job they'll need to keep that information private. But if you're concerned or you're in an industry where everyone knows everyone else, you may have to make a direct request for privacy.

Moving On: How to Leave Your Company in Ways That Promote Your Brand

I come across too many people who think that leaving an employer has to involve bad blood. I can tell you from personal and professional experience that it doesn't. The problem isn't *why* the employee is leaving: Forty-four percent of managers and 42 percent of young workers polled in my research said it was reasonable for an employee to leave a job if "any better opportunity comes along." Fifteen percent of managers and 14 percent of young workers said it was reasonable to quit if "an opportunity that pays more money comes along."

The key to leaving with your head held high (and a bunch of ringing endorsements you can leverage in your next job and for the rest of your life) has to do with timing the announcement. "Giving very little notice and/or going to a competitor are good ways to burn bridges," says Allan McKisson, VP of HR at Manpower. "But if someone is leaving for personal or career reasons and they've kept us in the loop, we're glad to help."

One important piece of advice: Don't pull the plug on your old job until you have a confirmed offer or a signed contract from the new one. Jumping the gun could leave you with no job at all.

When it comes time to make the actual announcement, tell the truth. You're not the only one with a network—and you never know when you're going to bump into someone you used to work with. Lying about what you're doing after you leave your current employer is just too risky.

Being honest about your plans—and offering to help fill your soon-to-be-former position with someone from your network—will make it a lot easier for you to get LinkedIn recommendations from the people you work with and for—something you should do as soon as possible so your smiling face and astonishing accomplishments will be fresh in their mind.

Finally, be sure to keep in touch with the people you worked with. Again, you never know when or where you'll see them again.

Should You Get an MBA?

Overall, 43 percent of the managers we interviewed in our study said that having an advanced degree would be an advantage, but it's not required. Only 10 percent say it's required. Interestingly, 60 percent of the young workers we interviewed felt that having an advanced degree is either recommended or strongly recommended (but not required), and 22 percent say it's required. Another case of a pretty big disconnect between perception and reality.

Aflac's Matt McDonald told me that it's more important that young people pursue their strengths, work to align those strengths with their passion, and work hard. "An MBA from a prestigious institution may open a few doors, but hard work will sustain the relationships you make and the reputation you build for yourself," he said. "Some theory is necessary, but practical experience, in my opinion, is more valuable."

There are, however, a number of factors you should consider when evaluating your options and making your decision. Of course, when it comes to making your own decision, statistics and personal stories aren't particularly helpful and, unfortunately, there's no right or wrong answer. In some specialized fields (such as accounting) an MBA or other advanced degree may be required. In other fields, an MBA could make you stand out in the market (unless everyone else has one—in that case, not having an MBA will make you stand out but not in the way you'd like). If you aspire to be a manager or you want to work for a big-name consulting firm, an MBA— especially if it comes from a top tier business school like Harvard or Wharton—will definitely help.

That said, depending on your situation, having an MBA might not help in the long run as much as you might think. Sixty-four percent of CEOs of the Fortune 100 companies do not have one. Bill Gates, Warren Buffett, Larry Ellison, Jeff Bezos, and Richard Branson don't have an MBA. The only U.S. president with one is George W. Bush.[2]

It's becoming hard to justify an MBA in today's' society when young people are strained by student loans and people aren't getting jobs. On average, people with a bachelor's degree earn $2.3 million over their lifetime. Those with MBAs earn $2.4 million. But the average tuition for a two-year MBA program is $82,147 (with books, housing, and other expenses you're up to $120,000), which makes the whole thing a wash.[3] Assuming you borrow most of that, paying your loans off over ten years will cost you $1,300 a month after interest and fees. Twenty percent of MBA graduates default on their loans and 40 percent of grads rely on their parents for loan assistance.[4]

Regardless of which way you're leaning, ask your manager or HR whether the company would pay for your program. Many employers will either foot the entire bill or offer full or partial tuition reimbursement programs. Also check out your alternatives. The Kauffman Foundation estimates that more than 2,000 colleges and universities in the U.S. offer entrepreneurship programs.

I know I've just given you a lot of information, but ultimately the decision to get an MBA is going to be a personal one, one that can have a major impact on your career and your ability to promote yourself. On the "get one" side, pursuing an MBA is a big commitment because it costs a lot of money and time. Depending on your situation, those sacrifices could pay off and lead you to better positions and higher salaries years out. On the "don't get one" side, MBAs are not for everyone—I don't have one. Colleges are evolving though, and you can take classes online from anywhere in the world now. Entrepreneurship classes can be particularly useful if you want to start a business someday or work for a start-up (you'll be with other entrepreneurial-minded people who might have companies already).

A Word on Job Hopping

I'm not a big fan of job hopping (which I define as repeatedly starting news jobs and then moving on six to twelve months later). It's really a perception issue. Having a series of short-term jobs on your résumé gives the impression that you're not terribly loyal and given how much it costs to hire and train new employees, a lot of companies won't want to invest a big chunk of cash in someone who may not be around long enough to produce a decent ROI. And, as I've said before, job hopping makes it pretty hard for you to earn your coworkers' trust and show them what a star you are.

In a survey of 1,500 hiring managers and recruiters conducted by Bullhorn, which makes recruiting software, 39 percent said that "the single biggest obstacle for an unemployed candidate in regaining employment is having a history of 'hopping jobs,' or leaving a company before one year of tenure."[5]

Here's what Donald Trump told me in an interview: "I look for somebody who has been at another job for a long period of time. If I see somebody who has had seven jobs in two years, I'm not interested because I know they'll probably be leaving me pretty soon." Liam Brown, COO of Marriott International, has a different take. "If we're looking externally, I don't pay much attention to job hopping unless it's rampant, like an every-six-months kind of thing," he told me. "It all depends on the interview and the conversation with the person. If they are the right person for us then we'll hire them." If you end up in a position where you quit or feel like you have no choice but to hop, then at least be able to articulate that in an interview. Tell them the honest truth as to why you're making a move and they will respect you more and won't look down on it.

Here's the kicker. Regardless of what anyone says, it's important to always be open to new opportunities. If something amazing comes along, get some advice from trusted friends, colleagues, and/or advisors. If it truly makes sense, take the leap.

How to Strategically Quit Your Job and Start Your Own Company or Freelance Business

In Chapter 10, we talked about intrapreneurship—how to develop a passion-driven business inside your company. In this section I want to talk about *entre*preneurship—quitting your job and building that passion-driven business without internal corporate backing.

Making the transition to the new business is pretty much the same whether you're doing it internally or externally. For example, you'll have to find a way to balance your full-time job and your other business. You'll be sacrificing your nights and weekends, and you'll have to make sure your side projects don't negatively affect your productivity or distract you from the job you were hired to do. For me, making all those sacrifices for a few years paid off because I was positioned to make the business I'd started on the side into a full-time career.

Entrepreneurship is all the rage—and Gen Y has what some are calling an unprecedented entrepreneurial spirit. According to a survey by Employers Insurance, 46 percent of Gen Yers want to start a business in the next five years.[6] Post–Gen Y people are jumping on the entrepreneurial bandwagon, with more and more people starting a business while they're still in college and becoming full-time entrepreneurs upon graduation.

Even businesses are taking note. My company did a study recently and found that nearly a third of employers are looking for entrepreneurship experience when hiring recent college grads.

Opening your own company sounds kind of glamorous, doesn't it—and there are plenty of really great things about doing it. But there are just as many challenges, which means that being an entrepreneur is most definitely *not* for everyone (as impressive as the stats above are, between 46 and 67 percent of people are *not* becoming entrepreneurs).

Not long ago you'd often hear that the entrepreneurial mind-set (especially in high-tech) was "Ready, Fire, Aim." As a result, a lot of people got the impression that becoming an entrepreneur was something you could just jump into without any preparation. Some who did, survived. But most didn't. So to keep you from going off half-cocked and quitting your job, I want you to take a few minutes to consider some of the pros and cons.

Pro: You're the boss and you set your own hours.
Con: You may be working twelve hours a day with no time off for months. You constantly have to sell yourself and drum up new business. You need to be self-directed, and the line between your personal and private lives can get awfully blurry.

Pro: If you succeed, you have a better chance of being recognized than if you were part of a big company.
Con: If you fail, there's no big brand or corporation to hide behind.

Pro: You keep a greater share of the profits.
Con: It's challenging, risky, income streams can be erratic, you have to finance your own taxes and benefits, and you absorb all the losses.

Pro: You get a chance to get your hands dirty in a number of areas.
Con: You may be put in a position of having to do work you have no experience doing.

Okay, let's assume that you've been through all this and you're sure that you want to get out there and launch your own company. Before you pull the trigger, take a long, deep breath and think about leveraging your job so you can learn everything you possibly can before you quit. The more skills you can learn on someone else's dime the easier your life as an entrepreneur will be. As Life Coach Jenny Blake, who quit her job at Google to start her own life coaching business, told me, "I absolutely loved working at Google and use the skills I gained over the five years every single day. Google is so fast-paced that it actually makes running my own business feel easy in comparison!" Jen Ortega, who left a job at Goldman Sachs to start her own online flooring business, goes even further: "At Goldman Sachs I learned very early on how to communicate, give presentations, operate with good customer service etiquette, create sound bites for important initiatives, build effective PowerPoint presentations, be disciplined with my time, set expectations with stakeholders, work with a global audience, manage large-scale initiatives, collaborate with people with differing personalities, and the list goes on and on." Wow! Start a business with a skill set like that and you're already miles ahead of the competition.

It's also a good idea to use blogs and social media as a platform to test a market before you enter it. Get feedback, see how your target market responds, retool, and build your company based on what customers want, not what you *think* they want. I did this a lot when I was still running my current business as a side project—and there's no way I would have been as successful if I hadn't done this kind of testing.

I strongly suggest that you not leave your job unless you're really ready. Then wait a bit more. Jerryanne Heath learned this lesson the hard way. After leaving her job as an analyst at Lehman Brothers, she had to move back in with her parents for two years before her start-up company, ConceptLink, was doing well enough that she could afford to pay herself. When starting a business, things always take longer and cost more than you anticipated. So it's critical that you have a big financial cushion that will allow you to pay for the expenses of running the new business while still keeping a roof over your head, food on the table, and your medical and dental insurance current.

On the other hand, don't wait too long. Here's what life coach Jenny Blake had to say: "I started my Web site in 2005, started working at Google in 2006, then started my blog, Life After College, in 2007. For four years I worked on my blog and a book of the same name on nights and weekends. For a long time that was sustainable and totally okay. But as the blog and book really started gaining momentum I realized I couldn't do both anymore. I kept hitting burnout points and feeling like I wasn't quite giving either one the time and attention it deserved."

Finally, don't do it alone. No matter how many skills you've got, handling every aspect of the business is probably not the best use of your time. So it's often a good idea to try to find business partners who are strong in areas where you're a little weaker. You may already know people like that. If you don't, there are lots of places to find them. Go to entrepreneurship events in your city. Check out South by Southwest (SXSW), TechCrunch Disrupt, Ignite, Startup Weekend, Global Entrepreneurship Week, Tech Cocktail, TEDx, Summit at Sea, and many others. The goal is to meet like-minded entrepreneurs and partners that will make your new business a success.

Whenever and however you decide to make the jump, do *not* let your boss know about the business and your intentions to leave before you're ready to quit. This is especially true if you're going to be competing with your soon-to-be-former employer in any way. Do *not* leave without giving plenty of notice and enough time for the company to find a suitable replacement. Do *not* use your employer's resources for your business. This includes spending time that should be your employer's on something to do with your side business. Do *not* steal company contacts and information, and do *not* burn bridges with the people you work with, as you might need them as you build your company.

Being an entrepreneur, from my own experience, is challenging, but also rewarding and exciting. You're creating your own dream and you're taking steps each day to make it happen. Based on your values, ideas, time management, work ethic, and determination, you can create something out of nothing. But keep in mind that if you're going to make it work, you'll need to be able to work independently and put in a lot of time. And even if you do all that, there's always the risk that things won't work out the way you want them to. So if you value raising a family, you like to be managed, or you want a bit more security in your life, hanging out your own shingle might not be for you—and that's fine. You can still act like an entrepreneur *within* your company and use their resources to help you make an impact.

Should I Stay or Should I Go?

The days of getting a job and staying there until retirement are long gone. But that doesn't mean you shouldn't have some loyalty to your company. After all, they hired you and gave you the opportunity to acquire experience, make connections, and develop yourself professionally.

When you're feeling like you're not getting anywhere at work and you're thinking about quitting, ask yourself why. What is the job lacking? Have you done everything you can to seek out new responsibilities or even turn your current job into your dream job? Then, think about the type of move you want to make: up, sideways, or out. The choice is yours.

But before you make any moves, be sure you'll be in a position to exercise your strengths and make good use of the skills you've worked so hard to develop. If not, you're heading into another dead end. On the other hand, if you're able to fit your skills and your personal brand into a new situation, you've got a recipe for success.

Your Career Is in Your Hands

Now that you've learned about the skills you need to get ahead, how to position yourself for success, and the different paths that can get you there, you're ready to put everything into action. Each step we've taken in this book will help take you closer to promoting yourself at work and getting ahead in your career. First, we walked through all the skills that you need in order to stand out, get recognized, and become an invaluable, go-to master of your trade. These included hard skills, soft skills, and online skills. We learned that soft skills are the most valued by management, that you have to be a specialist instead of a generalist, and that your online brand can be a tool to help you manage your career.

We then touched on the importance of gaining visibility at work without bragging and coming off as selfish. Take credit where credit is due but also share your successes with your team. Then we analyzed what managers are looking for when they decide whom to promote (the ability to prioritize work, having a positive attitude, and teamwork topped the list), and compared that with the Millennial view of workplace success.

Next, we talked about how different generations (Y, Z, X, and Boomers) operate and how to best manage those relationships. Then I showed you how to create a network both inside and outside the workplace and how to leverage your network to get ahead. We also explored two creative ways to take your career to the next level. First, by positioning yourself for a job that reflects your passions and talents. Second, by becoming an intrapreneur and coming up with creative solutions to problems—without leaving your job. Finally, because I know many of you are feeling stuck in your careers, we talked about how to explore your options and decide between moving up, sideways, or out.

This book is meant to be your reference for every stage of your career. It will help you differentiate yourself from your coworkers and set you on a path toward creating a meaningful, exciting, and impactful career. When you're at a bar and someone asks you what you do (which always happens), you'll be able to respond with confidence and pride, because your job is inextricably linked with who you are and who you're destined to become—someone who understands how to thrive in the new world of work and who creates his or her own future instead of relying on others.

Just reading a book and thinking about it won't get you to the next level in your career. I wake up every morning and say to myself "let's make something happen" and then I spend part of every day doing at least one thing that will help me get ahead.

When I graduated from college I never could have imagined how my career would develop. But if you believe in yourself, try new things, and spend some time outside your comfort zone, you can do anything you want. Who knows what you're meant to be or how you can impact your profession or even the world. You're part of a generation that has the potential to make a positive difference in the workplace *and* in the world. Within the next decade, we're going to become the majority of the workforce, which not only positions us to achieve greatness, but also to pass down our wisdom to the next generation. Careers are all about knowledge transfer: We learn from those who have been there before and we teach those who come up next. I firmly believe that you can become part of the Millennial movement and I want you to because we need people like you—people who care about their careers and won't be content to just sit on the couch waiting for their big break. Let others stay there while you start stockpiling achievements and skills that can't be ignored.

Now, how do you start?

Do one thing every day—add a new skill, share a new idea for your group, some thing—that will advance you. Developing this "One Step Forward a Day" habit will keep you current, make you feel more fulfilled and confident, and increase your value. It also will make you more creative and fulfilled when you're not working. And it will ensure that you do 365 things this year to improve yourself.

In this book, I have showed you how to begin that process. Now I will tell you when:
   Start right now!

Great things come to those who don't wait,

Dan Schawbel

ACKNOWLEDGMENTS

To my fearless agent

There would be no book deal without Jim Levine, one of the top literary agents on the planet. His vote of confidence as well as his knowledge of the publishing industry were pivotal in securing the book deal of my dreams.

To my team at St. Martin's

Matt Martz and Dan Weiss understood the book idea immediately and both brought years of experience and insight to improve the quality of the book.

To my research team

I started off as a research novice, but with the help of experts I was able to become an expert over the past few years. Thanks to Luke Williams and Tim Keiningham, both of whom are executives at Ipsos

Research, I was able to come up with a unique and interesting survey concept that supported the book. A very special thanks to Christina Schelling and Jason Gong at American Express for their support, feedback on the study, and excitement for the project.

To those who helped bring
the book together

I'd like to thank Armin Brott, who helped me organize my ideas and hone my voice. Carolyn Monaco and Robin Simons helped me take my original book proposal to the next level. Binyamin Cooper, Carrie Bowe, Jessica Wonczyk, and Jessica Kerch were great interns who helped me with many of the interviews I did for the book, as well as the promotional program.

To my friends

Bill Connolly has been a great asset, an even better friend, and I thank him for always putting things in perspective. Rachel Tuhro is always looking out for me and ensuring that I remain humble. Jon Mitman has been a loyal friend for over a decade, always telling me the honest truth regardless of how I might react. Angela Sanchioni, the proud friend, has always made me feel special.

Other friends who have supported me over the years include: Russell Wyner, Ken Pickard, Robert Quinn, Chloe Finklestein, Ryan Paugh, Caitlin McCabe, Ryan Benevides, Jessica Dunham, Scott Bradley, the Orkin Family, Katie Konrath, Deb Lalone, Regan McDowall, Corey Merrill, Ashly McPhillips, Sarah Parrish, Jason Kleinerman, Joe Crossett, Liz Yurkevicz, Ashley Meyer, Raymond Chan,

Acknowledgments

Adam Conrad, Jonathan Joe, Kenny Yee, Brendan Ross, Lauren Colby, Cody Clearwater, Joel Backaler, Pete Ziegler, Jeff Gabel, Joshua White, Maria Elena Duron, and Sam Glick.

To my mentors

Penelope Trunk, Jonathan Fields, Pam Slim, Sally Hogshead, Bob Burg, John Jantsch, David Meerman Scott, and Jill Konrath.

NOTES

Foreword

1. Trendera is a consulting company focusing on providing insights into future cultural trends.

2. http://business.time.com/2012/09/28/note-to-gen-y-workers-performance-on-the-job-actually-matters/.

1. The Future Is YOU

1. www.businessweek.com/managing/content/aug2010/ca20100820_173207.htm.

2. Bureau of Labor Statistics and The Business and Professional Women's Foundation.

3. www.prweb.com/releases/2012/8/prweb9817689.htm.

4. http://online.wsj.com/article/SB10000872396390443713704577603302382190374.html.

5. http://online.wsj.com/article/SB10000872396390443713704577603302382190374.html?mod=e2tw.

6. www.forbes.com/sites/ciocentral/2012/07/03/lets-play-to-keep-gen-y-staffers-gamify-their-work/.

7. http://edition.cnn.com/2012/08/20/business/generation-y-global-office-culture/index.html.

8. Edelman's 8095® 2.0 Study: www.edelman.com/news/study-finds-millennial-generations-power-to-influence-is-increasing/.

2. Discover What You Were Meant to Do

1. Quote from Anne Hubert, senior vice president at Scratch Media. "They're thinking about finding their life's work, their calling," she says. "Eighty-four percent of them believe they're going to get where they want to in life. . . ." finance.yahoo.com/blogs/daily-ticker/retirement-thing-past-millennials-164410760.html

2. Survey conducted by the insurer Aegon. qz.com/148051/twenty-somethings-have-incredibly-unrealistic-expectations-for-retirement/

3. Pew Research—pewsocialtrends.org/2013/08/01/a-rising-share-of-young-adults-live-in-their-parents-home/

4. Report from Georgetown University Center on Education and the Workforce, quoted in *The Wall Street Journal,* online.wsj.com/news/articles/SB10001424052702303643304579105450145516622

5. washingtonpost.com/blogs/wonkblog/wp/2013/05/20/only-27-percent-of-college-grads-have-a-job-related-to-their-major/

6. "Millennials at Work: Reshsaping the Workplace," Pricewaterhouse Coopers, pwc.com/en_M1/m1/services/consulting/documents/millennials-at-work.pdf

7. Report by PricewaterhouseCooper, pwc.blogs.com/milton-keynes/2011/10/next-generation-students-will-rent-for-longer.html

8. Study by NerdWallet, nerdwallet.com/blog/investing/2013/73-retirement-norm-millennials/

9. Eight percent had a parent accompany them to a job interview (PwC in *The Wall Street Journal*)

10. millennialbranding.com/2012/11/student-career-development -study/

11. finance.yahoo.com/news/71-millennials-want-co-workers-16150 0376.html

12. stevepavlina.com/articles/list-of-values.htm

13. online.wsj.com/news/articles/SB20001424127887323968704578 8652354071373238

14. probonoaustralia.com.au/news/2013/04/corporate-volunteering -delivers-leadership-development-report

15. northwestern.edu/magazine/summer2008/cover/seniorwatch_ sidebar/sidebar02.html

16. Beyond.com and *Millennial Branding*

17. blog.linkedin.com/2013/12/18/the-25-hottest-skills-that-got -people-hired-in-2013/

3. Hard Skills: Be More Than Your Job Description

1. Bureau of Labor Statistics: http://finance.yahoo.com/blogs/the -exchange/3-million-job-openings-tell-us-skills-gap-004026892.html.

2. www.usnews.com/education/best-graduate-schools/articles/2012/03 /22/youre-an-engineer-youre-hired.

3. Ibid.

4. Soft Skills: Make Every Impression Count

1. http://webscript.princeton.edu/~tlab/wp-content/publications /Willis&Todorov_PS2006.pdf.

2. www.businessmanagementdaily.com/20071/piercings-bad-breath-and-tattoos-oh-my.

3. http://conferenceconnexion.com/harvard-study-85-of-the-reason-a-person-gets-a-job-keeps-a-job-or-advances-has-to-do-with-people-skills/.

5. Online Skills: Use Social Media to Your Advantage

1. www.informationweek.com/news/security/privacy/227700369.

2. www.retrevo.com/content/blog/2011/06/posting-remorse.

3. www.ncircle.com/index.php?s=news_press_2010_04-22-Survey-71-percent-of-Companies-Able-to-Monitor-Employee-Social-Media-Use.

4. Technorati, "State of the Blogosphere," 2009.

5. http://mashable.com/2011/12/15/british-facebook-alcohol-photos/#23917Greater-Control-of-Status-Updates.

6. www.towson.edu/main/discovertowson/brianstelter.asp.

7. http://alexandralevit.typepad.com/wcw/2011/04/google-is-forever.html

6. Gain Visibility Without Being Known as a Self-Promotional Jerk

1. www.apa.org/monitor/2011/02/narcissism.aspx.

8. Develop Cross-Generational Relationships

1. Kit Yarrow and Jayne O'Donnell, *Gen BuY: How Tweens, Teens, and Twenty-Somethings Are Revolutionizing Retail,* (San Francisco: Jossey-Bass, 2009).

2. http://dl.dropbox.com/u/101899934/MTV%20millennial%20 makers%20(9-10-12)-01.jpg.

3. www.fdu.edu/newspubs/magazine/05ws/generations.htm; www .arthur-maxwell.com/articles/2011/09-generations.php; http://rtc.umn .edu/docs/2_18_Gen_diff_workplace.pdf.

12. Moving Up, Moving Sideways, or Moving On?

1. www.careerbuilder.com/JobPoster/Resources/page.aspx ?template=none&sc_cmp2=JP_Infographic_2012NewJobeHunt &pagever=2012NewJobHunt.

2. http://bestengagingcommunities.com/2012/04/20/is-an-mba -worth-it-this-infographic-says-no/.

3. Ibid.

4. Ibid.

5. www.ere.net/2012/09/18/want-a-job-you-can-commit-a-crime -just-dont-stay-unemployed-too-long/.

6. http://money.cnn.com/galleries/2012/smallbusiness/1206/gallery .gen-y-entrepreneurs.fortune/index.html.

INDEX

ABOUT THE AUTHOR

Dan Schawbel is the Managing Partner of Millennial Branding, a Gen Y research and consulting firm. Dan is a leader and supporter of his own generation, as well as a world renowned career and workplace expert. He is the author of *Me 2.0: 4 Steps to Building Your Future*, now in thirteen languages. *Me 2.0* made *The New York Times* summer reading list for job seekers, *The Washington Post* summer reading list for business leaders, and was the the *New York Post* number one career book of 2009.

Dan is the founder of the Personal Branding Blog, a *Forbes* "Top Web site for Your Career," and ranked as the number one job blog by CareerBuilder. He is a columnist at both *Time* and *Forbes*, a syndicated columnist at *Metro US,* and has contributed to *Fortune, The Wall Street Journal, The Guardian*, and *The Globe and Mail.* His research, insights, and advice have been covered in *Wired* magazine, CNN, *USA Today*, PBS's *Nightly Business Report, The Willis Report* on Fox Business, *Elle* magazine, and numerous others.

Through his research, he has helped companies like American Express, NBC Universal, Fidelity, and Monster better understand his generation. He's also spoken at some of the world's most prestigious companies, including Google, Fidelity, IBM, Time Warner, CitiGroup, and Siemens, as well as some of the most notable schools, including Harvard Business School, Stanford, Cornell, and MIT.

About the Author

Dan was named to the *Inc.* "30 Under 30 List" in 2010, the *Forbes* "30 Under 30 List in 2012," and *Business Week* cites him as someone entrepreneurs should follow on Twitter. He lives in Boston, Massachusetts, and graduated from Bentley University in 2006.

Connect with Dan Online

Web: DanSchawbel.com
Facebook.com/DanSchawbel
LinkedIn.com/In/DanSchawbel
Twitter.com/DanSchawbel